HOSTAGE NATION

HOSTAGE NATION

COLOMBIA'S GUERRILLA ARMY
AND THE FAILED WAR ON DRUGS

VICTORIA BRUCE AND KARIN HAYES

with Jorge Enrique Botero

ALFRED A. KNOPF   NEW YORK   2010

THIS IS A BORZOI BOOK
PUBLISHED BY ALFRED A. KNOPF

Copyright © 2010 by Victoria Bruce and Karin Hayes

All rights reserved.
Published in the United States by Alfred A. Knopf,
a division of Random House, Inc., New York,
and in Canada by Random House of Canada Limited, Toronto.
www.aaknopf.com

Knopf, Borzoi Books, and the colophon are registered
trademarks of Random House, Inc.

Library of Congress Cataloging-in-Publication Data
Bruce, Victoria.
Hostage nation: Colombia's guerrilla army and the failed war on drugs /
by Victoria Bruce and Karin Hayes, with Jorge Enrique Botero.—1st ed.
p. cm.
"A Borzoi Book."
ISBN 978-0-307-27115-0
1. Political kidnapping—Colombia. 2. Hostages—Colombia. 3. Fuerzas
Armadas Revolucionarias de Colombia. 4. Guerrillas—Colombia—History—
21st century. 5. Drug control—United States—History—21st century.
6. Colombia—Politics and government—21st century. I. Hayes, Karin.
II. Botero, Jorge Enrique, 1956– III. Title.
HV6604. C7B78 2010
986.106'35—dc22   2010003904

Manufactured in the United States of America
First Edition

To all the journalists who have died and to those who continue to risk
their lives covering the violence in Colombia and the war on drugs.

CONTENTS

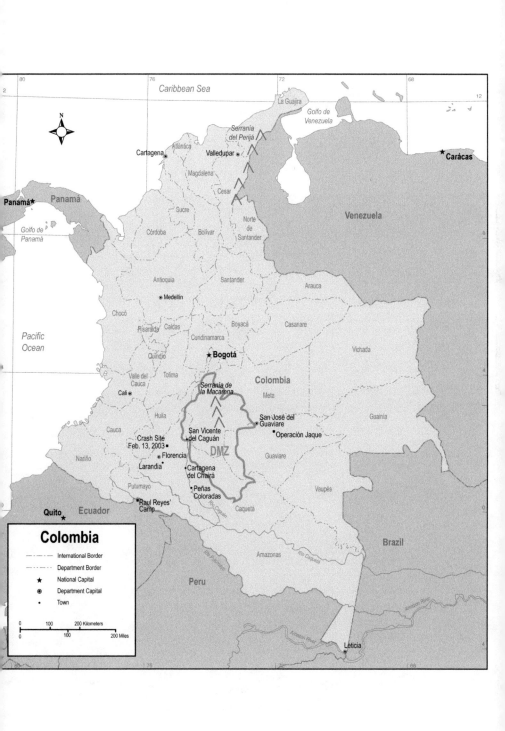

Caribbean Sea

La Guajira

Golfo de
Venezuela

Serranía
del Perijá

Cartagena

Atlántico

Valledupar

★ Carácas

Magdalena

Cesar

Panamá ★

Panamá

Sucre

Norte
de
Santander

Venezuela

Golfo de
Panamá

Córdoba

Bolívar

Antioquia

Santander

Arauca

⊙ Medellín

Chocó

Risaralda

Caldas

Boyacá

Casanare

Pacific
Ocean

Cundinamarca

Quindío

Vichada

★ Bogotá

Valle del
Cauca

Tolima

Colombia

Cali ⊙

Serranía de
la Macarena

Meta

Huila

San José del
Guaviare

Guainía

Cauca

San Vicente
del Caguán

Operación Jaque

Crash Site
Feb. 13, 2003

Florencia

DMZ

Guaviare

Nariño

Larandia

Cartagena
del Chairá

Putumayo

Peñas
Coloradas

Vaupés

Raul Reyes'
Camp

Río Caquetá

Caquetá

Quito ★

Ecuador

Brazil

Amazonas

Río Caquetá

Peru

Amazon River

Leticia

Colombia

- - - International Border
- - - Department Border
★ National Capital
⊙ Department Capital
• Town

0   100   200 Kilometers
0   100   200 Miles

PROLOGUE

In February 2003, a short news clip of a plane crash in the Colombian jungle grabbed our attention. We had spent the previous year making our first documentary film, *The Kidnapping of Ingrid Betancourt*. It was assumed that three of the American crew members survived the crash and had been captured by Fuerzas Armadas Revolucionarias de Colombia (FARC) guerrillas, the same group that had held Ingrid for over a year. A book on Ingrid and the American captives seemed like a logical journalistic extension after the documentary. At the time, we had only two sources: the mother of hostage Marc Gonsalves, who was the only family member who would speak to the press, and Gary Noesner, an FBI hostage-negotiation expert who had recently gone corporate. We'd had the good fortune to interview Gary several times in the past, so the coincidence that Gary's first case with his new employer turned out to be that of the three kidnapped Americans seemed like great serendipity.

Six months after the Americans had been kidnapped, a surprising symbiotic relationship began when we delivered proof to Gary's office in Washington, D.C. that the three Americans were still alive. On the video we carried back from Bogotá were interviews of the hostages; these had been shot by our Colombian colleague, Jorge Enrique Botero, who was the only journalist ever to be allowed into FARC hostage camps. At the time, no one in the U.S. government had any knowledge of the hostages' whereabouts or even whether they were still alive. Knowing that we were bringing the video, Gary had invited one of the lead FBI investigators in the case, a State Department counter-terrorism official, and the vice president of Northrop Grumman, the men's employer. And in what was surely one of the most surreal moments in both of our careers, we opened a laptop and showed them videos of Marc Gonsalves, Thomas Howes, and Keith Stansell pleading for their families not to forget them and begging the U.S. government not to attempt a rescue.

Shortly after, even with the publicity generated by Botero's footage of the men and our documentary film *Held Hostage in Colombia*, which aired on CBS's *60 Minutes II*, the History Channel, and in news reports around the world, there was little interest in the Americans' story. As our subjects remained in the jungle, the book, which we had worked on for six months, didn't seem to have either a market or an ending in sight. We shelved the proposal. Over the next few years, we would occasionally pull it out and dust it off—changing titles, reorganizing, and rewriting—only to discover that we still didn't have a book. With no news on the hostage situation and not even the slightest hint of a release, more than half a dozen half-finished proposals gathered dust on our office shelves, got lost in moves, or ended up in the recycled paper pile.

But the story was never far away. The hostages had become an unshakable part of our lives. We were on a first-name basis with Tom, Marc, Keith, and Ingrid. And for Botero, there were dozens more. They worked their way into our thoughts and our daily conversations. In Karin's dreams, Ingrid often appeared on the brink of liberation, only to disappear back into the jungle. We empathized with the frustra-tion of the family members, several of whom we spoke to often. We met with senators, congresspeople, members of NGOs, and anyone else we felt could help bring attention to the story or do something to help the three Americans and hundreds of other Colombian hostages. We stud-ied every bit of news about the FARC. We were, by turns, hopeful and fearful for the hostages when Colombian president Álvaro Uribe made conciliatory and then aggressive moves toward the guerrillas. For

Botero, covering the hostage stories was even more overwhelming than it was for us. He made so many trips into the jungle to try to gain access to the hostages that at times we feared he would collapse from exhaustion. What we all realized as the years went by was that there was little as journalists or filmmakers that we could do. All three of us attempted to escape the emotional grip of the difficult and consuming subject by taking on new projects, far away from the jungle prison camps.

More than a year into our hiatus from the hostage story, the three of us reunited on the topic when the trial of FARC commander Simón Trinidad took place in U.S. district court. It was during the fall of 2006 that we realized the scope of this book was so much greater than the story of the American hostages. Our book was the story of a four-decades-old guerrilla movement that grew to include the most wealthy and lethal insurgent army in the world. The FARC's extraordinary rise was linked to one of the most ill-fated policies of the United States in the last half century. The disastrous multibillion-dollar plan to wage war on an herbaceous shrub, *Erythroxylum coca*, lured Tom, Marc, and Keith into the war on drugs and led directly to their five-and-a-half-year internment in FARC prison camps.

Over the years, Botero had been an essential source, granting us hours and hours of his time, deliberately unfolding the history and culture of his complicated country. During those long conversations, he guided us into the mysterious world of the FARC with stories of his travels into the mountains and the jungle. We heard how he'd raised the ire of the Colombian government, how he'd infuriated the top FARC commanders, and how the mother of his children had been a victim of his country's violence. We realized that his contributions to the book were invaluable, and we invited him to coauthor it. The three of us worked together across continents for the next two years, until summer 2008, when Ingrid and the Americans were rescued by the Colombian military. To us, this seemed like a logical place to end a story we'd been covering for six and a half years. Botero, however, was packing for another trip to the jungle. We asked him what motivated him, what made him continue following the story of the remaining hostages, and what made him continue covering his country's endless civil war. It was then that we realized Botero was not only our most integral source and coauthor; he was a true protagonist, the person who fastened the book together.

It is admittedly difficult to craft a book with three colleagues in two languages over the course of six years and hundreds of hours. We spent a great deal of time flushing out the political complexities of Colombia and its relationship to the United States, and we worked diligently to maintain journalistic balance when our coauthor became part of the story. During the weaving of this tale, there were many events and challenges that would have derailed most other projects. Logistical, emotional, and political differences among us ping-ponged across continents via e-mail, video chats, and occasional meetings in D.C., Bogotá, New York, and Miami. Together, we hammered out the ideas behind this story. Our work was punctuated by fights about style, translations, and edits. In the end, we always remained dedicated to what we believe is an incredibly important story, and a book that could not have come about in any other way.

Victoria Bruce and Karin Hayes
October 2009

HOSTAGE NATION

1

"These Gringos Fell to Us from the Sky!"

On the morning of February 13, 2003, a group of sixteen guerrillas—part of an elite mobile unit of the Fuerzas Armadas Revolucionarias de Colombia (FARC)—were making their way across the foothills of Colombia's Eastern Cordillera. In the brilliant morning light, they could not see an airplane, but they were sure that one had circled above because of the familiar sound of a turboprop engine. Reynel, the commander of the group, told his unit that the plane was either a crop duster or a spy plane, because only fumigation and reconnaissance planes flew into the remote territories between the foot of the Andean mountain range and the low-lying Amazonian jungle. Fumigation planes were more common, and over the years, the guerrillas had shot down several. The crop dusters were manned by one pilot (usually an American or a foreigner from Central America under contract to a U.S. corporation) and equipped with tanks full of highly concentrated glyphosate—a toxic herbicide produced by the U.S. chemical company Monsanto. The targets were coca plants, which would wither and die if the chemical was applied correctly, but if pilots overshot the coca fields or the glyphosate drifted in the wind, it could wipe out rain forest or crops of yuca, soy, and corn. Occasionally, larger planes would fly over at altitudes out of reach of the guerrillas' automatic rifles. These crews

FARC (Fuerzas Armadas Revolucionarias de Colombia) "Special Forces" guerrillas trained to protect commanders at a camp in Caquetá, Colombia. Photo: Carlos Villalón.

were American, and the payloads were U.S.-supplied reconnaissance equipment designed to gather intelligence on FARC movements and identify drug labs and coca fields for the spray missions. The guerrillas knew that if the gringo "spies," with their high-tech instruments, were able to see or hear them under the jungle canopy, the Colombian army would not be far behind—and would be coming in to kill them. So it was with great satisfaction that an eighteen-year-old guerrilla named Jaison overheard his superior, a female guerrilla called "La Pilosa," receiving permission from her commander to shoot down the enemy plane:

> LA PILOSA: There is a bug flying by here, very low. . . . Hey, if it's a
> fumigator, could we burn it?
> EL PAISA: [Yes, if] it's low, burn that tail.

The Cessna crew had been in the air for an hour on their flight from Bogotá. Their next stop was the Larandia military base in southern Colombia, where they would refuel. With only thirty miles to go, "out of the blue the engine just spooled down . . . *pshhhheeew*," says copilot Thomas Howes.

"What's happening?" yelled Keith Stansell, a technician in the back of the plane.

"That's an engine failure, sir," pilot Tommy Janis shot back.

Stansell grabbed the radio to call the base:

"Magic Worker, Magic Worker, Mutt 01 is declaring Mayday. We have lost engine."

In the cockpit, Janis quickly calculated that the plane could not make it over the crest of the mountain range to land at the Larandia base. The terrain below was covered by densely forested hills. Howes knew the plane could glide on descent, but he didn't see any suitable place for a landing and didn't think they would survive the crash. Janis tried to restart the engine, but there was no response. "I cursed myself for trusting a single-engine plane for this type of work," Howes says. He'd logged thousands of hours of flight time in this aircraft and had had some very close calls. But never had he been so sure he would die. He pulled hard on his shoulder straps and reached over to secure Janis as the pilot scoured the ground, searching desperately for a place to land the plane. A second technician, Marc Gonsalves, hurried to secure the gear, making sure that all of it was tightly fastened so that they wouldn't be hit by flying equipment in the crash. Then he prayed to Jesus to forgive him for his sins and protect his wife and his three children.

STANSELL: Magic Worker, Magic Worker, Phoenix Ops, Phoenix Ops. Mutt 01, we are north 015617, west 0752958. Does not look like we are going to be able to find a suitable terrain. How copy?

GROUND CONTROL: That's right. I copy, sir. Activate your beacon?

STANSELL: Roger that. . . . Continue to update, sir. We are looking for a place on the ridge to set down.

Suddenly, looking out of the left side of the plane, Janis saw a clearing about the size of a soccer field in the middle of the forest and aimed for the spot. "We're going to hit very hard," Howes yelled to the crew in the back.

GROUND CONTROL: Mutt 01, this is Magic Worker, say, uh, say souls on board.

STANSELL: There are five souls on board, sir. Tom Howes, Tom Janis, pilots; Keith Stansell, Marc Gonsalves, operators. Four of us and one host-nation rider.

GROUND CONTROL: Copy.

STANSELL: We love you, buddy. Man, we're just lookin' for a spot here.

GROUND CONTROL: Mutt 01, Magic Worker, what you say again lat and long?

GONSALVES: 0151 north, 07530 west.

It was eerily quiet in the plane as Janis maneuvered the gliding aircraft in a wide arc. For a moment, Howes thought they had too much speed—that they would overshoot the site—and he pushed away thoughts of how his death would affect his five-year-old son. On the ground, the guerrillas, unaware of the engine failure and that the plane was about to crash-land, raised their weapons. The plane's metallic body reflected the sun, converting it into a sparkling target. In a matter of seconds, bullets crashed against the belly of the aircraft. The Colombian army picked up the guerrillas' radio transmissions as the insurgents shot at the plane:

EL PAISA: It sounds good over there. Can you hear?

GUERRILLA NUMBER TWO: Yes.

EL PAISA: I hope the SOB gets knocked down.

GUERRILLA NUMBER TWO: I hope they waste them.

Stansell was glad that he'd called home to Georgia that morning. He'd wanted to make sure that his two kids and his schoolteacher fiancée were awake and getting ready for school. Before he hung up, he told them that he loved them. Then he picked up the radio:

STANSELL: Down. We are going down now.

GONSALVES: 0152 north, 07530 west.

STANSELL: We are going in.

GROUND CONTROL: Mutt 01, Magic Worker . . . Mutt 01, Magic Worker. Say status. . . . Mutt 01, Magic Worker. Say status.

As the Cessna drew a mile-wide curve on its crash-landing approach, Derek Harvey, the mission's administrative coordinator at the American embassy in Bogotá, received Stansell's Mayday call and communicated by radio with him as the plane descended. On board, the Cessna's transponder relayed the same coordinates to Key West, Florida, where a Department of Defense (DOD) counternarcotics task force traced the path of the plane on a computer screen as it arced across the forest backdrop and came to an abrupt stop. After that, says Harvey, "we tried to call them on cell phones; we continued on their emergency radios. And we never heard from them."

From two hundred yards away, the guerrillas saw the plane crash-land, its fuselage splitting in two and its wings exploding. Inside the plane, the crew heard metal tearing away and felt an immense impact as the landing gear ripped off and the belly of the plane scraped the ground. "We were sliding and everything in my vision was bouncing," Gonsalves wrote in the book *Out of Captivity*. "I saw a slit of light pour through the front of the aircraft as the cabin was torn open like a can of tuna." The guerrillas watched as the plane continued rolling downhill, covered in a cloud of dirt and smoke, until everything suddenly stopped and all was silent. La Pilosa radioed her commander, El Paisa:

LA PILOSA: We knocked it down!

EL PAISA: Huh, uh-huh, son of a bitch, man, that fucking son of a bitch.

Believing they'd shot down the plane, the guerrillas were exuberant. "When we saw the plane fall to the ground and explode, we couldn't believe it. Many of us were unable to speak, as if we were frozen by the surprise," says Jaison. "Then we began to celebrate like crazy, raising our weapons and shouting victory cries." The celebration was interrupted by the commander, who shot his rifle into the air, scolding his subordinates. "He said that we were acting like kids with a piñata, and he ordered us to start running down to the remains of the airplane to see if there were any survivors. None of us thought that any-one would be alive after such a large impact, so we hurled ourselves, stumbling down the hill, thinking that we would have to pull some bod-ies from the remains of the plane." When the guerrillas came upon the wreckage, they saw one crew member emerge, then another, and then one more. To Jaison, it was like watching ghosts materialize from a cloud of dust.

At the Larandia military base—just seventeen minutes by air from where the plane crashed—Sfc. Juan Pérez and Sfc. Bo Wynn of the U.S. Special Forces team received orders from their commander at the U.S. Embassy in Bogotá to get to the helicopter fields. They hurriedly packed their SAR (search and rescue) gear—canteens, first-aid supplies, arms and ammunition, compasses, flares, radios, and GPS units—and rushed to the airfield. Special Forces commander Lt. Col. Duke Christie was aware that the Special Forces training team was not per-mitted to take on a rescue mission in enemy territory. "But since we had an SF capability so close by," Christie told journalist Robert Kaplan, "I wanted to give my superiors the option of changing the ROEs [rules of engagement] for this extraordinary circumstance." Pérez and Wynn had been training Colombian troops in antinarcotics missions and had actually been instructing the Colombians in precisely the type of SAR operation that now needed to commence.

Minutes went by, with no movement of the Special Forces team or call to action by the U.S. military commander, Col. P. K. Keen. The delay incensed a Colombian-American veteran of the U.S. Army who worked closely with the four aboard the Cessna. "I called the MILGROUP [military advisory group] commander and said, 'Get 'em!' Keen could have said, 'Here goes my career, but get them!' There were planes and people standing beside the aircraft from the State Department; U.S. Special Forces guys were standing by, ready to give their lives."

In the pile of debris at the crash site, Marc Gonsalves had no idea if he was hurt. He couldn't feel any pain, only the intoxicating force of adrenaline pulsing through his body. Frantically, he scrambled about the wreckage, searching the plane for their survival gear, their guns, and their mission orders—which he did not want to fall into the hands of the enemy. But everything was covered with dirt, and it was difficult to see. Stansell was already out of the plane when he heard the sound of rapid gunfire. He looked over his shoulder and saw the guerrillas coming toward them. The Colombian sergeant who was aboard the plane with the Americans wanted to run. "He kept yelling, '¡Guerrillas! ¡Guerrillas!' " Stansell says. "I told him in English that he could do what he had to do, that my only concern at that point was getting the pilots out of the plane."

As the guerrillas advanced, Stansell, terrified the plane would catch fire, shook Tommy Janis and yelled at him to get out of the plane. The pilot was barely coherent. "I told him that everyone was okay. I said, 'But the guerrillas are here, and they're going to take us.' " Janis's head was cut badly, and he could barely move. Next to him, Howes's body slumped forward in the cockpit, his face imbedded in the broken windshield. Stansell thought the copilot was dead, and he yelled for Gonsalves to help him pull both pilots from the plane. When they pulled Howes out, they were relieved to discover that he was alive and could walk, but his injuries looked grave. Blood poured from a gash above his eye and from another across his chin. Stansell was sure Howes would die. Stansell had already disposed of their guns, and as between fifty and sixty armed guerrillas approached them, pointing semiautomatic weapons, Stansell raised his hands to surrender, shouting, "No armas, no armas."

La Pilosa yelled for the guerrillas to surround the Americans. "What do you think, Reynel?" the delighted woman said to her superior. "These gringos fell to us from the sky!" Knowing the Americans would have called in their position as their plane went down, the guerrillas forced the men away from the crash site, pushing them up a steep hill as they stumbled on the pitted ground. Behind them, other guerrillas searched the plane and collected every piece of material that wasn't completely destroyed. Then they planted land mines around the site to impede the Colombian rescue troops, who would soon be on their way.

Howes, Gonsalves, and Stansell were forced down a hill, into a ravine, and up a slope, ahead of Tommy Janis and Colombian sergeant Luis Alcides Cruz. "We came to a small structure, a little building, and we were given some lemonade water to drink," Gonsalves says. One of the guerrillas told them not to worry, that they wouldn't be hurt. None of the three men actually believed it was true. Gonsalves was terrified. He expected that at any minute he would be tortured and killed. Stansell, too, thought they would die. "If you're going to kill us," he pleaded to one of the guerrillas, who he assumed was in charge, "please give us a respectable death."

The men sat for several minutes as the guerrillas assessed their condition and tended to Howes's head with a cloth bandage. Then from the distance came the unmistakable *tat-tat-tat* of helicopter rotors. The three men were shoved into a trench next to the hut. Stansell thought the helicopters probably carried members of the Colombian army—possibly accompanied by U.S. forces—responding to his Mayday call. Now he realized that having the Colombian army there would be the worst-possible thing. He was sure there was no way for a successful rescue. A dozen guerrillas surrounded them—all with guns ready. If the Colombian military got too close, it would be a massacre. For what seemed like a very long time, the guerrillas pinned the hostages to the ground.

Howes remembers climbing out of the trench when the helicopters finally left. He looked back toward the crash site and saw Tommy Janis and Sergeant Cruz being marched toward them down an uneven slope. Several guerrillas held guns to their backs as they walked, and a few more led the way. He thought that Janis seemed to be walking okay and hoped that he hadn't been injured too badly in the crash. He still couldn't believe that Janis had been able to land the plane and that they'd all lived through it. As Howes, Stansell, and Gonsalves were forced away from the hut, Howes expected that Janis and Cruz would arrive there a few minutes later and be given the same treatment: the guerrillas would give them lemonade to drink and assess their physical condition.

At the airfield in Larandia, Pérez, and Wynn were still waiting for orders from the U.S. Embassy to board the available Black Hawk helicopters. Several hours went by, but the order never came. Then the two Green Berets were told to "stand down." Colonel Keen, who was calling the shots from his office at the U.S. Embassy in Bogotá, would later explain his decision in a 2008 interview: "We weren't putting any U.S. military folks on the ground. It all unfolded very quickly. We were trying to determine where they went down, whether the area was secure or not. We discussed it in the embassy, that there were some Special Forces guys at Larandia. I don't recall when we decided to delay or hold them. We wanted the Colombian military to secure the area. We wanted to determine what situation we had on the ground there. We weren't running a military operation. We were interested in getting there quickly but didn't want to put more people at unnecessary risk."

2

Rules of Engagement

Within minutes of the crash, at the request of Keen and U.S. ambassador Anne Patterson, the Colombian military in Larandia embarked on a rescue attempt. But initial efforts would be feeble at best. "Our response was quite slow," Colombian army colonel Gustavo Enrique Avendaño said in a 2006 court testimony. "At nine a.m., we were informed about an incident relating to an aircraft, and that there had been individuals kidnapped. Immediately, we received the geographic coordinates." Avendaño contacted the Colombian National Police and readied his own troops at the base. (The National Police are responsible for civilian policing and are under the command of the minister of defense.) But there was a problem: In another part of the country, the Colombian health minister's plane had crashed, and Avendaño's fleet of helicopters had gone to assist in the rescue. The battalion normally had sixteen personnel-transport helicopters and four helicopters equipped with artillery. "Unfortunately, that morning we only had one personnel-transport helicopter," recalled Avendaño. The lone helicopter, which could carry only five troops, departed at 9:50 a.m. from Larandia and arrived at the crash scene at 10:17 a.m.—more than an hour after the plane had crashed. The Colombian troops found the burned wreckage of the plane, but the immediate area was deserted.

With the single transport helicopter, Avendaño began ferrying soldiers, five at a time, to the site. An hour later, several helicopters from a nearby military base arrived and began taking soldiers to the crash area. By 11:00 a.m., Avendaño joined sixty men on the ground. "When I arrived at the location, our main mission was to rescue the crew," he said. A local man who arrived in the area gave the troops information as to the direction that the guerrillas had taken when they left with the hostages. "We proceeded north of where the aircraft had crashed. At one p.m., two thousand meters from where the plane went down, we unfortunately found two bodies." One of the dead men wore blue jeans, a white T-shirt, and sneakers and appeared to be an American. He had been shot in the back of the head at close range, the bullet having entered the back of his neck and exited through his forehead. The other, a Colombian, had been shot twice—once through his clavicle and once through his back. There was no trace of the other three Americans. At the small house where Gonsalves, Stansell, and Howes had been just four hours earlier, soldiers found hundreds of shell casings for automatic rifles, and Avendaño deter-

On February 15, 2003, two days after the crash of the California Microwave Systems Cessna, locals investigate the wreckage. Photo: Reuters TV.

mined that was the position from which the guerrillas had shot at the plane.

"We continued to secure the scene," Avendaño said, "the area where the plane was found, where the house was, where the bodies were found, so that the national prosecutor's office and their personnel and a representative from the American government or the embassy in Colombia could do what they had to do." Avendaño then ordered his troops to search the perimeter two miles from the crash. Knowing the guerrillas would have planted land mines, the soldiers moved very slowly behind a demining unit. Their search netted a plethora of litter left by the guerrillas, who, it was obvious, had made an expeditious retreat. There were two backpacks belonging to the guerrillas, grenades, note cards with the code that the guerrillas used when communicating on the radio, and a 9mm gun. There were approximately 950 rounds from various-caliber semiautomatic rifles and machine guns, and twenty-three antipersonnel mines. Between the house and the bodies, the Colombian troops found two wallets. "So we gathered the wallets and put them into a bag to hand over to the prosecutor's office so that they could have the evidence gathered at the scene." Because the downing of the aircraft and the subsequent murder and kidnapping of civilians had not happened during military combat, the investigation of the crash would not be conducted by the Colombian army, but by the Colombian prosecutor's office. "The bodies remained on-site because we could not touch the bodies," said Avendaño. "All we could do is protect the scene."

During their first few hours of captivity, the guerrillas continued pushing Gonsalves, Howes, and Stansell away from the crash site. When they felt sufficiently safe from the immediate threat of the Colombian military, the guerrillas ordered the Americans to strip down to their underwear. Stansell was struck by the appearance of their captors. He'd been working on antidrug missions in Colombia for two years and had been briefed over and over on Colombian insurgent groups. He'd been told the FARC was an enormous and well-equipped army of narco-terrorists, but what he encountered hardly fit the image of a cohesive terrorist force. Most were no more than teenagers. Their uniforms were shabby. Each wore a different type of hat in a different way, and to Stansell, they all seemed incredibly ignorant—no more than bullies with anti-American attitudes and Russian guns. The guerrillas confiscated all of their belongings, including wallets and family photos. After a strip search, which, the guerrillas said, they conducted to look for possible transmitting microchips planted on the Americans' bodies, the men were given back their clothes and told to move out.

Several hours later, the group heard helicopters approaching in the distance. In a panic, the guerrillas ordered Stansell, Howes, and Gonsalves to cross a rough clearing and head toward a house on the other side. "The Colombian military couldn't open fire on our position because they would have killed us," wrote Howes in *Out of Captivity*. "The FARC didn't try to shoot the helo down because the gunner would have returned fire on them. So we were all standing there looking up at them, and they were looking down at us as they hovered overhead." The guerrillas shoved the men to the ground and forced them to crawl on their bellies under the tree cover until the helicopters lost sight of them and left the area.

The guerrillas regrouped and continued their march toward the mountains. As the initial shock of their crash and capture began to subside, the men's thoughts turned to their families and colleagues. How would their loved ones react to the news of the crash? What had happened to Tommy Janis and Sergeant Cruz? "The gringos asked about the other two guys that were in the plane," the young guerrilla Jaison recalls, "but the comrade did not answer them. They asked the same question several times, until the comrade broke the silence and told them not to worry about the situation of their friends, because they were dead." La Pilosa delivered the line to Tom Howes with a chill in her voice, almost proudly. As the only one of the three who could speak Spanish, Howes turned to Stansell and Gonsalves. "She says she killed Tommy J. herself, and she would kill us, too."

Without the capability to conduct a nighttime search, Colonel Avendaño airlifted his troops from the area at sunset. Throughout the day, Colonel Keen worked with a team at the U.S. Embassy in Bogotá. "We set up an operations center made up of officers from the MILGROUP, members of the country team [U.S. government personnel working out of the embassy], to monitor the situation," says Keen.

"We worked with the Colombians to focus on the situation. We had briefings to keep SOUTHCOM [Southern Command—a joint command of the U.S. Army, Navy, Air Force, Marine Corps, and Coast Guard that is in charge of military operations in Central and South America] informed of what we knew, and what the Colombians were finding. The Colombians were trying to get information from the FARC, trying to determine how to locate the Americans, trying to understand what the FARC's intentions were." By 12:30 a.m. on February 14, the embassy had issued an authorization order to put U.S. agents on the ground in the morning. At 4:00 a.m., Brig. Gen. Remo Butler, commander of Special Operations in Central and South America, arrived with a team of eight people. "We got there; we immediately checked into a hotel, got an hour or so of sleep, and then went over to the embassy for the first briefing. There was a great sense of urgency on getting those Americans back. I worked at the embassy for a while, got in contact with the people in SOUTHCOM, and at my headquarters in Puerto Rico, and kind of gave them my initial assessment."

Before 7:00 a.m. on February 14, Avendaño's troops returned, to find the crime scene compromised by some local men picking through the wreckage. By 10:45 a.m.—more than twenty-six hours after the crash—Butler, Lawrence "Steve" McCune (the site manager of the company responsible for the Cessna missions), and FBI agent Alejandro Barbeito arrived on the scene. McCune would identify the body of the dead American as that of pilot Tommy Janis, and Barbeito would take possession of the remains. Members of the Colombian prosecutor's office examined the crime scene and took possession of the body of Sgt. Luis Alcides Cruz. An Alcohol, Tobacco, Firearms, and Explosives (ATF) team inspected the equipment left in the wreckage and reported that it had been sufficiently destroyed by the crew before their capture. Within an hour, the bodies of Janis and Cruz were taken to the Larandia base and loaded onto a plane that would take them to Bogotá.

Author Robert Kaplan, who was on the scene in Larandia, writes in *Imperial Grunts* that the Green Berets stationed at Larandia were demoralized by not being allowed to take part in the rescue. "We lost the initiative after we were made to stand down the first night," Sergeant Pérez told Kaplan. "We were so afraid of getting our guys killed that we let 'em get captured." By midmorning of the fourteenth, the situation of the kidnapped Americans had turned from an emergency to a long-haul mission. Kaplan writes:

In a hostage situation akin to a kidnapping, the first 24 hours are crucial, particularly the first night following the abduction. It may be the only time when a rescue squad can effectively keep the perpetrators from moving their prey out of the vicinity. All the satellite and other high-tech surveillance that the Americans would subsequently bring to bear on the crisis would never make up for that original 24-hour delay. The middle level officers had been ready to move, but then "Washington" took over.

"You have to remember," argues General Butler, "Colombia is a sovereign nation and you do not just go into another sovereign nation and attempt to take over." Butler worked with several Colombian generals and was pleased with how aggressively they were handling the situation. "We all worked together trying to formulate a plan to prevent the FARC from getting the hostages out of the area. Time was of the essence. The Colombians set up a cordon around the area. It was very simple. You look at the terrain, and you say, Okay, there are hostages, don't know their condition. How fast can they move? So we put a cordon at a distance greater than possible for them to move. The strategy was to seal the guerrillas and hostages inside the zone and capture them. If they tried to break through the cordon, the Colombian troops would try to grab them on the way. That area is very dense. It's mountainous, jungles—very difficult terrain to move in. And it looked like no matter what we did, they were always just a half a step in front of us. The Colombians expended an incredible amount of assets. And when you look at the assets that they have, and what they expended, and the amount of money that they spent on this project, it was tremendous. We could not have asked for better support."

Butler also defends Colonel Keen's handling of the situation and the decision not to let the Special Forces in: "If you ran into there helter-skelter hell-bent, the chances are very great that the FARC would have ambushed them because they probably were expecting somebody to make an attempt to do that. You don't go into Colombia and just start shooting up. A Special Forces guy will never tell you he can't do something: 'We can do anything. Just give us a gun and some bullets, and we can do it.' I think it was a military decision, and a political decision, to keep the Special Forces there and let them advise the Colombians, because, *one*, they didn't know where the hostages were, and, *two*, they had no idea what they would've been walking into."

John McLaughlin, former commander of the State Department Air Wing that oversaw the antinarcotics missions, told BBC News that the poor initial response to the crash was the result of having no "pre-approved agreement among all the participants on how to launch a rescue team." Had the plane crash occurred in another combat zone outside of Colombia, the crew would likely have come under the protection of the U.S. military. The *Defense Federal Acquisition Regulation Supplement* states, "The government at its sole discretion may authorize or may require the use of certain Government-provided logistical or in-country support." In such hot spots as Bosnia and Somalia, contractors were commonly aided by U.S. troops. However, in Colombia, even though downed aircraft and hostage taking were not uncommon, the U.S. military actually had no direct responsibility to undertake a rescue, because the entirety of the antinarcotics work in Colombia was overseen by the State Department rather than the DOD.

McLaughlin also felt that the men's status as contractors, rather than as active-duty U.S. military personnel, was part of the reason the military refused to act immediately after the crash. "If you had military guys flying the mission, they would have the full weight of DOD behind them, ensuring that all the things needed for air safety would be in place before they take on such a mission," he said. In a 2008 interview in Germany, Keen, who had been promoted to major general, would argue that this was not the case. "It would be the same response," he said. "We would have the same capability to respond. If it was a downed aircraft, no one would be asking, 'Is this a contractor, DOD, military?' It would be 'Let's do what we can to locate and recover them.' "

In the days following the crash, the immediate response of the U.S.

government was to bury the story as quickly as possible. A former FBI hostage negotiator working on the case felt that there were several factors behind the government's desire to keep the kidnapping under wraps. "First and foremost was the government's belief that media coverage would only enhance Tom, Marc, and Keith's status, and thereby make them more valuable hostages for the FARC to leverage," he said. "But in this case, the FARC were clearly aware of their value from day one, regardless of what was or was not in the media. I also believe they kept the story under wraps to avoid bringing unwanted political or public attention to the classified program the guys were working on, and to avoid unwanted scrutiny and criticism of the government's activities in Colombia." Adam Isacson, director of the Center for International Policy in Washington, D.C., agreed with this assessment. "Obviously it's embarrassing to the U.S., because [the kidnapping] causes people to ask questions about the policy in Colombia and the role of contractors in general," he said. The men's role as contractors, rather than as active military personnel, also helped push the story from the headlines. Myles Frechette, the former U.S. ambassador to Colombia, had put it bluntly to the *St. Petersburg Times* in 2000: "It's very handy to have an outfit not part of the U.S. armed forces, obviously . . . if somebody gets killed or whatever, you can say it's not a member of the armed forces. Nobody wants to see American military men killed."

3

The Elegant Guerrilla

On December 31, 2004, nearly two years after the guerrillas marched Howes, Stansell, and Gonsalves off into mountains, a stocky middle-aged man, bald and bespectacled, sat handcuffed and shackled aboard a U.S. government Gulfstream jet, bound for the United States. He wore the clothing of a prisoner from the Cómbita maximum-security prison outside of Bogotá. He was flanked by six agents of the North American government: five FBI agents and one DEA agent. Before boarding the jet, fifty-four-year-old FARC commander Simón Trinidad, the highest-ranking FARC member ever to be captured, raised his fist in defiance and repeatedly yelled out to reporters, "*¡Viva las FARC! ¡Viva Manuel Marulanda! ¡Viva Simón Bolívar!*"

The 150 years of violence that prompted Simón Trinidad to join the FARC can be traced back to Simón Bolívar, the Venezuelan revolutionary who helped liberate South America from the Spanish. In 1821 Bolívar created Gran Colombia, an area encompassing present-day Colombia, Venezuela, Ecuador, and Panama. "The Liberator" named himself president and appointed one of his military generals, Francisco de Paula Santander, as vice president. The two men soon became bitter political rivals. Their followers split into two factions, which, by the late 1840s, became the Partido Liberal, whose adherents included those

FARC founder Manuel Marulanda in the early years of the guerrilla organization. Marulanda earned the nickname "Tirofijo" ("Sureshot") for his excellent aim with a rifle. Photo: Cuadernos de Campaña.

in the oligarchy who were aligned with Santander, and the Partido Conservador, whose members included the oligarchs who sided with Bolívar. While the parties took the names Liberal and Conservative, the titles did not correlate at all to the ideological meaning of the words *liberal* and *conservative* in the North American political vernacular. The Conservative party wanted a more centralized government, something that had never been achieved in Colombia due to a weak military, the country's treacherous geography, and a lack of cohesion among the country's departments (states). The Liberal party was more inclined toward decentralization. And although clergy members aligned with the Conservative party because of its platform to give more power to the Church, there were no great ideological, economic, or policy differences between the two parties. Within each party, there were those who leaned politically to the Left, those who were centrists, and those who were politically on the Right.

Over the nineteenth and twentieth centuries, one party would hold power for several four-year terms before losing the presidential election to the other party. The elected party would reap all the perks of incumbency, while members of the opposition party would be stripped of most ruling-class benefits. Periods of lasting violence were commonplace between Liberals and Conservatives from the parties' beginnings, with thousands killed in eleven major clashes before the dawn of the twentieth century. A civil war began in 1899, when Liberals declared war against the Conservative government after accusing the Conservative party of maintaining power through fraudulent elections. The Thousand Days' War claimed an estimated 250,000 lives, but it ultimately failed to overthrow the Conservatives. The Conservative party remained in power until 1930, when the Liberal party was able to convince a Colombian electorate, suffering from an economic depression, to elect Liberal candidate Alfonso López. The Liberals remained in power until the 1946 election of moderate Conservative Mariano Ospina.

During Ospina's term, conflict between the Liberals and Conservatives continued, resulting in increasing partisan hostility. Then in 1948, the assassination of Liberal party presidential candidate Jorge Eliécer Gaitán brought about a tremendous surge in violence, which would cause 300,000 deaths throughout the 1950s, earning the decade the name La Violencia. Killings became more and more sinister and grotesque. Bodies—mostly those of Liberals—turned up all over the country, mutilated, burned, and decapitated. Peasants who considered themselves members of the Liberal party (mainly because they followed the party of their *patrones*) were targeted by death squads sponsored by the Conservatives. Liberal peasants and members of an emerging Communist movement counterattacked, forming gangs and self-defense units. All the while, the Liberal elite in Bogotá, mostly unaffected by the violence, turned a blind eye to the bloodshed.

It was one of those rural Liberals, a young salesman in his late teens named Pedro Marín, who went into hiding in the hills of the Cordillera Central and emerged to become one of the most successful guerrilla leaders in history. Of that period, Marín later wrote, "The police and armed Conservatives would destroy the villages, kill inhabitants, burn their houses, take people prisoner and disappear them, steal livestock and rape the women. The goal of the Conservative groups was to inflict terror on the population and take advantage of the goods the peasants had." Rather than wait idly for his impending murder at the hands of Conservatives, Marín took the nom de guerre Manuel Marulanda (after a murdered union leader) and gathered the necessary tools to launch a guerrilla war. "The Liberals wanted to fight back," he wrote. In addition, Marín brought together Communist party members, who were also targets of the Conservatives. "Men and women formed groups that had little stability, but as the residents in the pueblos began to hear about these groups, more people joined. Like many newly founded groups, they lacked experience and adequate organization. But they made their way to the spine of the Cordillera Central, and for those who had been essentially condemned to death by Conservatives, this became a place of salvation."

Marulanda had very little formal education, but he quickly became a skilled leader and an excellent guerrilla tactician—his proficiency as a marksman earned him the nickname "Tirofijo," or "Sureshot." In 1953, after a military coup ousted the Conservative president Laureano Gómez, Gen. Gustavo Rojas offered amnesty to Liberals who had taken up arms. After many who turned themselves in were murdered, Marulanda and the majority of his guerrilla troops vowed never to return to civilian life and to continue their fight against the entrenched and corrupt political establishment. La Violencia came to a close at the end of 1957, when the Liberals and Conservatives joined together in a power-sharing relationship they called the National Front.

Unlike his charismatic contemporaries Fidel Castro and Che Guevara, Marulanda gave no rousing speeches. He lived an almost hermetic lifestyle and remained mostly an enigma to the general Colombian population and to many in his ranks. Physically, he was unassuming—short, stocky, and unsmiling—and in his later years, he had a profound slouch and sagging features, which gave the appearance of a grumpy grandfather rather than the commanding leader of a vast guerrilla army. While he demanded his troops be in full military uniform, Marulanda was most often photographed wearing the clothes of a campesino—

long-sleeved plaid shirts with white undershirts and loose blue work pants tucked into high rubber boots, a machete and a pistol tucked into a belt around his waist.

Marulanda's prowess in battle was legendary throughout Colombia and embellished to the point that he was said to have taken down entire battalions single-handedly. Over the years, his army grew into the thousands, becoming well disciplined and organized. The guerrillas adopted a Marxist ideology and considered themselves Communists, but remained unconnected to Cuba or the Soviet Union. The FARC commander presided over and was considered one of the members of the Secretariat, a five-member body that was responsible for all military and political decisions, but he also had to answer to a fairly cumbersome Central High Command of approximately twenty-five members. The Secretariat also controlled the guerrilla army's finances, coordination with other guerrilla groups, and military strategies. Except for Marulanda, members of the Secretariat were all of equal rank, and although some guerrilla leaders questioned the decision, Marulanda never appointed a second in command or a successor. In the field, FARC troops were divided into sixty fronts, each with a senior commander and a second in command. In 1993, the then seven Secretariat members were decentralized and placed in seven blocs spanning the entire country. The move was made for security reasons after a 1990 attack on Marulanda's headquarters, as well as to give the Secretariat a greater command over regional operations. In essence, by the mid-1990s, FARC troops were spread throughout almost all of rural Colombia. Smaller cells of guerrillas masqueraded as civilians in Bogotá, Medellín, and Cali—the major population centers situated among three Andean cordilleras that trisect the country from north to south. The land in the majority of FARC-controlled regions lacked any significant network of roads and thus was ideal for guerrilla warfare. It was extremely difficult for Colombian soldiers to fight the insurgents by conducting standard military operations. Also inhibiting the Colombian forces was the fact that for many decades, members of the poor rural civilian population, the campesinos, felt abandoned by the government and were mostly uncooperative when dealing with soldiers searching for guerrillas.

Although the guerrilla foot soldiers lived simply, in the mid-1990s, the FARC, after struggling for thirty years to fund its troops, grew to be the richest guerrilla army in the world by becoming a major player in the country's most lucrative black-market export. By 1998, estimations of the FARC's annual income from the taxing and trafficking of cocaine and heroin varied widely, but it was most often reported to be in the low hundreds of millions of dollars. To the guerrillas, money from the drug business was considered completely legitimate because the bounty was shared among a multitude of players, who crossed every level of Colombian society from street thug to oligarch. Drug money permeated every government agency, every branch of the military, every elected political level, including—at least in the case of Ernesto Samper in 1994—the president of Colombia. "Legitimate" banks or financial institutions were infiltrated, as well as many rural businesses and dozens of self-defense and paramilitary groups. Even the Catholic Church was not immune; in the 1980s, donations and newly constructed churches came compliments of Medellín drug boss Pablo Escobar. In essence, the term *narco* could be a prefix to groups or individuals from every category of Colombian citizenry. The remainder of the guerrillas' vast income in the late 1990s came from the kidnapping and extortion of over a thousand Colombian citizens a year. Ransoms paid ranged from several hundred to several million dollars.

In 2003, when Howes, Stansell, and Gonsalves were captured, the FARC was estimated to number between fifteen and twenty thousand troops. The rank and file came mostly from poor rural villages, where schools were ill-equipped or simply didn't exist. FARC soldiers, mostly in their teens and early twenties, both male and female, strolled freely through villages where for decades there had been no Colombian government presence. Impoverished children were in awe of the guerrillas, with their clean uniforms, military caps, and glistening rifles. Given the extreme poverty, the idea of joining the guerrillas held great allure. Most believed life in the FARC would be better than at home. Food was much better and always plentiful; teenage guerrilla soldiers were taught to read and write. FARC soldiers received no monetary compensation, but often, deep familial bonds formed between commanders and the young guerrillas.

The FARC's official minimum age for recruits is fifteen, but some are as young as thirteen, and journalists have reported seeing guerrillas as young as ten. Secretariat member Iván Ríos defended the recruitment of children in the book *El Orden de la Guerra*, arguing that with the horrors of Colombia and the realities of an endless civil war, the FARC is more of a salvation for children than a death sentence. Paramilitaries come into villages and massacre entire families they feel are aligned with the FARC. The constant battles among paramilitaries, the Colombian military, and the guerrillas have displaced more than four million people. And with the government unable to provide for the massive population of internal refugees, thousands of children are left with few options; they join the guerrillas or find their way to the major cities to beg, become child prostitutes, or spend days in dumps looking for food and desperately sniffing rags soaked with gasoline to stave off hunger. "The children love the guerrillas because here there is love, warmth for them," says Ríos. "We will not lie and say that there are no children in the organization. There are children in the organization, but they are particular cases and practically obligatory cases."

Upon entrée into the FARC, the youngest soldiers are made to prepare food, plant crops, tidy the encampments, and pass messages among commanders. They clean the large rifles but are given small pistols because the weight of the Russian-built AK-47s is too much for their small frames. For four hours a day, they are taught FARC ideology: The Colombian government is corrupt; the American government is imperialistic; FARC is the people's army; the FARC and the poor are persecuted by the state. With the FARC's form of limited Marxism having changed little in forty years, there is hardly more rhetoric to absorb. At sundown, they collapse onto plank beds. Above them, a black plastic tarp shields them from the ceaseless rain, and netting dissuades ravenous mosquitoes.

While nearly all FARC guerrillas—including those in commanding positions—entered the ranks from lives of destitute poverty, a handful of guerrillas came into the FARC from middle- or upper-class families, having university educations and deep ties to the oligarchy. And it was one of those few who in 2004 would become permanently entangled in the hostage drama of Howes, Stansell, and Gonsalves.

Simón Trinidad was born in Bogotá in 1950 as Ricardo Palmera, the pampered child of an upper-class family from Valledupar, a city of 350,000 in northeastern Colombia. Palmera was the seventh child of eleven sired by his father with five women. "It was a comfortable life financewise," Palmera says. "This allowed me to have a happy and pleasant childhood, go to school, to travel the country." There was a long tradition of political involvement in both his parents' families. His great-grandfather Federico Palmera was killed while fighting on the Liberal side during one of the many civil wars in the nineteenth century. His two grandfathers were active members of the Liberal party during the conflicts at the end of the nineteenth century and the beginning of the twentieth. His maternal grandfather, a successful textile businessman, Rodrigo Pineda, was the mayor of the large city of Bucaramanga in the 1930s.

In his early life, Palmera had little interest in politics or the elite formal education his family's social status afforded him. "Ricardo Palmera wasn't the most sensible of my schoolmates," says Luis Gabriel Jaramillo, "nor the most studious." Jaramillo remembers being in awe of Palmera's exceptional social skills, especially his prowess with the girls, when they attended the Swiss-Colombian School in Bogotá. "Already at our young age—ten, twelve, fourteen years—he presented himself as a successful man of the world. I admired him, and I was delighted with this miraculous sociability, with his grace of a distinguished Valentino." The schoolboys were all descendants of European immigrants, and most conducted themselves with inherited modesty and timidity. Palmera was the exception, Jaramillo says, "but he assumed his role without any presumption, which embodied him with the spirit of a brotherly leader."

Palmera was very close to his mother, Alix, who separated from his father in 1954. After the divorce, Ovidio Palmera would send Alix money each month from the proceeds of his two-hundred-acre farm, Los Mangos, on the outskirts of Valledupar. Although she was now a single mother, Alix never lacked an upper-class lifestyle. She employed a driver for her 1955 Chevrolet Bel Air, lived with her three children in a comfortable apartment in the north of Bogotá, and passed her days playing canasta. Palmera finished high school with terrible grades, but his social stature enabled him to attend and graduate from the private and left-leaning Jorge Tadeo Lozano University in Bogotá in 1975. After graduating, Palmera worked for an agrarian bank in Bogotá, the Caja de Crédito Agraria, Industrial y Minero, where he provided small loans to rural areas. By mid-1976, he returned to his father's home department of César with his new wife, Margarita. There, he helped manage the vast farms that belonged to his father, Valledupar's most prominent lawyer and a former senator from the Liberal party. According to Palmera's brother Jaime, it was during that period that Palmera and his father, who was a great admirer of Fidel Castro, became close political allies. "I believe that [the political positions of his father] not only influenced but were definitive," says Jaime. "Dad and Ricardo spent hours and hours talking about politics. I am sure that those chats marked my brother forever."

By the late 1970s, Palmera's wife, Margarita, opened a business in Valledupar, selling imported Italian jewelry. Palmera continued his career in banking and also took a teaching job at a state university. Even in the highest social circles, Palmera was considered a fancy man. He danced in the local clubs, rode horses for enjoyment, and loved the arts and theater. "He was so charming and intelligent," Lilián Castro, a Valledupar native and former friend of Palmera, told *The New York Times*. "Ricardo Palmera was every bit the gentleman." Friends would call him jovial, well mannered, and driven. But when it came to matters of social justice, there was a seriousness to Palmera's drive.

In 1979, Palmera and several of his university colleagues were captured at their homes and taken by the military to the Popa Battalion in Valledupar. That night, he was handcuffed, blindfolded, and taken in a cattle truck to a military headquarters in Barranquilla. "For five days, I was denied food. The first three days, I was denied anything to drink. I was also prevented from sleeping, and I was made to undergo questioning that was very fierce and that happened day or night. I was charged with supporting a guerrilla movement in Colombia." His interrogators accused Palmera of being a member of the ELN (Ejército de Liberación Nacional, the National Liberation Army, Colombia's second-largest guerrilla group), but at the time, Palmera had never met a member of any guerrilla group. He finally convinced the army of his innocence. After he had been forced to sign documents stating that he had been treated well and had not been tortured, the army released him. "When I returned to Valledupar, I learned that a few days after my capture they had also detained the doctor José David López, the lawyer René Costa, and the labor and syndicate director Víctor Mieles. Years later, the three were assassinated by the army."

Palmera's experience with the army fortified his rebellious spirit. By 1982, the Liberal party bifurcated, and the offshoot movement that Palmera joined, dubbed "New Liberalism," stood on the dangerous platform of antidrugs and anticorruption. "Basically, the program was to solve the problems of political corruption in the traditional parties, to fight against drugs, and to promote democracy," Palmera recalls. "Already in 1982, the drug problem had permeated throughout the entire Colombian society. The Atlantic region, the north region of the country, where I was living, had already suffered the negative consequences of drug trafficking very severely." Palmera became part of a civic movement that supported teachers and students from the university as candidates for the city council of Valledupar. Along with other left-leaning professionals, Palmera began to attend meetings to try to find ways to help the multitude of destitute Colombians who, they believed, were oppressed by the entrenched oligarchy. "It was all pure ideology for Ricardo," Edgardo Pupo, a close friend of Palmera told *The New York Times* in 2004. "He was convinced that the system here didn't work and that only a communist system would." Another friend and political colleague, Imelda Daza, remembers that Palmera became more and more fanatical in his views. "He was always criticizing us when he discovered us at parties, drinking rum and dancing. 'By drinking we are not going to change this country,' he'd say." Palmera was a known admirer of Joseph Stalin, and because of his increasingly severe nature, his contemporaries nicknamed him "the German."

In 1984, the FARC agreed to a cease-fire after successful negotiations with the government. For the first time since its formation, Manuel Marulanda's guerrilla army was gaining mainstream political acceptance. Out of the negotiations came a new political party, the Unión Patriótica. "It was not only the party of former guerrillas; it had a very wide political agenda," says Palmera, who immediately became a member. "Many people joined it—the Liberals, Conservatives, priests, democrats, patriots, people from many walks of life who were not necessarily Communist, socialist, or leftist." The new movement quickly became a political phenomenon; in 1986, its members were elected to seats in both houses of Congress and captured dozens of state and municipal executive and legislative offices. But the fragile peace that had come with the cease-fire and the FARC's induction into mainstream politics would not last long. The startling success of the Unión Patriótica was a threat to the Liberal and the Conservative parties, which had divided power for nearly two centuries, and the situation rapidly translated into violence. Unión Patriótica senators and mayors were assassinated, one after another. Party members were threatened with death and told to leave their cities or towns. Those who remained were brutally killed. Paid assassins committed the crimes. The military and the police looked the other way, and sometimes even acted as accomplices. According to a 2002 United Kingdom Home Office report, between 1985 and 1987, approximately 450 members of the Unión Patriótica were murdered. More recent reports estimate that between 3,500 and 4,000 Unión Patriótica members have been murdered since 1985. While the death squads acted anonymously, later investigations would prove that the social, economic, and political elites of both the Liberal and Conservative parties were behind the massacres.

Palmera, being an active member of the Unión Patriótica and a left-leaning university professor, also became a target. Death threats came frequently. "They were simple phone calls, or small notes that said 'Son of a bitch, you leave or you die,' " he recalls. Many of Palmera's colleagues left the region, and some abandoned the country. A month after the assassination of a close friend, Palmera's and Margarita's names appeared on a list of those next in line to be killed, and Palmera's father suggested the family move to Mexico or Paris for a few years. Margarita left immediately to find what they both hoped would be a temporary home in Mexico. Palmera stayed behind, getting his eight-year-old daughter and his eleven-year-old son ready for the move. He also needed to deal with his business affairs. "I stayed because there was property to be sold. We had to sell the jewelry store and other things. I also had to hand in all the university responsibilities and also the management of the Banco del Comercio, where I had been working the last five years." After the murder of another close friend, Palmera began to question his decision to leave. "I began to wonder whether it would be an act of cowardice to leave running, to hide myself outside of the country," says Palmera. "I loved Margarita. We had an excellent marriage, and of course my children were most precious and valuable to me. However, to go into exile was to flee, leaving behind a trail of cadavers of people who were friends, valued companions who sacrificed everything, even their lives."

The attacks against the Unión Patriótica came to a climax in October 1987 with the assassination of Jaime Pardo Leal, the party's presidential candidate. Some days prior to the killing, Palmera had traveled to Bogotá to speak with Leal. But instead, he ended up attending Leal's funeral. While a disillusioned and furious Manuel Marulanda recalled all Unión Patriótica FARC members back to the mountains, a grieving Palmera reached out to a FARC commander he had met during the political campaigning of Unión Patriótica candidates. "I wrote him a letter. I said I would not run away like a dog from my country—that I would stay. He replied. He told me to think about my decision, to think it over. And he recommended I go speak to the members of the FARC Secretariat, Jacobo Arenas and Manuel Marulanda, who had been the promoters of the Unión Patriótica movement." At the end of November, Palmera went deep into the hills in the department of Meta, in central Colombia, where the FARC Secretariat had their general headquarters. At the time, the Secretariat was made up of five top commanders, who were working on strategies to reorganize the guerrillas after the calamity of their entry into mainstream politics with the Unión Patriótica.

After arriving in the camp, Palmera personally met with Marulanda and Secretariat members Alfonso Cano, a former leader of the Juventud Comunista (Communist Youth movement), and Jacobo Arenas, who had been at Marulanda's side since the FARC's formative years. "I told them that I was not willing to leave, to flee, to go into exile, and I wanted to join the FARC. Jacobo Arenas said the idea was not to have people leaving the city to go to the mountains; that was crazy. He told

me, 'Stay here for a couple of days. Get to know this life. It's very difficult. Get to know some of the members. And while you're here, give us
some classes on Colombian economics.'" The didactic professor
eagerly accepted the position. The economic struggle of poor Colombians was proof that the armed conflict had a legitimate cause, and
Palmera's lessons, taught mostly to uneducated guerrilla recruits, consisted of the basics: The wealth and the land of Colombia is in the
hands of few. Capitalism is bad. Socialism and communism are good.
We are here in the mountains because the corrupt oligarchy won't let us
into the political arena. If they let us, then we can change the economic
situation of the country and wealth can be shared among the majority.

Days after Palmera's arrival, seven members of the Juventud
Comunista in Medellín were assassinated at the headquarters of the
Unión Patriótica. Apparently, the news was enough to change the mind
of Jacobo Arenas with regard to Palmera. "He told me, 'If you want to
continue alive and in the struggle, come to the FARC,' " Palmera says.
Although he accepted the invitation, Palmera still believed that it would
not be long before he was reunited with Margarita and his two children.
"The FARC, at that time, were in the peace process with President
Betancur. And the FARC, despite all the assassinations, the threats and
[having] some of its members in exile, still believed in the peace
process, and I believed in it, too." At thirty-seven, Palmera took the
nom de guerre Simón Trinidad, a name he felt gave respect to his idol,
Simón Bolívar, and joined the revolutionary army. (The practice of taking a nom de guerre was both to protect a recruit's family and to signify
the radical life change of becoming a guerrilla fighter.) He was assigned
to the Nineteenth Front on the northern coast of the country for basic
training. Jacobo Arenas and Alfonso Cano told him that although he
would be assigned a teaching position, he would have to comply with all
the duties and obligations of any guerrilla member. He was given the
job of training young uneducated guerrillas in politics and ideology.
Later, he was put in charge of a FARC radio station that broadcast from
the mountains, and finally he was made the second in command of over
one hundred guerrillas in the FARC's Forty-first Front in northern
Colombia. His territory covered a vast area of the Serranía de Perijá,

the northernmost part of the Eastern Cordillera, which extends along the border between Colombia and Venezuela.

Some guerrillas would say that Trinidad was forced to appear very militant to gain respect within the organization. "He had a certain complex because of his bourgeois origin, and that always forced him to take more radical positions," said one high-ranking guerrilla who knew him well. "He seemed to scream, 'Believe me, I am a revolutionary!' " And although Trinidad would spend many hard years in the jungle and mountains, he never lost the distinguished air of a college professor. His mother, though heartbroken when her son joined the guerrillas, sent him camouflage fatigues made by the same tailor who had sewn his aristocratic banker's suits. It would not only be his manner of dress, elocution, and education that would separate Trinidad from the vast majority of his comrades. Nearly all FARC guerrillas felt an intense level of detachment from the victims of the oligarchy and aristocracy whom they kidnapped or murdered. For Trinidad, those he once called friends were now terrorized by the organization to which he so fervently belonged. It was a circumstance of his dual life that he would never fully escape.

4

Friends and Neighbors

Cold and exhausted, Carmen Alicia Medina hiked alone in the rain along a *trocha*, a hidden guerrilla pathway in the Serranía de Perijá mountains, seventy miles from her home in Valledupar. She'd been to this place several times before, each time to meet a FARC guerrilla named Octavio. Sometimes she carried a heavy pack with boots, cell phones, medicine, batteries—anything they had demanded of her in exchange for a meeting. Each time she came hoping for "proof of life" and desperately seeking some kind of monetary demand from the guerrillas who had kidnapped her husband several months before, on March 22, 1998. As she made her way, Medina became anguished at the thought that she might have to turn back once again without evidence that her husband was still alive. When she arrived at her meeting place, "it was raining really hard," Medina recalled in a 2006 court testimony. "Octavio asked me to come close to the tent so that I wouldn't get wet. I said, 'No. I'm not moving from this stone until you promise me that you're going to tell me how Elías is. You have three options: You can kidnap me with Elías, you can give me the proof, or you can shoot me. But I'm not going to move.' "

Medina's gall was born of exhaustion and frustration. Her will and morale had been tested tremendously over the past several months in a game of cat and mouse that had been played since the day a group of seven FARC guerrillas took her husband, Elías Ochoa, and his brother, Eliécer, at gunpoint from their ranch in El Paso, a hundred miles south of Valledupar, near the Ariguaní River. Medina arrived at the ranch to find that one of the family's bodyguards had been shot, and she half carried, half dragged him back to the house to get help. Elías Ochoa, who had spent two years as the mayor of Valledupar, was taken with his brother to a FARC hideout in the mountains. Because the protocol for FARC kidnappings was very well known, Ochoa knew right away that he would be ransomed to his family. He hoped this would happen soon, of course, but the FARC's strategy in the business of kidnapping had always been one of extreme patience. With seldom any pressure from the military or police, hiding a hostage in Colombia was a relatively inexpensive and easy undertaking. Whenever there was a perceived threat, the guerrillas, competent at navigating difficult jungle and

Simón Trinidad and his partner, Lucero, speak with local campesinos in 2000 in San Vicente del Caguán (inside the demilitarized zone) about the FARC's plans. Photo: Salud Hernández-Mora.

mountain terrain, would simply march their hostages to another remote area. Taking their time to contact the victim's family was a strategy that the guerrillas felt helped immensely when it came time to negotiate a price for the hostage's freedom: The emotional turmoil brought about by the disappearance of a loved one was then exacerbated by the long silence that followed, sometimes for several months, sometimes for more than a year. Families suffered immeasurably, waiting moment by moment for any communication from the kidnappers. When it finally came, by way of a note, a visit, or a phone call, the family members were often so emotionally weakened that they were willing to agree immediately to the kidnappers' demands.

For the victim, the interrogation about one's fiscal capacity began almost immediately after capture: "We know that you stole five hundred million pesos of government money when you were mayor. How many cattle do you own? We saw that you sold a farm for three hundred million pesos. How much is your emerald mine worth?" Such research about an individual's life was something that the guerrillas undertook in order to estimate the value of their commodity and to plan a negotiation strategy. Commonly, the kidnappers would have some prior knowledge of their victim's financial affairs, as well as a general idea of what they could get for each hostage. For Ochoa and his brother, fifteen days passed, and they still had no idea what the guerrillas would ask for their release, so Ochoa decided to push the issue with commander Octavio. The commander had been part of the group who kidnapped him, and Ochoa had watched as Octavio shot their bodyguard with an R-15 rifle. Ochoa recalled the events surrounding his kidnapping in a 2006 court testimony. "I asked Commander Octavio whom we needed to speak to about the kidnapping, about accelerating the process. He was emphatic in telling me that the person who had to make the decision about the negotiations and the demands was Commander Simón Trinidad."

Ochoa was relieved and optimistic. "Everyone in Valledupar knew that Ricardo [Palmera] had become a FARC member, and that he was using the name of Simón Trinidad." Ochoa asked Octavio if Trinidad was still with the Forty-first Front of the FARC, which Ochoa knew was the group of guerrillas controlling the region where he was being

held. Octavio replied that, yes, he was. To Ochoa, it seemed like a terrific stroke of luck. "I was very happy to get the information that it was
Simón Trinidad who had to make the decision, because we had been
friends and known each other well when he was my colleague at the
university and he was general manager of Banco del Comercio. At that
time, my waterworks company had accounts with that bank." The two
men taught in the same department and saw each other quite frequently. "We would meet either at the administrative offices of the
bank or at the company, and we would talk on the phone frequently. We
did not have a social relationship, because he belonged to a socioeco-
nomic stratum that was much higher than mine."

Many would say that it was his social status and former banking
career that gave Trinidad inside information into which members of the
Valledupar elite were the biggest fish for FARC kidnappers. Colombia's
daily newspaper, *El Tiempo*, reported:

A few days after Trinidad went to the FARC in 1987, the most
wealthy men of Valledupar carried a blank check in their pock-
ets. It was christened "the Simón check." It was a sort of insurance policy to prevent oneself from becoming a guest at the
"Sierra Nevada Hilton" or "Serranía de Perijá Hilton," tragi-
comic names with which the people of [the department of]
César baptized the FARC camps.

Trinidad was reported to have stolen thirty million pesos
($125,000) from the Banco del Comercio before he left, along with
financial records. The newspaper *El Espectador* quoted the governor of
the department of César, Hernando Molina, in a 2003 article: "Extortion and kidnapping appeared like a plague in Valledupar, naturally
orchestrated by Palmera." Molina told *The New York Times*, "Because
he knew us, he could say how much each of us had. It was a bill come
due, but we never understood why, because we had never done anything to him." The charges that Trinidad used stolen bank records to
kidnap his former friends and colleagues were vehemently denied by
Jaime Palmera, Trinidad's eldest brother: "One didn't have to be a manager of a bank to know who had money in Valledupar at the end of the

eighties and beginning of the nineties." Jaime was harshly critical of the FARC's policy of kidnapping, and he had been devastated by his brother's decision to enter the ranks of the guerrilla group.

Although public opinion mostly considered a friendship with Trinidad to be a liability, Ochoa still believed that his relationship with his former colleague would help free him. "I asked to speak with him, because I thought that would facilitate the negotiations greatly," he says. Ochoa asked one of the FARC captors, a man named Dumar, to speak with Trinidad, and Ochoa was close enough to hear the radio transmission. Ochoa believed he heard Trinidad say that his case would soon be resolved. Still, Trinidad did not agree to speak with Ochoa.

Weeks into his kidnapping, a new commander appeared in the camp. "He told me that he came on behalf of Simón Trinidad to speak with me." This was when Ochoa would find out what the FARC would demand for his freedom. Ochoa remembers that "the expression used was 'You have to make a contribution to the war.' And the contribution that they mentioned was one million *dollars*." Ochoa was stunned. "[I told him] that even if I sold all my assets and my family's assets, I could not raise that amount. And that would include my children's, my wife's, and all my relatives'. I offered ten million pesos [seven thousand dollars]." Ochoa's insulting offer infuriated the commander, who admonished him for his lack of respect to the FARC and gave him a lesson in the business of extortion and kidnapping. He told Ochoa that the FARC would, under no circumstances, release anyone for less than fifty million pesos. In fact, if the FARC needed fifty million pesos, it would just go to a rural area where the big landowners lived and demand it from any one of them. If they didn't pay, it would simply take away two or three hundred head of cattle. A few days later, the landowner would seek out the FARC, willing to pay the money so that the cattle would be returned.

Eight days after Ochoa learned of the demand, he and his brother were moved out of their original camp. They began a march that lasted over forty-seven nights. Each day, they walked for six to ten hours— much of it in the rain. Their captors were mostly between thirteen and seventeen years old, and all were armed with semiautomatic rifles.

Ochoa continued to believe that his relationship with Trinidad would help free him, and not a day went by that he didn't asked to speak with his former friend. When the group of captors and hostages finally arrived in a camp, Ochoa and his brother were allowed to listen to the radio, but it was taken away immediately when the broadcast contained news about their kidnapping. "I complained about why it had been taken away from me, and the answer that I was given was that it was an instruction given by Simón Trinidad," Ochoa says. But there was always a radio somewhere in the camp tuned to a news station, and Ochoa stealthily moved as close as possible to hear any news. "Commander Dumar would lower the volume so that I could not hear it. But he would allow me to hear other national and regional news broadcasts on the radio." Ochoa also listened intently to the radio communications among the guerrillas, hoping to glean some insight into his future. The guerrillas spoke in code to one another over the radio, but it was soon apparent which words referred to what. One code word he heard over and over: "Whenever they referred to us, they would say the 'calves' or the 'merchandise.' "

What Ochoa did not hear or know, but could only painfully imagine, was what his wife of fifteen years, Carmen Alicia Medina, was going through to try to free him. After the kidnapping, the guerrillas contacted Medina and told her that she would have to hike alone into the Perijá mountains for a meeting with a midlevel commander named Octavio. Medina, who endured chronic pain from an injured leg, made several excruciating trips. "I had to go up a mountain, many hours, sometimes just to be listened to, just to be given an opportunity, asking God to give me strength. Not only to overcome the situation but also because I am deathly afraid of snakes. I was asking God to just please not let me find a snake." Each time, she begged for information, but the guerrillas had nothing for her—no proof of life and no demand for money. Medina felt that the guerrillas were interested in her only because she continued to deliver the items that they requested, such as cell phones with prepaid cards, batteries, and medicine. But she had no choice other than to make the trip each time they requested her to do so. "The several occasions that I went up, they would ask me for something. Sometimes they would leave a list down below. I even sent medicine for Elías for his high blood pressure, because he suffers from high blood pressure, and that worried me."

After several meetings, Octavio told Medina that he had participated in the kidnapping of her husband, that the two Ochoa brothers were being held in a hostage camp, and that they were alive and doing all right. "And that was when he told me that Professor Ricardo [Palmera] was also in that front. That made me very happy. He was my teacher—my professor for four semesters—teaching me Colombian economics and economic history. We had friends in common at the university, and I also knew him as the head of the bank. I knew his family, all his siblings, brothers and sisters, and I knew his wife, Margarita." Medina felt very strongly that her many connections to Trinidad would help. "I always felt that he was my way out—that he was the person from whom I was going to obtain Elías's release." Medina asked Octavio to facilitate a conversation with Trinidad.

Months later, Medina heard a rumor that her husband and his brother had been killed. After several more fruitless trips, she found herself at the meeting with Octavio in the pouring rain. "I was determined, and he realized that I wasn't going to budge," says Medina. When the rain lightened up a bit, Octavio came out of the tent and walked toward Medina. "That's when he told me he was going to help me; that he was going to ask for authorization from Commander Simón to get the proof of life." Octavio went back to the tent and began to speak over the radio. He used some code words, and at first Medina didn't understand, but she moved closer to the tent, where she could hear. Medina heard Octavio call Trinidad by name. "He [Octavio] said that I was insisting on the proof of life, and that I was getting very annoying." And then she heard the voice of her former professor come through over the radio: "Yeah, tell her that we'll give it to her in two weeks."

Two weeks later, Medina again went to see Octavio and received the proof of life (the exact contents of the proof of life were never reported). "On the same day that I got the proof of life, we were also told that we needed to pay a million dollars. I held my head, and I started crying. I was saying, 'We don't have that money.' And I asked

Octavio, 'Why are you talking about *dollars*? You don't like Americans.' And he said, 'Well, it's a million dollars.' After they said it was going to be a million dollars, I anguished because it was unreachable, unobtainable." For some time, Medina heard nothing more.

"Finally, one day, Octavio called me on the cell phone, and even though I had insisted to talk to Simón Trinidad, I understood that that wasn't going to be possible, because they were asking me for money— lots of money. They said the agreement was reached; they said it would be one hundred million pesos [seventy thousand dollars]. And I said to him, 'We don't have that money,' and he said, 'If you don't have the money, send two coffins, because we're going to kill him.' It must have been God that gave me the strength. I said to him, 'Kill him, eat him, and rot with him, because I don't have that money.' "

Again, Medina agonized during a long, deafening silence from the guerrillas, at which time the tragedy touched everyone in her family, even the youngest members. Her six-year-old son was having nightmares, and Medina appealed to País Libre (a Colombian foundation that offers help to the families of kidnapped victims) to give the boy psychological counseling. Medina was tormented by the fact she had baited Octavio to kill her husband, but felt she hadn't had any other choice. "I think that was the way to make them understand that we didn't have that kind of money. Besides, Simón Trinidad knew it." She continued to communicate with Octavio and was finally given another demand—twice as high as the last. "They were asking for two hundred million pesos [$140,000] to free them." With no option, Medina did everything she could think of to secure the amount. "My mother-in-law sold her house. I quit my job in order to get the severance pay. We got a mortgage on our house. We took loans from friends to gather the money. And I went to pay that amount in cash. And they told me on that day that the two would be freed."

In the camp where Elías and Eliécer Ochoa were being held, the two men heard an order given over the radio to "bring in the hostages." Medina had received word that her husband and his brother would be released and was told to go to a location where the guerrillas would deliver the two men. Along with several family members, Medina traveled to an area in the mountains. "We went there early in the morning.

That night, they released Eliécer. When I saw that it was only Eliécer who was freed, it was very hard for me. I tried not to make him feel bad when I did not see Elías. Eliécer was crying, telling me that he didn't want to leave him, but they forced him to leave and leave Elías."

Medina was enraged. "I wanted to go out looking for Octavio to confront him with the fact that he had lied to me, because he said that they would turn both of them over, and they did not. The next day, I went back to the area where we had been meeting, looking for Octavio, but he wasn't there. He didn't want to face me." Instead, Medina spoke to the guerrilla in charge. "I complained to him that after I had been asked to provide so many provisions such as food, meat, rice, et cetera—all things that they had asked me for, that Eliécer had told me that all they had been fed was rice and spaghetti and *cacharina* [a cracker made of flour and water]." Medina implored the guerrilla: "How could that be? How could they do that?" And then she asked the question that was most important to her: What were they to do about freeing Elías? "He told me that if I wanted Elías, I'd have to pay an additional one hundred million pesos." Perhaps Simón Trinidad had changed his mind about the additional ransom for Ochoa, or maybe it was another high commander, because five days after Eliécer's release and seven months after the two had been kidnapped, Elías Ochoa was set free.

Whether the kidnapping of the Ochoas or other members of the Valledupar elite bothered Trinidad's conscience was impossible to determine. But he would later write about the painful consequences that his decision to enter the FARC had for his family. "The disloyalty to my dad hurt a lot," Trinidad wrote. "He proposed my departure into exile thinking about the well-being of the whole family. So I wrote him a letter explaining why I made the decision to join the FARC. I didn't imagine that my decision was going to affect them so much. His house was raided several times by the military, and he received multiple death threats."

Trinidad's abandonment of his social position to join the FARC turned the Palmeras into pariahs in Valledupar—the same city that a few years earlier had bestowed his father with the title of "Legal Conscience of the Department of César" and had considered this family one of the most prominent and respected in the region. According to the eldest son, Jaime, many of the attacks that his father and mother had to put up with were instigated by their old friends from Valledupar society. "It came to the point where the old man was prevented from entering the Valledupar Club," he says.

In 1996, Trinidad's sister, Leonor Palmera, was kidnapped for seven months by AUC (Autodefensas Unidas de Colombia, United Self-Defense Forces of Colombia) paramilitary leader Carlos Castaño in a show of force and retaliation against the FARC and against Trinidad. After gaining her freedom, for her own security and for the security of her family, Leonor left Colombia for Paraguay with her two children and her parents, doña Alix and don Ovidio. By then, don Ovidio was succumbing to the effects of Alzheimer's disease. He died in 2003, as Trinidad says, "far from the land of his birth and from his homeland."

5

Contractor

When Keith Stansell, Marc Gonsalves, and Thomas Howes were captured by FARC guerrillas, they were working as military contractors for a small company called California Microwave Systems (CMS), a subsidiary of contractor giant Northrop Grumman. The work that CMS was doing was part of an eight-million-dollar contract to gather information on drug production and trafficking. There were a handful of employees tasked for the job—pilots, systems analysts who operated the surveillance equipment, and mechanics who maintained the company's two Cessnas. The company rented a small office and hangar space from an American army veteran who had created a successful business catering to the many North American contractors working under Plan Colombia—the half-billion-dollar-a-year Colombian component of the U.S.-funded war on drugs.

While Plan Colombia was certainly the most expensive program in the history of U.S. relations with Colombia, a deep interest in this strategic nation runs back nearly a century. In 1903, the Colombian government refused to sign a treaty that would hand over "all rights, power and authority" of the Panama Canal to the United States in perpetuity (Panama had been a state within Colombia since the Bolivarian revolution, with varying levels of cooperation with the central govern-

Colombian antinarcotics police patrol a coca field while an American contractor spray plane fumigates coca crops near Tumaco, Nariño, southwest of Bogotá. September 12, 2000. Photo: AP Images/Scott Dalton.

ment in Bogotá). With control of the canal in doubt, the United States seized the opportunity to back Panamanian separatists to fight against Colombian troops heading toward Panama City. Panama gained independence in a military junta (partially financed by the French company building the canal) on November 6, 1903. Panama's ambassador to the United States quickly signed the Hay-Bunau-Varilla Treaty, granting the United States the right to build and indefinitely control the canal. The United States and Colombia repaired relations with a reconciliatory treaty in 1921, and for the rest of the century, the United States would sit squarely on the side of the Colombian government in South American political disputes, especially when it came to matters of the burgeoning communism that had made its way to the western hemisphere.

In April 1948, the ninth Pan-American Conference (an annual meeting of U.S. and Latin American leaders) was being presided over by the U.S. secretary of state, George C. Marshall, in Bogotá. The conference—attended by representatives from more than a dozen countries—had two goals: to put a stop to a perceived Soviet-inspired Communist movement throughout Latin America and to form the Organization of American States (OAS), which would widen the U.S. government's economic and political influence in South America. On the third day of the conference, popular presidential candidate Jorge Eliécer Gaitán was shot and killed in central Bogotá. Members of Gaitán's Liberal party took to the streets, rioting and looting shops for weapons. The assassin was killed by a mob, his body dragged to the steps of the presidential palace. Army tanks advanced on the palace, and students took over a radio station, demanding the incumbent president, Mariano Ospina, resign and flee. Possibly to fuel the case of the strongly anti-Communist coalition at the conference and remove suspicion from Ospina's ruling Conservative party, Ospina immediately accused Gaitán's shooter of being a Communist. Kremlin-inspired revolutionaries were said to be responsible for orchestrating the violence. But in reality, there was no proven Communist link to the assassination or to the unrest. A 1960s declassified CIA document analyzing the violent uprising—referred to as "El Bogotazo"—reported, "The government preferred to blame the riots on communist agitation and foreign intrigue, rather than to address itself to the underlying causes of popular discontent." About the assassin, the document stated, "The murderer was apparently one of those fanatics or psychopaths we say may never be excluded from calculations on the safety of dignitaries. His motives cannot be known for certain, for he was battered to death on the spot by frenzied bystanders. Inevitably, charges were raised of the complicity of the Conservative Party, of the Communists, and of the U.S. But no strong evidence of a political plot has ever been produced."

By 1960, after continuing to come up empty for more than a decade in its pursuit of the Red threat, the U.S. government believed it had found proof of a real Communist rebellion in Colombia—a ragged group of fighters in the central Colombian mountains, led by peasant revolutionary Pedro Marín. To help Colombia fight the rebels (whose ideology at the time was more nationalist and anticapitalist than Communist), President Alberto Lleras signed a military-aid agreement with the United States. The Colombian military received twenty-five fighter jets and sixteen light bombers and lessons from U.S. pilots in how to napalm insurgent settlements. In 1964, the Colombian army, trained and funded by the United States, went to wipe out Marín and his cohorts with a bombing raid on their camp. When troops arrived on the ground, the rebels were nowhere to be found. The raid had forced Marín and forty of his men to become mobile guerrilla warriors, disappearing into the impenetrable Colombian countryside. It was the beginning of a new kind of war, one that the Colombian government—for more than four decades—would be powerless to end.

The United States remained dedicated to helping keep communism in check, and in 1962, the government developed a counterinsurgency program called Plan Lazo. The policy included a dramatic increase in aid and the training of Colombian soldiers and citizens "to perform counter-agent and counter-propaganda functions, and as necessary, execute paramilitary, sabotage and/or terrorist activities against known communist proponents." The relationship between the two countries morphed in the late 1970s when the sale and use of illicit marijuana and cocaine trafficked through Colombia became a social crisis and a fiscal drain in the United States.

In the early 1980s, the white powder that had once been a white-collar drug exploded into American inner cities in the form of crack cocaine. By 1985, use of cocaine among young adults reached an all-time high with over 8 percent of those between the ages of eighteen and twenty-four and 6 percent of those between the ages of twenty-five and thirty-four admitting to using the drug. In 1986, President Ronald Reagan called drug abuse "a repudiation of everything America is" and implored Americans to join a "national crusade against drugs." With the increasing fervor over this issue, the U.S. House of Representatives voted overwhelmingly (378–16) in favor of a $1.7 billion Omnibus Drug Bill. While the money and military aid allocated in the bill seemed extreme to some, the political climate in the United States gave lawmakers little option. "This is such an emotional issue—I mean, we're at war here—that voting no would be too difficult to explain," said Arizona senator John McCain. "By voting against it, you'd be voting against the war on drugs. Nobody wants to do that." Ninety-seven million dollars was allocated to build prisons, $200 million for drug education, and $241 million for treatment. The bill was accompanied by an aggressive campaign to attack the drug business at its source.

Peru and Bolivia were the initial targets of the $200 million U.S. effort to find a supply-side fix to the problem. At the time, both Andean countries were the main growers of coca and producers of cocaine. The drug trade then traveled to Colombia, where smugglers took advantage of the Caribbean Sea, the Pacific Ocean, and the narrow land bridge through Panama to ship the illegal export through Costa Rica, Nicaragua, Honduras, or El Salvador, then from Guatemala to Mexico. A second passage ran northeast to Florida, directly or via Haiti, the Dominican Republic, Puerto Rico, or the Lesser Antilles. Planes, boats, and trucks carried the powder north, with transport accomplished easily and mostly with impunity. Eradication efforts began at the ground level, with local contract workers or government troops spraying herbicides or cutting down the coca plants. To help the thousands of coca farmers who were put out of work by the eradication programs, the United States Agency for International Development (USAID) earmarked $131 million between 1987 and 1998 for crop substitution and alternative development for Bolivia and Peru. In both countries, the programs failed miserably, with the total area of coca cultivation decreasing by less than 5 percent. In another ill-fated attempt to stop cultivation, Bolivian growers were paid two thousand dollars per year by the U.S. Embassy's Narcotics Affairs Section not to grow coca. According to a 2002 report by the U.S. General Accounting Office, the $100 million program to pay farmers was rife with corruption, as many ineligible beneficiaries collected payoffs, and farmers who collected funds just moved to other areas and continued to grow coca. Even in those early years, the idea of trying to wipe out cocaine by eradicating coca plants seemed pointless to many critics. Paul Boeker, president of the Institute of the Americas at the University of California, San Diego, told *The New York Times* in 1991 that the land in the Andes suitable to growing coca was virtually unlimited. "Nibbling around the edges of the leaf market," he said, "is terribly inefficient." Traffickers in Colombia soon realized the same thing: coca could just as easily be grown and processed in Colombia as in Peru and Bolivia. And toward the late

1980s, the bulk of the cultivation business was firmly planted in Colombian soil.

In a secondary method designed to dampen the flow of illegal imports, the United States put pressure on the Colombian government to extradite captured drug dealers. A bilateral extradition treaty between Colombia and the United States had come into effect in 1979 under Presidents Jimmy Carter and Julio César Turbay. The treaty—along with $26 million in U.S. aid—launched what Washington thought would be a model antinarcotics program. A snag was hit when President Belisario Betancur, elected in 1982, refused to extradite Colombian nationals as a matter of principle. But two years later, following the murder of the Colombian minister of justice by Pablo Escobar's men, Betancur relented and began approving the extradition requests. From November 1984 to June 1987, Colombia extradited thirteen accused narco-traffickers, including Carlos Lehder, who was believed to have amassed a net worth of $2.5 billion. The thirty-eight-year-old Lehder was sentenced in the United States to life without parole, plus an additional 135 years. But in a major setback for Washington's antidrug effort, in June 1987, the Colombian Supreme Court declared the extradition treaty unconstitutional. More than seventy extradition requests were shelved, including one for Medellín cartel CEO Pablo Escobar—arguably one of the most successful drug bosses who ever lived.

In the late 1980s and early 1990s, the reign of the big cartel bosses continued to fuel ever-increasing violence. Bogotá, Cali, and Medellín were repeatedly racked by bomb attacks, kidnappings, and shootings intended to intimidate government officials into changing laws to favor the drug traffickers. Brutal conflicts also erupted among the big cartels and reached a pinnacle in 1993, when a war broke out between Pablo Escobar and a rival vigilante group, Los Pepes. Although the cartels were a scourge for the Colombian government, some in the general population, reaping the benefits of a drug economy and of generous cartel bosses who sought to improve their communities, had a more favorable feeling toward the cartels. Soccer stadiums, churches, schools, and low-income housing were built compliments of drug money. All the while, the Colombian government and justice system became increasingly impotent and permeated with rampant corruption.

The FARC and other armed groups were also capitalizing on the new profits. At the time, guerrillas controlled many of the coca-growing regions in central and southern Colombia, while the cartels managed much of the cocaine production and trafficking. The guerrillas operated by taxing the cartels and drug producers for protection and services. According to a Rand Corporation report, fees (which fluctuated depending on market value) were approximately $15 per kilogram for production of coca paste and $10.50 per kilogram for cocaine shipments. The FARC demanded $5,200 for international drug flights and $2,600 for domestic drug flights. They also charged "protection" fees for each laboratory, landing strip, and acre of coca and poppy fields. This economic alliance began to collapse when the leaders of the cartels in Medellín and Cali began investing their newfound wealth in property, primarily large cattle ranches, which placed them firmly in the ranks of the guerrillas' traditional enemy—the landowning elite. Beginning in the early 1980s, family-based drug empires invested millions of dollars to buy more than 2.5 million acres—more than one-twelfth of Colombia's productive farmland. In turn, the guerrillas began a policy of kidnapping and extortion of the cartel members. For protection and retaliation, the drug lords organized and financed their own paramilitary armies. Politicians, ranchers, and peasants tired of guerrilla attacks helped form the "self-defense" groups. Most notorious were two organizations using the same name: Muerte a Secuestradores, or MAS (Death to Kidnappers). One group was formed as a death squad for the Medellín cartel; the other was formed by army officers and ranchers.

At the time, the units were actually sanctioned by the government and military leaders, who had called for peasant self-defense groups to rise up against the guerrillas. The policy initiated Colombia's "Dirty War" as paramilitary groups linked to drug cartels worked closely with the Colombian military to brutally torture and murder suspected guerrillas, guerrilla sympathizers, and peasant union leaders. At the same time, the self-defense units attacked police and authorities investigating drug trafficking and paramilitary activity. Throughout the 1980s, paramilitary groups were implicated in the assassinations of hundreds of police officers, judges, and political leaders, including Minister of Justice Rodrigo Lara Bonilla in 1984.

By 1993, with strongly antidrug president César Gaviria in office, the cartel bosses began to fall. Escobar was murdered in December 1993 by Colombian Special Forces, with the help of U.S. intelligence agents, who firmly believed that they had put a nail in the coffin of not just a wanted drug boss but the war on drugs. There were fifteen more top cartel leaders left. "We felt like it was one down, fifteen to go," John Carnevale, director of planning and budget at the White House Office of National Drug Control Policy (ONDCP), told *Rolling Stone* in 2007. "There was this feeling that if we got all 16, it's not like the whole thing would be over, but that was a big part of how we would go about winning the War on Drugs." Shortly after Escobar was taken out of the business, the remaining fifteen cartel bosses were either killed or safely out of circulation in U.S. prisons. There were copious pats on the back and champagne toasts from Bogotá to Washington.

It soon became apparent that the celebration had been premature. By the mid-1990s, a multitude of factions—guerrillas, paramilitaries, local peasants, city drug dealers, and street gangs—entered the business to fill the power vacuum. The proliferation of new drug regimes made the trafficking business more robust than ever. Manuel Marulanda's guerrilla army, with an estimated eighteen thousand soldiers controlling more than 50 percent of rural Colombia, was well positioned to take a large percentage of the new market strategy. Although the FARC was only one of several larger shareholders in a much bigger export operation, the regime change from cartels to insurgent armies was not lost on U.S. president Bill Clinton, who repeatedly linked the FARC to drug trafficking by referring to them as "narco-guerrillas." Manuel Marulanda, who did not appreciate the "narco" label, would continually downplay his organization's role in the drug trade and claim he could eradicate coca production in three to five years with crop-substitution programs if supplied with economic aid from the government and international organizations. All the while, his army was making a fortune and steadily increasing its military armament strength and troop levels, and launching successful offensives and attacks throughout the country.

When it was apparent both that the drug flow was actually increasing and that Colombia—the United States' strongest ally in South America—was losing its fight against the guerrillas, the United States stepped up its funding to the tune of $309 million in 1999, followed by $765 million in 2000. The behemoth offshoot of the war on drugs was a six-year program dubbed "Plan Colombia" by the Clinton administration, which argued that wiping out the guerrillas was crucial to ending the flow of drug imports. To prop up the Colombian military, the State Department—which is responsible for antidrug operations abroad—turned to U.S. defense contractors to supply the Colombian military with weapons, military training, and equipment to fight the guerrillas. As Colombia continued to enjoy its status as the third-largest recipient of U.S. aid, the military components of Plan Colombia were substantially downplayed publicly, while the coca eradication and fumigation program became its touted centerpiece. (USAID began a $52.5 million alternative development program in 2000 to coincide with the military and eradication components of Plan Colombia. The funds were to be administered through the Colombian government. But because nearly all of the coca-growing regions were completely under the control of insurgents, the programs had little success.)

As with other military contracts, the outsourcing of the war on drugs in Colombia was designed to protect the U.S. government from liability should anything go awry. And to complicate an already-confusing picture, larger corporations would frequently subcontract to smaller companies in order to distance themselves from accountability. The military's SOUTHCOM Reconnaissance System (SRS) program that employed Thomas Howes, Keith Stansell, and Marc Gonsalves in 2003 was no different. Lockheed Martin was selected by the DOD as the prime contractor, which then subcontracted to Northrop Grumman, which then subcontracted to California Microwave Systems. The practice created an absence of oversight or protocols for the CMS employees. A 2003 U.S. Navy investigation found that there had been no written set of standard operating procedures at CMS. Pilots and systems operators had to learn procedures largely by word of mouth. DynCorp (which ran the fumigation missions) was the biggest U.S. contractor in Colombia and had the largest budget, the most planes, and a fleet of SAR helicopters. However, the positions at CMS were coveted because they paid nearly 25 percent more than what the DynCorp pilots were making for similar work. (According to former CMS pilot Doug Cockes, pilots were paid $160,000 per year and systems analyst, slightly more.)

Although they considered the drug-interdiction work they were doing an important part of America's war on drugs, most of the men took the job for one reason, according to Stansell. "If it weren't for the money," he wrote in *Out of Captivity*, "we wouldn't have been in Colombia. We were making good coin, and that was important to us— what it brought to our egos, what it might mean down the line for our kids and our retirement. I wasn't so much interested in being a hero with a capital H, as I was being a hero to my family and in my own mind by bringing down some big bucks. Call me shallow. Call me greedy. Call me what you want. I didn't care. I still don't really. All I was doing was living the American dream." Stansell and his colleagues were hired to work four weeks in Colombia and then be home in the States for two weeks. In Colombia, the men lived in La Fontana, an upscale apartment complex in northern Bogotá. Although most of them weren't single, four weeks away from home was a long time. Many found the local Colombian women—legendary for their beauty and sensuality— irresistible.

The men were tasked with finding drug labs and smuggling routes used by the FARC. They used photographic equipment during the day and infrared remote sensing gear at night. But from five thousand feet, differentiating coca labs from farmers' huts in an endless sea of green wasn't easy. Growers had become so accustomed to the planes that they'd found dozens of ways of disguising labs, including covering them with rain-forest vegetation or building them alongside working farmhouses. The contractors also looked for coca fields. The homogeneous swaths of bright green leaves were easily identifiable in aerial photographs from directly overhead. However, the acreage was so great throughout the region controlled by the FARC, and the crops were so widely distributed, that finding all of the coca planted in Colombia with the two CMS platform planes was an impossible task. Flying at lower altitudes would make their reconnoitering job easier, but it would also mean that the planes were more vulnerable to guerrilla fire. Because guerrillas had shot down half a dozen crop-dusting planes since the beginning of aerial fumigation in the 1990s, DynCorp made it a policy to have the spray planes followed by SAR forces in Black Hawk or Huey helicopters, ready to intervene in case of a crash or hostile fire. For the CMS missions, however, there were no SAR capabilities at all.

Several of the pilots had complained that the planes they flew on the reconnaissance missions, loaded with heavy equipment, far exceeded the weight limit for the Cessna. In fact, two CMS pilots, Douglas Cockes and Paul Hooper, who had worked for the company for more than two years, had written lengthy letters in November and December 2002 to Northrop Grumman, detailing the problems with the planes and the missions: "The mission aircraft could not reach any suitable landing area if the engine failed over most of the terrain over which the SRS mission is flown. The continued use of this platform invites a catastrophic impact in mountainous terrain if there is an engine failure. . . ." Cockes and Hooper asked that Northrop Grumman immediately replace the single-engine Caravan with a more powerful dual-engine Beechcraft King Air 300 series aircraft. "This is uniquely an issue of safety and a recommendation that will possibly save lives, limit the companies' exposure and enhance the mission's performance."

The concerns of Hooper and Cockes were ignored. The two pilots had tried to rally support from Thomas Howes and Tommy Janis (the pilot who was killed by the guerrillas after his successful crash landing on February 13, 2003), but Howes and Janis, although agreeing with Hooper and Cockes to some extent, refused to add their names to the complaint and continued to fly missions. Their decision and the company's refusal to upgrade the aircraft to a dual-engine plane made Hooper and Cockes furious. According to those working at the airport hangars where CMS had its Bogotá offices, the single-engine problem was already well known. In August 2001, the Cessna that Janis was flying lost power at thirteen thousand feet, twenty miles out over the

Caribbean Sea. He was an excellent pilot and was able to glide the plane to a safe landing at the airport in Santa Marta, in northern Colombia. Because Janis had been on a flight to Miami for aircraft maintenance and not on an official reconnaissance mission at the time, there was no report filed or any investigation into the cause of the engine failure.

Although the pilots continued to fly missions, infighting between the pilots and CMS management about safety issues was rampant. Thomas Schmidt, who was a Vietnam veteran, had nearly come to blows with the CMS site manager, Steve McCune, who Schmidt believed had no idea about flying and therefore no business telling pilots what to do. The animosity between the two resulted in write-ups for Schmidt for flying too close to a mountain and endangering the crew. "They never asked for Tommy's side of the story," says Sharon Schmidt, Tommy Schmidt's wife. "Tommy was pretty angry about that. He said, 'Why not talk to the guys who were *in* the plane?' But they reprimanded Tommy, which was *really* stupid. It was just another reason why there was so much animosity there."

At the base where many of the contracting companies had offices, several who knew McCune saw it differently. "McCune was a professional. He was very strict, very competent," one of McCune's business colleagues said. "Hooper and Cockes were well paid, but they were disconnected because of the way they would rotate in and out of the country. The pilots only flew. They didn't check the airplanes. They would fly, go home, and not work any more than that." Another point of contention had to do with handguns that had been issued by Northrop Grumman. Although U.S. military Joint Doctrine recommends against giving contractors arms and uniforms, the air force provides that arms should be issued "only in the most unusual circumstances" and states that carrying firearms is strictly voluntary. "It was basically that we would only be issued the weapons when we went out to fly," says Hooper. "Our position was that we needed them flying and certainly driving around in Bogotá." Many were afraid that the hour-long commute from their apartments to the airport could turn deadly, since bandits commonly approached drivers in traffic and robbed them at knifepoint, sometimes kidnapping people from their cars. According to Hooper and others, McCune was not happy that his employees were always armed, especially given the very volatile nature of his relationship with several of them. In early 2002, McCune told his employees that he needed to take away their guns and that they could use them only when they were on an SRS mission. Hooper felt that it was a retaliatory move by the CMS boss. "He just wanted to twist our tails for not agreeing with their inane policies."

The controversy that erupted because of the safety issues and the handguns stimulated McCune to issue a flurry of write-ups for bad behavior on the part of several of the pilots. In rebuttal, Hooper and Cockes sent a letter to Kent Kresa, chairman and CEO of Northrop Grumman, in December 2002, expounding on the intolerable conditions that those connected with the SRS mission faced. They dubbed the group apartment where the original site manager (McCune's predecessor), sensor operators, and a technician lived together from 2000 to 2001 as the "Animal House," and blamed the program director, James Hollaway, for failing to correct a toxic working environment that included drug and alcohol abuse by CMS managers, sloppy security with classified documents, and, in one case, the hiring of a local prostitute as a secretary for the company. (Cockes says that after the crash, he had the letter faxed to the U.S. military at SOUTHCOM. He later heard that the U.S. ambassador to Colombia, Anne Patterson, had also been given the letter, but he says he was not contacted by anyone from the military or the embassy.)

Hooper and Cockes also complained that when they objected to an operation that they found dangerous, they were threatened with termination. "In our opinion, the Program Director and Site Manager seem to believe that since we are 'well compensated,' we should accept ever-increasing risks as simply a fact of doing business. They continue to hold this view even though neither of them has ever been on a mission deep into hostile territory. We are not paid to accept an ever-increasing amount of risk, but rather to use our professional training and experience to mitigate risk as much as possible." The pilots proposed a meeting to discuss their concerns at some mutually agreed-upon location in North Carolina, Tennessee, or Alabama. Northrop Grumman executives invited Hooper and Cockes to meet at the company's headquarters in Maryland but refused to let the Northrop Grumman/CMS flight-operations manager Douglas Tait (who Cockes said agreed completely with his and Hooper's assessments) attend the meeting. Believing that he would be railroaded into giving a deposition to the corporation's attorneys, Hooper declined to attend the meeting. And with the meeting set to coincide with a two-month trip out of the country, Cockes, who says he would have loved to give a deposition had he been available to, did not attend either.

Despite internal tensions, the missions were considered extremely successful and returned a high yield of reconnaissance data on drug labs and FARC movements, which, in turn, gave credence to the idea that progress was being made in the war on drugs. Orders for missions were coming in from every direction—the U.S. Embassy in Bogotá, the U.S. Army, and the Department of Defense, among others. Unfortunately, there was no clear chain of command, and Northrop Grumman and CMS never truly addressed the pilots' concerns about flying single-engine planes that exceeded weight and altitude limits. Cockes and Hooper had planned to work for the company another five years—enough to secure a Northrop Grumman pension—but the dangers of their job mounted, and in December 2002, Cockes and Hooper quit before being fired and left a trail of bad blood behind them.

Two months later, their former colleagues Tommy Janis, Thomas Howes, Keith Stansell, and Marc Gonsalves crashed into the Colombian frontier. For all of the hundreds of hours they had flown over this terrain, the rain forest was completely unknown to the Americans. In the initial days after their capture, the guerrillas constantly pushed the Americans to keep moving to evade the Colombian military. They stumbled on the rough, muddy ground, their hands grasping at thorny tree branches covered with biting ants. Their feet throbbed and blistered. As they moved higher up in the mountains, the temperature dropped and the cold became unbearable. Stansell, who was suffering from broken ribs and constant diarrhea, remembered a conversation he'd recently had regarding a survival course that Northrop Grumman demanded he take. "I told this company guy that I wouldn't do it," Stansell wrote. "When he asked why, all I said was, 'With this piece-of-shit aircraft we've been asked to fly in, there's no way I'm going to survive a crash. A dead man doesn't need to know how to survive.'"

6

Making Deals

On February 14, 2003, the families of Keith Stansell, Tom Howes, and Marc Gonsalves were informed of the crash by a Northrop Grumman representative and told that there was no information on the men's whereabouts. For three more days, the status of the Americans remained unknown, but it was assumed that they had been taken hostage by the FARC. For Gary Noesner, who was assisting in handling the situation for Northrop Grumman, the case itself wasn't anything out of the ordinary. Noesner had spent over two decades with the FBI, dealing with terrorism cases and hostage negotiations. Only one month earlier, he'd retired from his position as chief of the Crisis Negotiation Unit of the FBI and taken a civilian position with Control Risks, an international security company that had been under contract to provide security services to Northrop Grumman. What Noesner expected would happen next in the case of the three American contractors was something much like what had been played out dozens of times over the past thirteen years under a protocol that Noesner himself had painstakingly developed.

In 1980, after eight years with the FBI, twenty-nine-year-old Noesner began working as a negotiator. At the time, hostage negotiation was still a fairly new discipline in law enforcement and was essentially an auxiliary function to SWAT (Special Weapons and Tactics). There were no full-time negotiators, so Noesner's Washington, D.C.–based job was twofold: He trained agents in the art of negotiation and he investigated terrorism cases overseas, mostly in the Middle East, where in the 1980s, he led the investigations of the hijackings of TWA Flight 847 and the Italian cruise ship *Achille Lauro* and many other such incidents. During the same period, Noesner honed his negotiating skills, dealing with prison riots, skyjackings, and militia standoffs in the United States. Then on December 21, 1988, Pan Am Flight 103 exploded over Lockerbie, Scotland, killing all 270 people on board. One hundred and eighty-nine of the passengers were Americans, making the attack against American citizens the deadliest on record. It was a turning point for Noesner, who, after so much time abroad, was burned out on terrorism cases. With his wife and three young children at home in Virginia, Noesner decided to take an offer he had turned down several times and become part of an FBI operational and teaching unit based in Quantico, Virginia. In 1990, the ten-year veteran of terrorism and

Gary Noesner on an FBI mission to train Jordanian police at the Dead Sea in 1995. Photo: Gary Noesner.

hostage cases became one of only three full-time hostage negotiators for the FBI.

That same year, the FBI began to investigate international kidnapping cases involving American citizens under the Comprehensive Crime Control Act passed by Congress in 1984. Any such incident would be considered a federal crime and therefore under the jurisdiction of the FBI. What had been Noesner's forte domestically was now under his domain globally. The first two overseas hostage cases were handled by Noesner's colleagues. One involved a coal mine employee in Ecuador; the other, a Peace Corps worker in the Philippines. Both cases ended in successful negotiations and hostage releases. At the end of 1990, Noesner was deployed on the FBI's third international hostage case. Brent Swan, a U.S. helicopter mechanic with Chevron Corporation, was kidnapped in Cabinda, Angola, by separatist rebels. While the rebels demanded a large ransom for Swan's release, the Angolan government threatened that if Chevron paid a ransom, the company would be thrown out of the country and cut off from significant investments in oil exploration and extraction infrastructure. For Noesner, the negotiation was a challenge he was eager to take on, and for eight weeks he worked alongside negotiators from Control Risks, the private security company hired by Chevron (and the company that Noesner would later work for). "What was eventually structured," explains Noesner, "was instead of giving them money or weapons, we gave them blankets, medical supplies, two vehicles, and office equipment." Swan was released. "The oil company got its employee back, and it was able to continue to operate in Cabinda. The Angolan government did not object to the agreement, because they weren't going to get hurt by these guys buying guns to fight against them. The U.S. government was happy. Everybody was happy. It was creative problem solving."

Noesner continued working on both overseas kidnappings and domestic cases, and he felt good about the FBI's new role in dealing with international crimes against American citizens. Although Noesner was a physically commanding man with a very strong personality, he realized that the role of a good negotiator was not to act as a sole operator in a hostage situation. Credit was something he could do without. The payoff was finding nonviolent ends to the crises, and Noesner had

perfected the art of persuasion, even in the most volatile of circumstances. Over the next several years, Noesner and his colleagues worked
quietly on international cases; all during this time, the U.S. government
claimed that it would not negotiate with terrorists while silently con-
senting to the FBI's involvement. Each hostage case was assigned two
FBI negotiators until an outcome was achieved. "We were helping
companies in South America, Asia, Africa," says Noesner. "If the company had to pay ransom, the FBI would say, 'Okay, we don't condone it.
We're not going to give you the money. We have to officially tell you
that paying ransom encourages more kidnapping. But if you're gonna
do it, let us help you do it smart so you don't get ripped off.' "

The successes were mounting for the FBI's hostage negotiators,
who were also considered "behaviorists" because of their intense training and understanding of criminal minds in hostage situations. However, negotiators were still subordinate to FBI tactical agents from the
hostage rescue team (HRT) during hostage crises. It was this power differential that would bring about what Noesner would consider the single worst day in the history of the FBI.

In February 1993, after a year watching a religious sect called the
Branch Davidians stockpile weapons at their headquarters in Waco,
Texas, agents from the Bureau of Alcohol, Tobacco and Firearms
attacked the compound. Inside, cult leader David Koresh sent women
and children to take cover and launched a counterassault on the federal agents. Four ATF agents were shot and killed and another sixteen
were wounded. Koresh allowed the bodies of five Branch Davidians
killed in the gun battle to be removed from the compound, and he
held fire as the ATF retreated. He then hunkered down with more
than one hundred followers, including women and children, and
refused to surrender.

Noesner was immediately deployed to Waco. Jeff Jamar, the head
of the FBI's San Antonio office, was the FBI's on-scene commander. He
was to rely on Noesner, the chief negotiator, and Dick Rogers, the head
of the HRT. For the first twenty-five days of the siege, Koresh proved
difficult, but Noesner and his team of negotiators were having success
almost daily. The day Noesner arrived, he and his team of negotiators
convinced Koresh to release four children. A total of twenty-one chil-

dren and two elderly women were released between February 28 and March 3. Noesner and his team's continuing strategy was chronicled in a Department of Justice (DOJ) report:

> The first theme was to appeal to the parents inside to join their released children by sending photographs and videotapes of the children into the compound, passing messages from the children to their parents and vice versa, and demonstrating that the children needed the parents, missed them and awaited their reunion. The second theme involved continued reassurance to all those inside the compound that they would not be harmed and would be treated fairly if they came out. The next theme was to use twice-daily FBI press conferences to accentuate the positive reasons for the individuals to come out, to demonstrate concern for their safety, to clarify press distortions or inaccurate speculation about persons inside the compound, and to use psychology to get the Davidians to doubt Koresh's leadership. In this regard, the negotiators also attempted to "drive a wedge" between Koresh and Steve Schneider, his second-in-command. The negotiators constantly urged Schneider to take charge and to bring the people out. Finally, the last theme was to pursue discussions aimed at providing Koresh with an incentive to come out, including discussing and implying weaknesses in a prosecution of Koresh, and pointing out to Koresh the opportunity to expand his following and promote his views through book and movie deals.

According to Noesner, Jamar and Rogers were not happy with what they considered slow progress. "There was an element, in my judgment, within the FBI that was frustrated it was taking so long. They felt it made them look weak and ineffective. They wanted to use force. They were embracing the concept 'We can make people do what we want them to do.' It seemed like every time we got hostages out, they would do something stupid on the outside. I was in charge of the negotiations. I'd have to dig us out of the hole again, and we'd get a few more people out."

The Department of Justice report cited some of what Noesner and other negotiators felt was undercutting the negotiations:

In the case of Waco, the negotiators felt that the negotiating and tactical components of the FBI's strategy were more often contradictory than complementary. The negotiators' goal was to establish a rapport with the Branch Davidians in order to win their trust. As part of this effort, negotiators emphasized to Branch Davidians the "dignity" and fair treatment the group would receive upon its exit from the compound. By contrast, the negotiators felt that the efforts of the tactical personnel were directed toward intimidation and harassment. In the negotiators' judgment, those aggressive tactics undermined their own attempts to gain Koresh's trust as a prelude to a peaceful surrender.

In particular, some of the negotiators objected to: (1) the loud music, noise, and chants used as "psychological warfare"; (2) the shut-off of electricity to the compound on March 12 shortly after two people exited the compound; and (3) the removal of automobiles from the compound on March 21 after seven people exited the compound. All of these actions were viewed by the negotiators as counter-productive to their efforts. The electricity shut-off and the removal of cars were seen as particularly unwarranted since these actions in effect "punished" Koresh for permitting the departure of compound members.

Of working the crisis with Agents Jamar and Rogers, Noesner says, "Dealing with David Koresh was easier. I'm more proud of anything that I've done in the FBI that we got thirty-five people out under incredibly difficult circumstances, *internally*."

After five weeks on the job, FBI bosses removed Noesner and replaced him with another negotiation coordinator. "They wanted to bring in another guy, Clint Van Zandt. He was really close friends with one of the more tactical-oriented guys high up in the Bureau. They never told me it was because I was thwarting their efforts." The official explanation from headquarters was that they were taking Noesner out of Waco because everybody else had rotated out. "They said, 'You've been there five weeks. It's time for you to get a rest.' " Noesner was told that when he returned from his scheduled trip to the Middle East, he would be brought back to handle the negotiations at Waco.

Over the next twenty-six days, not a single person came out of the Branch Davidian complex. On April 19, the day that Noesner returned to the United States, a combination of tear gas and ammunition rounds started a fire that destroyed the compound. Seventy-six people died in the fire, including David Koresh, twenty-one children, and two pregnant women. Finger-pointing ensued in the immediate aftermath, and the official blame was put solely on Koresh and the Branch Davidians. But many, including Noesner, who were critical of the handling of the incident demanded and got an investigation, something that angered many in the Bureau. The reports that came out shed light on what had essentially been an FBI debacle of epic proportion. The devastating and very public failure at Waco catapulted the idea of negotiation to the forefront of the FBI's agenda and brought Noesner's position as a negotiator to the same level as that of tactical leaders who would be deployed in such cases. "All these commissions said, 'You've got to prop up the negotiation programs,' " says Noesner. For the rest of his career as an FBI agent, Noesner headed up the Crisis Negotiation Unit and never again took a subordinate role in a hostage crisis.

FBI agent Chris Voss, a lead international kidnapping negotiator until November 2007, remembers Noesner's proclivity to cause a stir within the agency. "He only seemed like a maverick because he knew what the right thing was to do; he wasn't afraid to push ahead with it at any given point in time. He would often scare the government bureaucrats who would be around us in the different interagencies." Voss says that Noesner could be incredibly insistent on pushing for what he believed in, but he was extremely skilled and artful when using a method Noesner called the "soft touch." "So, yes, Gary was a maverick, but he was also a tremendous leader, and he knew his business."

After Waco, the importance of well-planned and well-thought-out policy on dealing with international hostage situations was recognized across government agencies at the highest levels. And in 2002,

President Bush signed the National Security Presidential Directive (NSPD-12), which would offer a set of guidelines for dealing with Americans held hostage abroad. "Gary Noesner was a principal architect of NSPD-12," says Voss. The Hostage Working Group, a subcommittee chaired by the National Security Council, was given the charge to implement the directive. Standing members of the group included the FBI, State Department Counterterrorism, Department of Defense, and CIA. "Gary was present when the heads of the agencies, [Secretary of State] Colin Powell, [Secretary of Defense] Donald Rumsfeld, [CIA director] George Tenet, sat in a room and agreed to it." The committee would meet either on an "as needed" basis, which was as much as once a month, or more frequently if international kidnappings called for it.

In January 2003, Noesner retired from the FBI, and Voss moved into his mentor's seat within the Hostage Working Group. A month later, Noesner, now a senior vice president for Control Risks (which was under contract to Northrop Grumman to handle the kidnapping of Howes, Stansell, and Gonsalves), was put on his first case as a civilian negotiator. By then, the seasoned negotiator had worked on over 120 hostage cases with the FBI. He didn't expect this case to bring anything he hadn't dealt with in the past. Working in Colombia would be nothing new for him, either. In Noesner's tenure with the FBI, he'd worked more Colombian kidnapping cases than any other type of case (mostly managing them from the States while sending a full-time agent to the country).

For more than a decade before Howes, Stansell, and Gonsalves were kidnapped, Colombia held the dubious distinction of having the highest kidnapping rate in the world, and the problem plagued not only Colombian citizens but also foreigners. Because Colombia has a wealth of as-yet-untapped oil and mineral reserves and there are hundreds of millions of U.S. government dollars earmarked to fight drug cultivation and production, numerous U.S. and foreign companies have employees in Colombia who have commonly been the target of kidnappers. The corporations have become accustomed to dealing with abductions, and dozens of hostage situations have been settled by dropping caseloads of American currency into jungle and mountain terrain. By early 2003, the process of dealing with kidnappings of foreigners in Colombia had been repeated so many times that there was an expected protocol—a commonly played-out exchange between kidnapper and negotiator that usually began as soon as the kidnapping took place.

Immediately after an employee was kidnapped, a negotiator from a security company was deployed to Colombia to try to establish contact with the kidnappers. In the United States, security companies such as the Florida-based Ackerman Group and the Washington, D.C., office of Control Risks provided operational guidance to clients as part of what was commonly referred to as "kidnapping and ransom insurance," underwritten by large insurers such as Lloyd's of London. The kidnappers might have been from one of the guerrilla groups—most notably, the FARC or the ELN—they might have been linked to paramilitary groups, or they could have been common criminals. The guerrillas had become so much of a problem that some North American companies were accused of paying illegal paramilitary groups for "protection" of their investments. In 2007, Chiquita Banana Company admitted to paying "protection" money to Colombian paramilitary groups— identified by the U.S. government as known terrorist organizations. (The company agreed to pay a $25 million fine to end a federal investigation.) Although the U.S. State Department forbids government concessions to terrorists or kidnappers, in all cases that Noesner had handled since 1990, a full-time FBI negotiator worked alongside and assisted the private security consultants to secure the safe release of hostages.

"Historically, FARC would grab an oil-exploration worker, a mining guy, an agriculture worker or someone like that and hold them for money," says Noesner. "Then they communicate with the family or the company. The company would sometimes have a relationship with a [company like] Control Risks, sometimes not. If it's an American citizen being held, even if it's a Colombian with dual citizenship, the FBI would deploy. Not to take over the negotiations but to say, 'Here's what we recommend; here's the issues as we see them.'" The security company's negotiator and the FBI agent would then appoint a family member or someone close to the case, who, after coaching, would act as a communicator to speak directly with the kidnappers. "The U.S. ambassador to Colombia would be informed of what was going on, but they pretty much gave the FBI free rein to assist and help the families as long as they reported back to the embassy."

If the kidnappers had already made a monetary demand, the negotiations would be fairly straightforward. The communicator would ask for proof of life, such as a video or photo of the victim. If the kidnappers refused, the negotiators would try to establish whether the victim was alive by asking questions that only the victim could answer. Once proof of life was established, the negotiations for money would begin. At the time of the kidnapping of Howes, Stansell, and Gonsalves, a common rule of thumb for Colombian kidnappings was that payment would likely be about 10 percent of the initial demand. Just under four years earlier, in a 1999 case, a $3.5 million ransom was paid for seven Canadians and one American oil worker seized in the Ecuadorian village of Tarapoa—the original demand had been $35 million. The settlement was a tremendous boon for the kidnappers. In the aftermath, the kidnapping of foreigners turned into large-scale and well-planned operations for various guerrillas and paramilitary groups, and negotiations became increasingly difficult to manage because of the enormous stakes.

One of the most ill-fated cases that Noesner oversaw from his Quantico, Virginia, headquarters began on October 12, 2000, when nine foreign workers were captured in Ecuador near an oil-drilling area close to the Colombian border. Forty men, dressed in fatigues and armed with assault rifles, surrounded the site. The victims—four Americans, a New Zealander, an Argentinean, a Chilean, and two French citizens—were forced into a helicopter, which the kidnappers then stole from the site and flew off to a jungle prison camp. Four days later, the two French helicopter pilots escaped. The seven remaining hostages had been working for three different corporations, each of which was represented by its own security company. The security companies' representatives had varying degrees of experience in hostage negotiations and held vastly differing views on how to proceed.

From the beginning, the negotiations were tense. The first contact from the kidnappers came over VHF radio to the large group of negotiators who were based in Quito, Ecuador. The group included an FBI agent, members of the Ecuadorian Police Anti-Kidnapping and Extortion Unit, three security officials from Chile and Argentina, and three private security consultants representing Erickson Air-Crane, a heavy-lift helicopter company; Helmerich & Payne, Inc., an oil-drilling firm; and Schlumberger, a New York oil-services firm. The kidnappers identified themselves as the "Free America Commando" and launched into a tirade against the role of the United States in Colombia's narcotics industry. The kidnappers, who were believed to be associated with FARC guerrillas, demanded eighty million dollars for the release of the seven men. It was a ridiculous and unprecedented demand. The negotiators went quiet and then broke out in nervous laughter. As the bargaining began, tensions grew. "There were arguments about who should lead the negotiations, what to offer, how quickly to offer it . . . all kinds of complications," an employee of one of the security firms told a local reporter after the crisis was over.

By early November, with the kidnappers sticking to their eighty-million-dollar demand, the negotiating team began considering the risky option of a rescue attempt. A thirty-five-member team from the U.S. military (SOUTHCOM) concluded that a rescue attempt would be too risky because the hostages were being held in the deepest part of the Amazon jungle. For more than two months, the heated negotiations went back and forth. The team of quarreling negotiators hadn't received any proof of life, and the kidnappers weren't budging on their first demand. Negotiators from one of the security companies argued that the $3.5 million that had been paid in 1999 was too high, and that by taking a tough stance with a lower offer, they could curb the guerrillas' outrageous demands. After twenty different communication exchanges between the kidnappers and the security companies, the kidnappers demanded that a counteroffer be made. Without conferring with the others, a representative from one of the security companies spit out a number: $500,000. Before anyone could stop him, the flustered intermediary repeated the number into the radio. The paltry sum was ridiculous—an absolute insult to the kidnappers. The blunder resulted in the kidnappers screaming expletives and terminating the conversation. "It was an ungodly mess. And sadly, the lack of effective communication between all the parties led to the execution of hostage Ronald Sander, the American," says Noesner. On January 31, 2001, the body of Sander, a fifty-four-year-old Helmerich & Payne employee, turned up full of bullet holes; he'd been shot five times in the back with a semiautomatic rifle. His body was wrapped in a white sheet, on which was scrawled, "I am a gringo. For nonpayment of ransom."

Days later, a deal was brokered. The security companies and their insurers would pay thirteen million dollars to the kidnappers. Logistics were worked out over the following weeks. The money, packed in seven boxes weighing more than nine hundred pounds, was shoved off a helicopter as it hovered over a jungle clearing that was marked by a red oilcloth. The hostages were given their freedom and arrived in Quito six days later, on March 1, 2001, after 141 days in captivity.

It was the high-dollar precedent set by this case that had Noesner expecting the FARC to demand a ransom in the tens of millions for the three Americans. The company was well aware of the possibility, too, and even before there was a demand of any kind, a Northrop Grumman representative told Howes's and Gonsalves's wives and Stansell's fiancée that the company might not be able to pay the ransom amount. Noesner assumed that in his new role as a civilian negotiator, he would work with the FBI and Colombian intelligence to negotiate a safe release. But Noesner was wrong. Since the attacks of September 11, 2001, the Bush administration had turned the word *negotiate* into a statement of weakness, a sign of failure. And this new paradigm would completely shut down any interest on the part of the U.S. government in looking for a diplomatic solution for the hostages' freedom. Confounding the situation even more, the FARC made an unprecedented demand. The ultimatum was posted on the FARC's official Web site on February 24, 2003: "Three Gringos in the custody of our organization will be liberated, along with other Colombian prisoners of war, once a prisoner exchange materializes in a large demilitarized zone between the government of Uribe and the FARC."

The FARC statement came as a complete shock to Noesner, to U.S. military bosses at SOUTHCOM, to politicians in Washington, and to the FBI agents, who had grown accustomed to helping negotiate for hostage releases in Colombia. It was especially shocking to the Northrop Grumman brass, who, although the company had acquired CMS four years earlier, claimed that they didn't have any idea that

Northrop Grumman had employees running such dangerous missions. (A source within the company would later defend the company's ignorance, arguing that companies like Northrop Grumman are so enormous that it is sometimes impossible to keep track of subordinate companies or to learn about every aspect of the company for sale before purchasing it.) The FARC's statement was even a shock to Colombian president Álvaro Uribe; never before had Americans in Colombia been considered spoils of the country's civil war. The "other Colombian prisoners of war" the FARC was referring to had been captured over the last half decade. They included Colombian politicians, military and National Police officers, and soldiers.

As far as FARC high commander Manuel Marulanda was concerned, Stansell, Gonsalves, and Howes were invading mercenaries fighting alongside the heavy-handed, hard-line administration of Álvaro Uribe. And because Marulanda considered *spies* more valuable than regular civilians, for whom the FARC mandate was to demand cash payments, the FARC's offer was to trade the gringos for guerrillas who had been captured and were serving time in Colombian prisons. For Marulanda, the idea of liberating his soldiers was driven by a strong paternal nature to protect his own. Above everything else, it was a question of honor. It was his number one goal, the thing that he was most passionate about. In 2001, under President Andrés Pastrana, deals such as this had been negotiated between the government and the guerrillas, resulting in prisoner exchanges, and Marulanda was hoping for a similar scenario this time around. But the political climate had changed in both Colombia and Washington, and both governments were now taking a much tougher stance against the FARC, which had the official U.S. designation of "terrorist organization." The second part of the demand, what the guerrillas referred to as "a large demilitarized zone," meant that the guerrillas wanted the government to guarantee there would be no Colombian troops in a 44,000-square-mile area covering the departments of Caquetá and Putumayo. Uribe announced that he had no intention of releasing FARC guerrillas from prison in an exchange or ceding a demilitarized zone to the FARC. (The FARC had persuaded Uribe's predecessor, President Pastrana, to demilitarize a

16,000-square-mile area for more than three years, with disastrous results for the government.)

For all his experience, Noesner was about to face a completely different landscape, one that he would have to navigate for a longer time than any other kidnapping case in his career. The case would pit him against the State Department, the Department of Justice, and even his former friends and subordinates at the FBI. Noesner would fume that the classified National Security Presidential Directive (which he had helped author) signed by George W. Bush, which included the passage "The U.S. Government will make every effort, including contact with representatives of the captors, to obtain the release of hostages without making concessions to the hostage takers," would be tossed aside as the government turned its back on the art of negotiation. Months after the kidnapping, the overarching dismissal of what Noesner had spent his entire career perfecting would lead him to conclude angrily, "Some in our government would just as soon see these guys dead as rescued."

7

The River Queen

The roots of *Erythroxylum coca* and its white powder derivative, cocaine, are deeply imbedded in the history of the northern Andes, the mountain chain that runs the length of the South American continent. As early as 500 B.C., Incan tribes in the areas of present-day Peru, Bolivia, and Ecuador used the plant in religious ceremonies. Shamans burned the leaves—which were thought to have magical powers—to see the future and purify places inhabited by evil spirits. In the late 1500s, Spanish physician and botanist Nicolás Monardes wrote about South American indigenous people who would chew a mixture of tobacco and coca leaves as a stimulant. When Spanish conquistadors took over land from the native tribes, they levied a 10 percent tax on coca production. The plant's medicinal benefits were widely known throughout South America, and in 1609, a Peruvian priest, Padre Blas Valera, wrote:

> Coca protects the body from many ailments, and our doctors use it in powdered form to reduce the swelling of wounds, to strengthen broken bones, to expel cold from the body or prevent it from entering, and to cure rotten wounds or sores that

*The town of Peñas Coloradas, on the Caguán River, under control of FARC comman-
der Sonia until her arrest in 2004. The community was very prosperous thanks to
cocaine commerce. The military took it over in 2004 and all the residents left. Photo:
Carlos Villalón.*

are full of maggots. And if it does so much for outward ail-
ments, will not its singular virtue have even greater effect in the
entrails of those who eat it?

Cocaine alkaloid was first isolated in 1855 and purified in 1860 by
German chemists, becoming commonly used in the late part of the century as a pain reliever and as an anesthetic during dental and eye
surgery. Because of its other neurological effects, such as increased
energy, lack of hunger, euphoria, and exhilaration (a result of its effect
of blocking the brain's ability to take up released dopamine), cocaine
was soon popular in a variety of medical practices. Sigmund Freud was
a well-known proponent of the drug as an antidepressant and for the
treatment of morphine addiction.

Peru supplied most of the world's raw coca leaf and became a major industrial producer of semirefined cocaine, *cocaína bruta*, for export to the United States and Europe by the 1880s. Because of the growing demand, Peruvian producers began to modernize production for large-scale commercial exportation. By the turn of the century, Peru was shipping ten metric tons of semirefined cocaine to the United States, France, and Germany annually. However, the drug's harmful effects, such as addiction, high blood pressure, and weight loss, were becoming apparent, and in 1914, the U.S. Congress regulated and taxed cocaine and opium imports, sales, and distribution under the Harrison Narcotics Tax Act. By the 1920s, a combination of prohibition and bad press about the negative effects of the drug caused demand to slow to a trickle, even though cocaine remained available and cheap. With the start of World War II, the availability of cocaine in the United States decreased and the price skyrocketed. Traditional trafficking routes were cut off by the war and remained disrupted well into the 1950s. The lack of cocaine made the drug an expensive indulgence, one for only the very rich.

By the late 1960s, President Richard Nixon believed that illegal drug abuse in the United States had reached epidemic proportions. The boom was blamed on a variety of sources: Vietnam, paraphernalia shops, media coverage, and youthful disenchantment with mainstream culture. While marijuana and heroin were the lead characters, cocaine was steadily making a comeback, but it still remained out of the financial reach of the majority of drug users. In 1970, Nixon signed the Controlled Substances Act—officially making cocaine illegal in the United States as a Schedule II drug (with only limited use by physicians). And in a 1971 press conference, Nixon named drug abuse as "public enemy number one," officially beginning the United States' decades-long war on drugs, which would prove increasingly futile as the years wore on.

By the late 1970s, with an exponentially increasing demand for cocaine among U.S. users, entrepreneurs in Colombia recognized that coca could be grown and processed in the most remote regions of the country, far away from the watchful eyes of Bogotá and Washington. Until the mid-twentieth century, a third of Colombia—the Amazon jungle, which reaches from the Eastern Cordillera to the southern border—was virgin land inhabited by small nomadic tribes. The demographic began to change in the 1950s, during La Violencia, when thousands of campesino families escaped from the bloodshed of their villages into the remote departments of Caquetá, Putumayo, Guaviare, Guainía, Vaupés, and Amazonas. They came from many regions of the country, seeking new lands to cultivate, slashing and burning the indigenous forest to clear small plots where they cultivated banana, yuca, rubber, and cacao (used to make chocolate) and tended to small herds of livestock. The jungle was colonized without the knowledge of the Colombian government, and without any central authority, the campesinos created their own laws to regulate their villages. Democratically elected community boards made major decisions regarding the welfare of the settlers. Makeshift schools, health clinics, markets, and bars sprouted from the jungle soil, and an Amazonian culture emerged—mixing the languages, the music, and the foods from many regions of Colombia.

In the mid-1970s, missionary Catholic priests—almost all Italian— arrived in the region, celebrating Mass and constructing small churches in Cartagena del Chairá, Remolinos del Caguán, and some other more populated villages in the region. News from outside, what was referred to as "the other country," arrived by radio or by word of mouth from those who traveled the Caguán River—known as the "gateway to the Colombian Amazon." It was during that period that the first groups of FARC soldiers appeared. For the guerrillas, the Amazon was a safe haven—a place to erect permanent camps, where they could increase their ranks without fear of the Colombian military. As far as the campesinos were concerned, the guerrillas were not intimidating. On the contrary, they offered some order and were a comforting, protective presence.

In the late 1970s and early 1980s, coca buyers, seeing endless opportunity in the remote jungle, came with seeds from the high-altitude coca shrub and distributed them among the Amazon farmers. The plants thrived in the jungle. Coca increased the farmers' incomes thirty- to fortyfold; a kilo of coca base paid $250, far more than what the farmers could get for twenty-five kilos of yuca or *plátano*. The coca was harvested as often as four times each year, and money flowed into the region. Villages on the shores of the Caguán River multiplied, but the coca boom also brought misfortune. Small farms were converted into huge plantations, which resulted in the need for manual labor to pick the crops. Men from all over the country came to the area, attracted by stories of "white gold." The promise was of better wages and a good life without government and without laws. The newcomers were the poorest of the poor, almost all illiterate and accustomed to solving their problems through violence. Many of the men who came to the Amazon were fleeing from justice, delinquents who had committed crimes and were now seeking refuge in the jungle.

The migrants lived in horrible conditions in camps near the plantations. The work they did was backbreaking labor; in the blazing sun and stifling humidity, they held the coca shrubs between their knees, *raspando* (scraping) the coca branches with their hands to pull off the leaves, then tossing the leaves into burlap sacks on their backs. The method earned the coca pickers the name *raspachines*. During the harvests, *raspachines* worked from 6:00 a.m. until 5:00 p.m. The workweek began on Monday and ended Saturday, when at dusk, thousands of men with thickly callused hands descended on the nearby pueblos. The bars pumped out the favorite music of the *raspachines*, "*narco-corridos*"— Mexican ballads chronicling violent epics of great narco-traffickers— and the migrant workers spent all of their wages on *aguardiente* (an anise-flavored liqueur), beer, and prostitutes. Sexually transmitted diseases spread quickly throughout the region. By Sunday night, most of the men were drunk and looking for a fight. On Monday, after the tumult of the weekend, those killed in drunken brawls were counted by the dozens.

By the mid-1980s, with escalating violence and no official entity to deal with the chaos, the FARC guerrillas stepped into the role of law enforcement and began to govern the region. At the time, the growers were still directly employed by the major drug cartels in Cali and Medellín, and the cartels would send out buyers to gather the merchandise by the ton. Because the guerrillas now had control over the area, they were able to tax the coca growers and the buyers. The new funding source was practically limitless and provided the guerrillas with money for weapons, as well as the ability to greatly increase their ranks. By the late 1990s and early 2000s, with the cartels long out of the picture in the

Amazon after their demise at the hands of Colombian and U.S. forces, the FARC had become the de facto government in all of the coca-growing regions in southern Colombia.

It was the task of a midlevel FARC guerrilla commander named Sonia to take care of business in Peñas Coloradas, a rugged outpost on the banks of the Caguán River in the department of Caquetá. Peñas Coloradas had become a commercial center on the river "highway," and boasted three bars, two whorehouses, one pharmacy, a health clinic, a school, a small park, and about fifty houses. The village was nearly identical to about twenty others that lined the Caguán River. Campesino farmers—worn and cragged old men in cowboy hats— young housewives, dusty children, and tattooed prostitutes all had a hand in the lowest level of the international cocaine trade. All over town, bright blue tarps were spread out, covered by coca base drying in the sun. (Base is the result of the first stage of processing, when kerosene, sodium carbonate, and sulfuric acid are used to turn the coca leaves into a thick paste.) In the rainy season, when coca crops flourished, FARC soldiers would come to town weekly and buy the base, and the campesinos would have handfuls of cash, as a kilo of base at the time could earn a farmer about one thousand dollars. In the dry season, the FARC buyers would come by infrequently, and coca base became the only currency in the village. At the local pharmacy, the white powder paid for dry goods, and the clerk weighed the base with a scale on the counter, collected the bags, and made change in pesos. Prostitutes, whom the FARC required to have weekly medical checkups, took bags of base to the doctor to pay for examinations and treatment. Kilos of coca base were traded for clothing, food, liquor, and medicine.

Sonia's assignment as the *comandante* of Peñas Coloradas and other nearby outposts was a testament to the toughness and determination of this woman in her early thirties who came from the department of Huila, in the foothills of the Andes. Born Anayibe Rojas Valderrama, she had lived in stifling poverty with her parents and twelve siblings. "In my house there wasn't enough money for my siblings and me to have shoes. I wore my first pair of shoes the day of my First Communion," she recalls. FARC soldiers were a common presence in the village, and given Valderrama's limited education and lack of future

possibilities, the young, clean, and well-fed soldiers were like gods to
her. In 1987, when she was twenty years old, without telling anyone or
leaving a note explaining her decision, Valderrama left to join the revolutionary army and took the nom de guerre Sonia.

At first, guerrilla life was difficult for the young woman. She would
wake up at 4:30 a.m. for chores and training. She cooked, planted and
cultivated crops, exercised, and studied reading, writing, FARC ideology, and weapons for at least two hours a day. In the evenings, all FARC
camps had a "cultural hour," when they would discuss the news and politics or sing and play music. Occasionally, Sonia would memorize
poems and recite them during the cultural hour. Afterward, she would
stand guard for two hours before being allowed to sleep briefly. Then
she would awake and repeat the identical tasks the next day.

Many of the male guerrillas in her unit courted her. "They compli-
mented me for being so *pilosa* [active and energized]," she says. Often
one of her comrades would ask her to be his girlfriend. "I always
refused." And the frustrated suitors began spreading rumors. "They
said I was stuck-up; that I thought I was a queen, hoping to conquer a
commander." Sonia was frustrated and felt underutilized. She hadn't
joined the FARC to find a man or to "peel potatoes or learn to be a dental hygienist," as they had been training her to do. She sincerely wanted
to be a soldier, and she would regularly request that she be sent into
combat. So Sonia was thrilled when she was taught how to operate
some new radios that had arrived. She was fascinated with the study of
communications, and she excelled in her class. Soon after, she was chosen to be the radio operator for a commander called Perdomo.
"Finally," she says, "I was on the road to the battlefields."

Meanwhile, a young guerrilla named Wilson was subtly working on
stealing her heart. "When the sun went down and everyone returned to
camp, Wilson would accompany me as I bathed in the river; he helped
me organize my small *caleta* [a tentlike structure] and tutored me in my
studies." If she had kitchen duty, he showed up and kept her company
while she dripped with sweat in front of the boiling pots. "He became
my guardian angel," she says. But still, Sonia refused his romantic
advances. It wasn't until Wilson was sent away to an explosives course
that she realized she was falling for him. Rumors that Wilson had

become cozy with a very pretty guerrilla in his class made their way to Sonia's camp. "I was tortured," she says. This torture, she believed, was love. So when Wilson finished his course and returned to the camp, Sonia threw him into her *caleta*, gave herself to him, and begged him never to leave. As was mandatory, they requested permission from their superior to become a couple, a state synonymous with marriage in the FARC. A top commander named Fabián Ramírez, who was visiting the camp, did the honors and gave his official blessing to the union.

Sonia quickly and accidentally became pregnant, which was prohibited in every level of the guerrilla army. She escaped punishment or being thrown out of the movement because Wilson was a high-ranking soldier and was very respected by the commanders. Sonia spent her pregnancy in the camp but left to give birth in Cartagena del Chairá, the largest pueblo along the edge of the Caguán River. She returned with the baby and was able to spend almost a year with Wilson and her son. Then the day came when her heart would break. The commander in charge gave Sonia the option to leave and raise the boy with her family, where she knew she would struggle just to feed him; but if Sonia wanted to continue her life as a guerrilla, which was the only way she and Wilson could be together, she would have to give up the child. Tortured, she and Wilson chose to send the boy to the same family who had raised Wilson in a remote area of Caquetá.

Sonia's military career flourished, and in 1998 she received orders, along with two hundred other guerrillas, to attack a military base in Caquetá. Sonia stayed back to coordinate the radio communications. Wilson was sent to the front, where he fell under the first barrage. For almost eight hours, Wilson lay on the ground, his stomach ripped open by shrapnel. She heard his terrible cries for help over the radio, but because the frequency was reserved only for commanders communicating battle plans, Sonia could not say a word as Wilson lay dying. "It was such anguish and helplessness that I felt, not being able to speak to him or to help him," she says. Finally, when his comrades were able to get to him, Wilson was near death. Sonia saw Wilson briefly when he was carried to a jungle hospital. A few days after, she learned that he had died and been buried in a temporary grave. Months later, some of Wilson's guerrilla friends brought Sonia a bag containing his remains. She washed the bones and put them in a clean bag, which she carried around for almost a year as her unit was moved from camp to camp, until she was able to return the bones to Peñas Coloradas, the place that Wilson had called home.

After giving Wilson's remains a decent burial, Sonia continued her work on the banks of the Caguán River. Never having had many close friends, she was very lonely. But many of Wilson's friends came to her, offering help. "Everyone loved him," she says. "And they knew how much he loved me, so I was inheriting what people felt for Wilson." As she traveled up and down the river, her mind would constantly go back to Wilson's last words to her as he lay dying: "You have to continue on, and take care of yourself, dear. And you must tell our son who his father was. So that he, too, will be strong—a warrior like his parents."

Her dedication to the movement and her great competence as a radio operator in the course of dozens of battles did not go unnoticed. The high commanders put her in charge of Peñas Coloradas. Sonia's duties, like other midlevel commanders, included finding teachers for the school and nurses for the health clinic. She mandated that all of the prostitutes carry a card stating that they did not have any sexually transmitted diseases. She controlled the quantity of gasoline that could be sold to boat owners, and anyone wanting to travel on the river had to ask her for authorization. Sonia was well liked and respected by the people. "She was our 'government,' because we never knew anyone from Bogotá," said one resident of Peñas Coloradas. Outsiders who arrived in the area had to register with her or with her subordinate guerrillas. She ran a tight ship, which was especially difficult during the weekends, when after a weeklong enforced sobriety, nearly everyone got drunk. She was also the town banker, the person who gave loans to the campesinos, a loving Santa Claus who bought all of the children Christmas presents, and a mediator who helped settle family squabbles and doled out punishment for bad behavior. The village had to be well run, because it was a large source of income for the FARC, and Sonia's most important responsibility was to keep track of all of the buying and selling of coca base in the region.

By 2003, Sonia's success and that of all the players in the massively diversified drug trade had caused the cocaine business to explode.

Street values in the United States reached a new low, with a gram of cocaine averaging one hundred dollars—an 89 percent drop in price since 1975. Sonia felt confident in her abilities and optimistic about her future in the guerrilla army. What she had no idea of at the time was that others besides her commanders had recognized her dedication. With the use of bugged satellite phones, Colombian military intelligence officers had infiltrated communications along the Caguán River and were closely following the goings-on of Sonia and her comrades. And what she could never have imagined then was that just one year later, her high profile in the FARC and involvement in the coca trade would link her fate to that of Marc Gonsalves, Keith Stansell, and Thomas Howes—the three American hostages whose goal had been to shut the pervasive business down.

8

El Caguán

Two years after Simón Trinidad joined the FARC, friends close to him say that he received word that his wife, who was living in Mexico with their children, had moved on with another man. The betrayal was the impetus for his decision to remain in the guerrilla army. The following year, in December 1990, during a meeting between the FARC and ELN commanders in the region, Trinidad met with a group of high school students who were part of the Juventud Comunista. When fifteen-year-old Lucero saw the forty-year-old guerrilla commander, her reaction was immediate. "I don't know if it was love at first sight, but, yes, there was attraction," she recalls. "I was an ordinary citizen, and I looked at the guerrillas and it was like seeing pure Che Guevaras." Lucero idolized the renowned Argentinean revolutionary from images and propaganda that she'd seen all of her life. Guevara was the perfect hero, someone who could have saved the world. "I felt more than a physical attraction toward the guerrillas. It was an admiration for them, for what they represented." Trinidad stood out from the others because of his elegant manner. But more than that, Lucero says, "was how I admired his beliefs that he defended in every word. In each one of us, he left a seed planted. The way he expressed himself, the way he reached each of us was very strong."

For Trinidad, the young Lucero was impossible to forget, as well. The two began to see each other occasionally, when Trinidad could get away from his duties, or when Lucero could concoct a lie that her widowed mother would believe to explain a three-day absence. "One day, he took my hand, and we became boyfriend and girlfriend," she says. There was a six-hour distance between Trinidad's camp and Lucero's farm, so the two spent most of their time apart. Over the next year, the guerrilla commander sent romantic letters. "When I was far away, a little card would arrive with a seed—whatever little seed—because, he said, 'You place a seed anywhere, and the seed is sown. Since I have thrown my love in your field, love will bloom there, because I have planted it there.' "

After a year, Lucero told Trinidad that she wanted to join the FARC. He was hesitant. "Simón feared that I only wanted to join the guer-

FARC commander Simón Trinidad and a United Nations envoy, American James LeMoyne, meet in San Vicente del Caguán during the negotiations between the Colombian government and the FARC on January 11, 2002. Photo: AP Images/Scott Dalton.

rillas because I was in love with him. He thought that after the first week, I would be begging them to let me return to my house." But Lucero was adamant. Her life had been spent on a small farm in Becerril, in the department of César, near the Venezuelan border. Lucero called it a "feudalistic society," where rich landowners controlled the political system and hired paramilitaries to kill poor farmers they accused of rebellion. Several of Lucero's childhood friends were killed in the violence, which made her greatly admire the guerrillas who fought back against the repressive oligarchy. On her third trip to visit Trinidad at his encampment, Lucero was adamant. "I said, 'Simón, I'm going to stay here.' " When Trinidad told her that she couldn't, "I told him, 'Then I'm going to the ELN.' " Whether or not Trinidad took her threat seriously, he conceded that she could join the FARC and stay with him in the camp. When Lucero failed to return home, her mother and brother set out to find her, and when they did, they pleaded that she leave with them. When they realized Lucero would not listen, they sought out Trinidad. "She is a spoiled girl," her mother told him. "She won't be able to handle this." But neither the young woman nor the guerrilla commander, both of whom had fallen completely in love, could be swayed. Lucero stayed.

"For me, it was very hard physically," says Lucero, who had to carry heavy equipment on her back. The black rubber boots, the *pantaneras*, were terribly heavy and blisteringly hot on the long hikes up the sierra. "I was fifteen years old, almost sixteen, and I was weak, thin. I fell while I walked, and I was very afraid of the dark. So it hit me very hard." She missed her mother, her sisters, her brother, and her friends. She missed the food she was accustomed to, seeing movies, and dancing to popular music. She missed the freedom of being a civilian. But to the teenager whose family had always considered her spoiled, it was all worth it. "You leave everything. You change everything for a new life. It's like a rebirth, but into a life of much more sacrifice. The advantage is that you know that the sacrifice will all be worth it after the triumph of the revolution." And with that thought, Lucero was content.

After taking basic military courses and studying FARC ideology for the first year, Lucero was allowed to be with Trinidad, and she soon became pregnant. She didn't know how to tell Trinidad. When she did, he was livid. "He told me, 'I spend my life telling young men and women that they better not get pregnant. Tell me: With what face am I going to tell them that I'm going to be a father?' " Lucero gave birth to a healthy daughter but was able to keep the infant with her for only four months. Then Lucero was given an ultimatum. Stay with your child or continue to be a *guerrillera* and send the child away. "There are your feelings as a mother," Lucero said of the difficult decision in a 2005 interview, "but also your feelings as a revolutionary. What weighs more? I made the choice to return to the guerrillas, with pain, with my heart in my throat, but with the conviction, the desire to continue fighting." Lucero took the baby to live with her mother, who was overjoyed to care for her granddaughter. Lucero was heartbroken as she said good-bye to the child, but she felt convinced that returning to the mountains and to Trinidad was the right thing to do. The two continued to live together in the camp, Trinidad as the second in command of the Forty-first Front, and Lucero, like many other young women who were romantic partners with older commanders, as "Trinidad's woman." But Lucero took her role in the guerrilla army and in its defense of poor Colombians very seriously. "You see the soldier's treatment of the civilians; the soldier sees the enemy in the civilian population. We treat the civilian population with love, with love and affection—because if they are not our relatives, they are our companions. It is for them that we are giving our lives, our youth, our joys. For them we made the decision to come here."

The bond between Trinidad and Lucero continued to grow with their intense belief in the cause. And in early 1999, when Trinidad received orders from the Secretariat to travel to the south of the country and take part in the first dialogues between the FARC and the Colombian government in fifteen years, there was no question that Lucero would go, as well. Trinidad was one of only nine commanders chosen for the honor by the commander in chief, Marulanda. He was extremely proud of the appointment.

The negotiations had come about because by 1998, the guerrillas had brought the Colombian government nearly to its knees. In 1996, the FARC had launched a new phase of the war with multifront attacks on military objectives, using 60mm and 81mm mortars and improvised cylinder bombs. In August of that year, the FARC attacked and destroyed a military base in Putumayo, leaving fifty-four Colombian soldiers dead, seventeen wounded, and sixty captured. On December 20, 1997, the FARC attacked an army communications base, kidnapping eighteen soldiers. In March 1998, the FARC wiped out an elite army unit in southern Caquetá after local sympathizers provided the guerrillas with intelligence on the battalion's movements. Within two days, 107 of the battalion's 154 soldiers were dead. On August 3, 1998, the FARC attacked an antinarcotics base, kidnapping twenty-four members of the National Police. All told, in the departments of Caquetá, Putumayo, and Nariño, guerrillas overtook Colombian troops and captured approximately five hundred soldiers and members of the National Police.

Emboldened by the success of his army, Marulanda set his sights on taking over the large cities and then the entire country—a long-range plan, for which he concluded he would need at least forty thousand guerrillas. But in 1998, with less than twenty thousand troops spread out across Colombia, Marulanda knew he was far from powerful enough to take Bogotá or any other big city. Instead, his strategy was to scare the populace into thinking that it *might* be possible for the FARC to capture the major cities. To do so, the guerrillas embarked on a campaign of bombing civilian and military targets around Bogotá, destroying electrical towers to cut off power, and impeding transportation routes into the city.

With the country paralyzed by the constant guerrilla violence, and the growing perception that the FARC could take over at any time, presidential candidate Andrés Pastrana campaigned in early 1998 with the promise of setting a stage for peace negotiations with the FARC. Pastrana won the election in June and took office in August. An enormous coup for the guerrillas came very soon after Pastrana's inauguration. In October, the new president traveled to the mountains to meet the FARC Secretariat members, who convinced Pastrana, as a precondition to the peace dialogues, to cede temporarily a vast demilitarized zone of more than sixteen thousand square miles of high plains and Amazonian jungle. The demilitarized zone, or DMZ, which became official on November 7, 1998, was like a FARC state within the country of Colombia, and the press was soon referring to it as "Farclandia" or simply as "El Caguán," because much of the DMZ rested in the Caguán River Basin. Residents in the area, which was composed of five municipalities within the departments of Meta and Caquetá, were now legally under the rule of the FARC.

The official talks began in January 1999 with lots of fanfare but with seemingly little momentum to come to a cease-fire. Three months later, while the dialogues were still in their infancy, Trinidad and Lucero arrived from the mountains of Perijá after a grueling six-hundred-mile journey. Marulanda gave Trinidad the assignment of managing journalists who would be covering the talks and giving a sort of media training to the local people in San Vicente del Caguán, an impoverished municipality that had become the ad hoc capital of the DMZ. Marulanda wanted a positive spin from the town's residents, who were likely to be asked their opinion about treatment under the guerrillas, who had been the unofficial government for years. Trinidad was also asked to handle economic topics that the FARC would discuss in the dialogues. The refined commander had yet to prove his worth to Marulanda, who had always been suspicious about the few in his ranks who weren't from *el campo*, but, rather, from the educated elite. But Marulanda could not have predicted how great an asset Trinidad would be.

Since there were no hostilities allowed between government and FARC troops in the zone, delegates arrived from a dozen countries, including Canada, France, Switzerland, and Spain, to participate in the talks. Trinidad, wearing a uniform of camouflage fatigues with a bright green scarf around his neck, sporting stylish aviator sunglasses, and carrying a semiautomatic rifle, received many of those visitors and moved easily among delegates sent by U.N. Secretary-General Kofi Annan, ambassadors from many countries, and even with the then president of the New York Stock Exchange, Richard Grasso, who had come to discuss investment opportunities for the guerrillas.

In June 1999, the Washington, D.C.–based Center for International Policy sent a delegation from the U.S. Congress, led by Massachusetts Democrat William Delahunt. Trinidad attended the talks with the Americans and the FARC lead negotiator and commander of the Southern Bloc, Raúl Reyes. The topics discussed included illegal drugs, kidnapping, and the recent assassination of three Americans who had been working with Colombian indigenous tribes. But the talks failed to produce any concrete proposals to deal with the ongoing violence. In one of the most surreal photo ops of the talks, America Online founder Jim Kinsey arrived for a meeting with Marulanda, hugged the guerrilla, and swapped his baseball cap for Marulanda's rumpled *cachucha*. After the meeting, Kinsey said that he felt that Marulanda was "very much interested in achieving peace. He understands, I think, that foreign investment is critical to the prosperity of this country, and I think is willing to negotiate and to discuss possible solutions that will move this country into the 21st century."

The meetings were a tremendous slap in the face for Pastrana and a great embarrassment to many Colombians, who felt that the outside world was legitimizing the violent insurgents while ignoring the elected Colombian government. The great pomp that surrounded the dialogues created an enormous economic boon for San Vicente del Caguán; journalists and diplomats came with plentiful dollars. Hotels, restaurants, and local prostitutes were the first beneficiaries of the "peace" dialogues. For the FARC, it was an oasis. After years of living separately, confined by the wild Colombian geography and hounded by the Colombian army, the Secretariat members were all together. The sanctuary allowed them to refine their plans and chart new strategies. Nearly ten thousand guerrillas moved about freely in the DMZ. The guerrillas felt empowered, invincible—the revolutionary esprit de corps was at its greatest point in the history of the rebel army.

As weeks turned into months, Pastrana continued to push for discussions on disarmament. FARC negotiators danced around the topic, preferring instead to talk about economic and social issues and land reform. In due time, they said, they would speak about peace—when those other topics were solved. Day and night, Colombian news broadcasts reported on the dialogues. Over time, as it became apparent that the FARC was not interested in a cease-fire, Pastrana's team began to look more and more impotent. While the government returned again and again to negotiate, the FARC continued to commit terrorist attacks outside the DMZ. Canisters packed with gunpowder and shrapnel were tossed into areas with civilian populations. Planes were hijacked, roads blocked off. Police and soldiers who surrendered in gun battles were taken prisoner or executed. The guerrillas remained unrepentant, even when civilians appeared to be targets or were caught in the cross fire. In a Human Rights Watch interview, Simón Trinidad referred to international humanitarian law as a "bourgeois concept." In July 1999, four thousand fighters emerged from El Caguán to attack bases and towns in five regions. In December 2000, FARC guerrillas ambushed and killed Diego Turbay, the head of the Congressional Peace Commission. Five others were also murdered, including Turbay's mother.

Amid the escalating violence, the government continued to cede the DMZ to the guerrillas, and dialogues carried on without progress toward a peace accord. It had become painfully obvious to most that the FARC had no intention of ending the war. Many would say the Colombian government was also uninterested in achieving peace. While the FARC attacked military targets, paramilitary units linked to the legitimate military committed horrible atrocities as well. In January 1999, paramilitaries killed 136 civilians in four days. The victims were accused of supporting the FARC, then shot in the head. In the town of El Tigre in central Colombia, four truckloads of militia forces began breaking down residents' doors. Twenty-six bodies were found, some beheaded. Twenty-five more disappeared. Witnesses later reported that the paramilitaries arrived in trucks belonging to the army's Twenty-fourth Brigade. Such events had been going on for decades; the Colombian Peace Commission reported that from 1988 to 1997, of the more than twenty thousand murders committed by illegal armed groups, paramilitaries and drug cartels were responsible for more than 80 percent of the killings, while guerrilla groups accounted for 20 percent.

Even as Pastrana waxed poetic about peace, he cozied up to Bill Clinton and $1.3 billion in military aid to fight the FARC in order to win the war on drugs. Critics claimed that the money allocated to Plan Colombia was being spent to fight a Colombian civil war tantamount to U.S. involvement in Vietnam. Rand Beers, assistant secretary of state for International Narcotics and Law Enforcement Affairs, denied the charges in 2001: "Plan Colombia is a plan for peace, and the United States supports President Pastrana's peace efforts," he wrote. "From the beginning, we have stated that there is no military solution to Colombia's problems. Colombia's ills go well beyond drug production and trafficking. That is why Plan Colombia is aimed at bolstering democracy, improving the economy, and respecting human rights while at the same time attacking narcotics. As a democratic neighbor in need, Colombia deserves our help. And we are providing it through a comprehensive, balanced assistance package in support of Plan Colombia." The balance, however, was heavily skewed on the side of military spending. In 2000, 78 percent ($765 million) and in 2001, 97 percent ($242 million) of Plan Colombia aid went to bolster Colombia's military forces, with the remainder earmarked for "economic and social assistance programs."

The money did not go to waste. With burgeoning war coffers, Pastrana formed a command team of generals and completely restructured and invigorated his flailing army. Terms for recruits were extended and conscripts were turned into professional soldiers. Troops were retrained and battalions modernized into swiftly deployable war-fighting outfits. The Colombian army purchased Black Hawks and Russian transport helicopters and modernized their aircraft, riverine, and combat equipment. According to a Stratfor intelligence report, with the new money and innovation, "the military was able, in but a few years, to field a revitalized force able to be employed in a manner more appropriate in the new phase the conflict had entered, that of mobile warfare." But perhaps the most important factor that would later be brought to bear against the FARC was the streamlining and bolstering of the army's intelligence operations (which were put under the direct command of a brigadier general) and its psychological operations division (which was responsible for inundating the guerrillas with messages and propaganda to encourage them to defect). The bulk of Pastrana's new and improved military came compliments of American taxpayers, with the Clinton and then Bush administrations arguing Plan Colombia's essential role in stopping cocaine from making its way to the United States. And although many illegal armed groups were involved in the drug trade at a level perhaps equal to the guerrillas, Plan Colombia funds were not used to aggressively fight drug production and smuggling by paramilitaries or to help prevent atrocities by the AUC or the military-paramilitary alliances. In 2000, Carlos Castaño, the head of the largest paramilitary coalition, admitted that the AUC received 70 percent of its financing from drug trafficking. And a leaked Colombian government report in 2003 put the paramilitary groups' share in the entire Colombian drug trade at 40 percent.

Publicly, the FARC blamed the failure of the negotiations on the government, claiming Pastrana wanted peace for free—without reforms and without social, economic, and political changes for the country. However, internally, Secretariat members congratulated themselves on the charade of the dialogues, which covered up a twofold plan to move the FARC toward its ultimate goal: overtaking the country. The first step was an unprecedented weapons buildup—the result of a creative arms deal for tens of thousands of Russian weapons. The guns came from Siberia and were brokered by both the Russian mafia and the Russian military. Aboard Russian cargo planes, the arms passed through the Canary Islands, Jordan, and finally into Colombia by way of Peru's remote jungle. Thousands of automatic rifles were smuggled by land; a reported twenty to thirty thousand more floated into El Caguán by parachute from Russian planes. In April 2000, MSNBC.com broke the story and reported that the FARC paid for the guns with huge shipments (about forty thousand kilograms) of cocaine—ferried back to Russia in the same planes that had delivered the weapons. (While it first appeared that Vladimiro Montesinos, head of Peru's intelligence service, had broken the smuggling ring, the spy chief was later implicated in the dealings.)

With the FARC flush with weapons, what Marulanda needed was more troops. So behind the smoke screen of the peace negotiations, the FARC Secretariat began a tremendous and wholesale recruitment effort that spanned the entire country, with the idea of doubling the FARC ranks to forty thousand troops. With the greatly inflated ranks, Marulanda believed he could actually overthrow the Colombian government. The new recruitment strategy was an extraordinary paradigmatic shift, one that would prove to be a catastrophic failure. In its thirty-five-year history, the FARC had always had standards for recruits: New troops came from families with Communist sympathies, or they came from areas where the FARC had been the only presence for decades. But in the frenzy to recruit enough bodies to match the number of arms, standards slackened. The majority of new recruits came from the massive glut of humanity that had arrived in the jungle to eek out a living in a lawless land—the *raspachines*, the coca pickers. The FARC also recruited destitute city dwellers. With no former background or tie to the guerrillas in any way, the new recruits lacked significant passion or commitment to revolutionary ideology.

Many political analysts in Washington, D.C., and around the world would credit the FARC's involvement in the drug trade as the reason for its eventual unraveling a decade later. But it was here, on this open playing field of a demilitarized zone, that Marulanda and his six top commanders would agree that they made their ultimate mistake: During the incredibly sloppy and careless recruitment campaign that flourished during the three years of the DMZ, not only did the FARC end up with recruits who were incompetent and undisciplined soldiers but the guerrillas were deeply infiltrated as well. The requirements to join the FARC had been set so low that the Colombian military took the opportunity to place many subversives within the FARC ranks. The number of infiltrators who entered the guerrilla army with the approximately ten thousand new recruits is impossible to know, but it could have reached into the hundreds. The true effect would not be realized for several years, when, blow by blow, with brilliant incremental plans carried out with great stealth by Colombian intelligence forces, Marulanda's forty-five-year-old army would begin to crumble.

9

The Exchangeables

At the beginning of 2002, a furious and demoralized President Pastrana finally seemed to realize that the endless posturing by the FARC was going nowhere. On January 12, he gave an ultimatum, demanding that the FARC evacuate the demilitarized zone or face military action. The FARC Secretariat responded with a long communiqué, in which they agreed to leave, telling the Colombian people:

> The 48-hour ultimatum, which will expire on the 14th at 9:30 p.m., established by Mr. President, unilaterally changes everything that has been agreed upon in the past three years. . . . Once again the selfish interests of a privileged and rich minority are being placed above the interests of 40 million Colombians. For the time being, the warmongers have won out to obstruct the possibilities of achieving peace with social justice. . . . To the country and the world we reaffirm our willingness to continue using all forms of struggle to achieve the changes that Colombia needs to in order to achieve reconciliation and reconstruction of the homeland. . . .

Presidential candidate Ingrid Betancourt hands out campaign material to FARC commanders during a meeting between the FARC and presidential candidates in Los Pozos, Colombia (a town within the demilitarized zone), on February 14, 2002. She was kidnapped by FARC guerrillas nine days later. Photo: AP Images/Ariana Cubillos.

The communiqué was signed by Raúl Reyes, Joaquín Gómez, Carlos Antonio Lozada, Andrés París, and Simón Trinidad in the mountains of Colombia on January 13, 2002. From his base in El Caguán, Trinidad read it live in its entirety on a national news broadcast.

Although the guerrillas had said they would vacate the DMZ, there was little evidence to suggest they were doing so. Pastrana's forty-eight-hour deadline passed, but, clearly wanting to avoid armed conflict, he held back from sending in troops for more than a month. Then on February 20, FARC guerrillas hijacked a Colombian airliner and took Senator Jorge Gechem hostage. The hijackers forced the plane down on a rough asphalt road in FARC territory, where dozens of guerrillas awaited the senator's arrival. It was the last straw for Pastrana, who went on television to tell the guerrillas they had a three-hour deadline to evacuate the DMZ. Pastrana, who had ordered thirteen thousand troops to encircle the zone, commanded the army to retake El Caguán, and the war returned with full intensity. As his disastrous four-year term came to an end, Pastrana was characterized as a wimp, an imbecile for what was seen as an incredible failure to deal with the country's civil war. For those vying to replace the beleaguered president, finding a way to beat the FARC and bring peace to the country was the number one issue on all the candidates' agendas.

Six days before Gechem's kidnapping, three presidential candidates met in Los Pozos and made very public bids to the FARC to end the war. The meeting room at a local community center teemed with Colombian news media, and campesinos clambered for a view of the candidates and the FARC commanders. Most dynamic at the televised meeting was Ingrid Betancourt, a spitfire senator from Bogotá. Betancourt wore her usual campaign outfit—jeans and a simple yellow T-shirt bearing her campaign slogan, COLOMBIA NUEVA. Her hair hung plainly to her shoulders, held back from her face by a pair of brown sunglasses. Across the table from Betancourt, wearing a military uniform with an armband in the colors of the Colombian flag, was Simón Trinidad. He shook Betancourt's hand warmly upon arrival, then stared at her smugly as she gave her pitch to the FARC guerrillas who sat across from the candidates at the table. Betancourt, by now a seasoned politician known for her passionately delivered calls for justice, spoke directly to the high-ranking guerrilla commanders: "When each one of you decided 'I'm going to the mountains to fight,' what was your intention? Was your intention to take water and electricity from the people whom you wanted to defend?" The FARC representatives, both men and women, sat expressionless as they listened to Betancourt's speech. At the end, Betancourt begged the FARC to make "a unilateral gesture toward peace: *no more kidnappings.*" Betancourt repeated the point for emphasis: "*No more kidnappings. . . . Stop kidnapping, and free the hostages.*"

Her plea may have resonated more with the voting public than with Trinidad and his fellow guerrilla commanders. Media reports and government propaganda against the armed factions constantly reminded the general populace that kidnappings were garnering hundreds of millions of dollars for the FARC, the ELN, the paramilitaries, and common criminals. From 1998 to 2002, the number of kidnappings each year reportedly averaged three thousand—a third of which were carried out by the FARC. Historically, the kidnappings had been almost exclusively for financial gain, but by 2000, many FARC hostage takings had taken a political turn. Increased success attacking Colombian military bases—which began in the mid-1990s—netted a massive increase in military prisoners. At first, because these prisoners weren't considered "economic" hostages for the guerrillas, FARC policy was to hold them for a few days, a couple of weeks, possibly as long as a month. Then the hostages would be handed over to a town priest, the Red Cross, or another humanitarian organization. During the increased fighting, many guerrillas were also taken captive; prisons were full of FARC guerrillas—almost a thousand in all of Colombia.

In 1997, Marulanda proposed an exchange of prisoners and publicly asked the Colombian Congress to approve a permanent "law of exchange" to be in force for the duration of the war. The FARC's proposal initially included exchanging captured government soldiers—whom the FARC deemed prisoners of war—for guerrillas in jail. But in 2000, the FARC Secretariat decided that captured elected officials would also be considered prisoners of war. They announced the change of tactic in an online communiqué: Politicians who entered FARC areas of influence would be captured and included on the list of what the FARC called the "exchangeables." The exchangeables differed from the hundreds of other hostages who were being held by the FARC for ransom payments, and they could be released only through an exchange of prisoners. Reacting to the crisis, the government passed a law in December 2001 that made it legal for a politician to run in absentia. Several families responded by actually running campaigns for their missing candidates. In 2002, this bizarre policy would be played out in one of the strangest presidential campaigns in history, the candidacy of Ingrid Betancourt.

In 1994, after leaving her comfortable life and her French diplomat husband, the thirty-two-year-old Betancourt entered a Colombian political scene that had for years been infused by drug money. As a congresswoman (and later senator), Betancourt was quick to "out" fellow legislators she felt were corrupt, immediately turning herself into an outsider in the House of Representatives. She ignored her detractors, and in 1996, she made a name for herself by exposing incumbent president Ernesto Samper for accepting campaign money from the Cali cartel. Her tenacity earned her a series of death threats and assassination attempts. In a 2002 interview, Ingrid described the threat that made her decide to send her two young children out of the country to live with her ex-husband. "A man came to my office. He said, 'I am here to warn you; we have paid the *sicarios* [assassins] to kill you and your family.' " Betancourt took her family out of the country but could not resist the lure of Colombian politics, and she returned to the country alone. In 1998, she received more votes in the nationwide senate election than any other candidate. But by 2002, as she began her presidential campaign, Betancourt had lost a great amount of support. She had published her autobiography in France, and within its pages was a hard indictment of the pervasive corruption in Colombia, fueled by the massive cash flow from cocaine trafficking. To the average Colombian, it was like airing dirty laundry in an international forum, and she was highly criticized.

On February 23, Betancourt, who was lagging far behind in the polls, and her campaign team traveled to Florencia—a steamy jungle town on the perimeter of what had been the DMZ just three days before. Her idea was to get to San Vicente del Caguán, where the military had gone to retake the town. It was reported that paramilitaries had also arrived and were "disappearing" anyone they deemed sympathetic to the guerrillas. A local priest interviewed by *The Observer* gave this account: "There was a local administration and police force in San Vicente, but when the DMZ ended, they all left or were murdered. The town hall is closed, the police station was blown up and the area left without any form of non-military government. Then [paramilitaries] arrived in town one night, and the next day there were five bodies in the Caguán river." According to Betancourt's second husband, Juan Carlos Lecompte, Betancourt had received a call from the mayor of San Vicente del Caguán, who was a member of her independent political party. "He told her, 'Ingrid, you have to come here. People are disappearing.' " Lecompte didn't hesitate to support his wife's decision. "She told me it was her duty to go."

Betancourt and her team were first told by a military general that they would have helicopter transport to San Vicente del Caguán. The road, everyone knew, was far too dangerous to travel. Hours passed, and several aircraft left Florencia, including one carrying President Pastrana, who was accompanied by dozens of members of the international and Colombian press for his visit to San Vicente del Caguán. Some felt that it was no more than a publicity opportunity to show the beleaguered president "liberating" the zone from the guerrillas, to whom he had given legitimate reign over the area for three years. Pastrana, who had once been a close friend of Betancourt's family, ignored her on his way to board the plane. Shortly after, Lecompte received a call from his wife. "She told me they would not take her by helicopter, but they had offered her a car, and she was going."

An hour later, Betancourt and four colleagues were traveling south toward San Vicente del Caguán. Adair Lamprea, the logistics coordinator for her campaign, drove the government pickup truck, and Betancourt sat in the passenger seat. There were three others in back. The two-lane asphalt road cut through the jungle in an area of El Caguán that was still very much controlled by the FARC guerrillas, but now Colombian troops were on the attack, making it incredibly dangerous. The mood in the car was somber as they pulled behind a white Red Cross truck stopped on the road. Twenty yards farther up, a colorful school bus spray-painted with the words BUS BOMB was parked perpendicular to the road, blocking traffic from both sides. It was a guerrilla roadblock—something that was to be expected in this part of Colombia. Lamprea recognized the roadblock as a method that the FARC used to capture people—one that had become so widespread that Colombians had actually given it a name: "Miraculous Fishing." The guerrillas would set up a roadblock and pull over any vehicle that tried to pass. If the victims had money or political prominence, they were taken away. The rest, they tossed back, often burning victims' vehicles or forcing them back the way they had come.

Lamprea stared at the bus and clenched the steering wheel. Ahead, a teenage guerrilla carried an automatic rifle over his shoulder and casually munched on a triangle of ripe watermelon as he told the Red Cross truck's driver to turn around and go back toward Florencia. Then he directed a young woman on a motorcycle to do the same. Lamprea was ordered to shut off the truck's ignition. Alain Keler, a French photojournalist, sat nervously in the backseat. Keler had joined the group to shoot photos of Betancourt's campaign for a magazine article in the French edition of *Marie Claire*. Betancourt, who had dual French and Colombian citizenship and had been raised in France, had become hugely popular in France over the last few years. But after traveling for a week with Betancourt, Keler's opinion of her differed greatly from that of her fans in France, who often referred to her as "Joan of Arc." He found her very arrogant and difficult to be around. And although he had made the decision to go, even after being warned it was very dangerous, he still resented being dragged along into the danger. The other two in the car were Mauricio Mesa, the campaign's cameraman, and Clara Rojas, an attorney and friend of Betancourt, who had helped her with her previous campaigns and the Samper impeachment trial.

A second guerrilla demanded all of the passengers' cell phones and Mesa's video camera. Keler didn't understand Spanish, and he continued to photograph the tense scene. One of the guerrillas yelled at him to stop, but he continued to shoot, and Mesa saw the photographer quickly unload the film from his camera and stealthily tuck it into his vest pocket. The soldier then ordered the white flags and placards that read INGRID BETANCOURT and PRENSA INTERNACIONAL stripped from the truck's exterior, and Lamprea was ordered to drive around the bus. On the other side was a second bus, sandwiching the small pickup. The woman on the motorcycle had made her way around the bus as well and was stubbornly refusing the orders of a second group of guerrillas to turn back. "Our car was parked, and we were looking to the side at the young woman," Lamprea recalls. "They grabbed her motorcycle, threw gasoline on it, and lit it on fire." Lamprea hated the brutal methods the guerrillas used to terrorize the local civilians. He felt sick as he watched the motorcycle go up in flames and saw the anger and desperation on the young woman's face.

Seconds later, an explosion rattled the group. "All I felt was a *BOOOM*, and everything shook," says Lamprea. Everyone in the truck screamed and ducked for cover, thinking they were under attack from the Colombian military. Lamprea assumed the buses were loaded with explosives, and he thought that another blast would set them off. Peering through a cloud of dust and debris, Lamprea saw blood pouring down the face of one of the guerrillas, who was screaming, "My leg, my leg, my leg." His shrieks gave Lamprea a moment of relief. The explosion had been caused by a land mine, not by a bomb from an air attack. The boy's left leg was now a bloody stump of shredded bone and muscle below the knee. However, none of the guerrillas went to help the injured boy. "If you don't put the guy in the truck, I'm going to get out and do it myself," Lamprea yelled at them. Still, none of the guerrillas moved to help. Betancourt and Lamprea couldn't ignore the injured soldier. "The fear, at that moment . . . it completely left me. There was a human being who had a wounded leg, and we had to help," Lamprea says. The young guerrilla shrieked in agony, and Betancourt insisted that they help get him to a hospital.

The guerrillas lifted the boy into the back of the pickup, and Lamprea thought that they would be taking the boy to a local hospital or to a local doctor sympathetic to the FARC. Unfamiliar with the territory, Lamprea asked the guerrillas for a guide. Several guerrillas climbed into the truck and ordered Lamprea to drive. Betancourt and the others remained quiet as the walls of the jungle rose up along the road, blocking the sun and wiping out any sense of direction. Eventually, two vehicles barreled toward them from the opposite direction and came to an abrupt stop. Together, the vehicles carried more than a dozen guerrillas, and cameraman Mesa realized immediately that they wouldn't need so many guerrillas to pick up one injured soldier. Mesa's hand shook as he lit his last cigarette and watched the guerrillas approach. They were much more forbidding than the first group, and they immediately ordered Betancourt out of the truck. "Ingrid told us not to worry, that everything would be okay," Mesa says. Betancourt reluctantly got out on the passenger side, and the guerrillas forced her to the driver's side. "Then the guy told us to get out on the other side, and he told another guerrilla to move us away from Ingrid," Lamprea says. Clara Rojas stepped out of the pickup with Lamprea, Mesa, and Keler. As they were herded away, Rojas asked where they were taking Betancourt. According to Rojas, the guerrillas became angry and forced her to join Betancourt. Lamprea felt a deep pang of guilt, knowing he should be with them as well. But his feet were frozen to the ground.

The soldiers forced Lamprea, Mesa, and Keler to move farther away from Betancourt and Rojas. "They wouldn't let us see Ingrid because they said that we would get upset. At that moment, I felt really scared because I didn't know what was going to happen. I didn't know if they were going to kill me there, or going to kill Ingrid, or going to kill Clara," Lamprea says. A guerrilla named Uni radioed his commander to report the capture of Betancourt and her colleague Clara Rojas. "Betancourt at first thought the uniformed guerrillas who stopped her vehicle were soldiers," Uni later told the Associated Press. He described the moment when she learned they were going to detain her: "Her face changed color. Only then did Rojas and Betancourt realize the extent of the trouble they were in," he said. Lamprea watched Betancourt standing defiantly as the guerrillas ordered her into their vehicle. Even as they became angry, she remained calm. One of the guerrillas became livid. "Lady, lady, get in! Get in now!" he yelled at her. Finally, with no other option, Betancourt climbed into the vehicle, and it drove away. Rojas stood for a moment, her face drawn. Then she was ordered into the other truck. "She said good-bye to us," Lamprea recalls. "She blew us a kiss. We stayed there, waiting to see what they were going to do with us. It was a terrifying moment."

Twenty minutes later, Lamprea, Mesa, and Keler were forced into the backseat of their truck with one of the guerrilla soldiers. The young guerrilla who'd stepped on a land mine was still lying in the truck bed, moaning and yelling for water. Five more guerrillas piled in back with him. The commander, who continued talking on a handheld radio, got into the driver's seat, and two more guerrillas squeezed into the front. Lamprea was trying to ignore the injured guerrilla's constant screams from the back of the truck, when his attention was diverted by a conversation between the two FARC soldiers in the front seat. "They said Ingrid was a politician just like all the others. That it was a good thing that they had captured her. That the country was going to know that they had a presidential candidate." Lamprea couldn't stand it. He had completely dedicated the last three years of his life to helping Betancourt in her political fight. "I said, 'If you guys think this, you're completely wrong, because this is not the person that you have just captured. This is a person who has been radical, who has been against corruption, who is in favor of land reform, who is truly for the poor in this country.' " Finally, the driver slammed on the breaks. "He turned around and yelled at me. He said, 'Don't tell me this shit. All politicians are the same.' " Twenty-four hours later, Lamprea, Keler, and Mesa were released on a deserted road. They walked throughout the night and finally came upon a group of Colombian soldiers who helped them get back to Bogotá. Lamprea prayed that Ingrid would be coming right behind them, and he was consumed by guilt that he was free while Betancourt and Rojas were still captive.

In Bogotá, Betancourt's husband was initially numbed by the news. The advertising executive, who had no experience in politics, was about to embark on an odyssey that he felt totally unprepared for. Believing that it would be the most important thing to her, Lecompte vowed to continue her presidential campaign. In the weeks that followed, Lecompte became a surrogate candidate for his hostage wife. He made a striking picture, both heartbroken and defiant, attending campaign events with a life-size poster of Betancourt held in his arms. He pleaded with the media not to forget her and begged Colombians to cast their votes for her—as a symbolic gesture for her freedom and the freedom of Rojas and all of the hostages. But the apathy of a hardened country was apparent. A local journalist echoed a common Colombian attitude in an interview several weeks after her capture. "She took her own risks," said *El Tiempo* sports editor Mauricio Bayona, "and she's paying for that now."

On May 26, 2002, Álvaro Uribe, a hard-liner who vowed to quash the FARC by any means necessary, won the presidential election. (Uribe, a former member of the Liberal party, had won the election as an independent candidate.) During the campaign, the FARC tried to assassinate Uribe by detonating a bomb in a bus near his motorcade. Uribe was unhurt, due to his armored vehicle, but three others were killed and thirteen injured. People across the country—especially those in areas with a large population—were invigorated by Uribe's tough talk, and he won in a landslide, becoming the only Colombian president ever to get more than 50 percent of the vote in the primary election. On inauguration day, FARC guerrillas in Bogotá, attempting an attack on the presidential palace, missed their target and shelled an area to the south, killing nineteen homeless people and injuring sixty. Because Uribe's father had been killed by FARC guerrillas in a 1983 kidnapping attempt, those who opposed his candidacy were afraid that the hard-liner's term would be a violent four-year vendetta. Uribe was also known to have openly supported self-defense forces in Antioquia when he served as the department's governor from 1995 to 1997. (Medellín, home to Pablo Escobar's cartel and the site of terrible drug-related violence in the early 1990s, is the capital of Antioquia.) Between 1994 and 1997, Private Security and Vigilance Cooperatives, or CON-VIVIR, its Spanish acronym, had been legal under a national program created by the Defense Ministry to use private citizens to combat guerrilla activity. But after reports of human rights abuses, the Colombian Constitutional Court stripped CONVIVIR of its ability to use military-grade weapons or to collect intelligence. While the official CONVIVIR units disappeared, many former members united with other vigilante gangs. The most prominent, the Autodefensas Campesinas de Córdoba y Urabá, or ACCU (which later combined with other groups to form the Autodefensas Unidas de Colombia, or AUC), was led by Carlos Castaño, whose father had also been killed by FARC guerrillas. The groups (which all were referred to under the umbrella term *paramilitaries*) built up troops and amassed weapons and cash from kidnapping, extortion, and narco-trafficking and were implicated in brutal acts against civilians, guerrillas, union leaders, and left-leaning politicians. What failed to disappear with the CONVIVIR were the accusations that Uribe maintained strong ties to the paramilitaries and their leaders.

On the day the votes were tallied and Uribe supporters took their celebration to the streets by the thousands, Betancourt and Rojas remained together in the jungle, with no news of the outside world. They did not know that Lecompte had named Rojas as Betancourt's vice presidential pick, and that Betancourt's small but dedicated group of supporters and family members had been able to convince more than fifty thousand Colombians to cast their votes for the missing candidates—barely saving Betancourt's fledgling political party.

10

Fallout

Three days after the February 13, 2003, kidnapping of Stansell, Gonsalves, and Howes, Colombian military rescue teams had completely lost the guerrillas' trail and had no intelligence on which to base a rescue attempt. "What [the Colombian army] tried to do was to develop a wall of human flesh around an area so that no one could get through it. But if you look at the landscape, it's mountainous, and it's jungle terrain. And it's possible to be fifteen feet from someone and not see them and not hear them. So it's very, very difficult," says Brig. Gen. Remo Butler, retired commander of the U.S. Army Special Operations Command South. The guerrillas knew they had barely managed to evade the army, and they continued to force the injured men to march for twenty-one days—first through the foothills of the Eastern Cordillera and then deep into the jungle. At times, Stansell was carried on a mule. An intestinal ailment and an injury to his ribs that he sustained in the crash made it impossible for him to walk. Other times, the three would be loaded into trucks and driven along makeshift jungle roads. On the last day of their grueling march, the group landed in a small clearing with a sixteen-by-twenty-foot structure. The sight of the rustic bungalow with three solid wood sides and a chain-link fence on the fourth side was incredibly discouraging. "As we walked up to the structure,"

Stansell wrote, "I knew immediately that this marked the end of our days as kidnapped contract workers and began our life as prisoners."

Their more than three weeks in captivity had been marked by many political conversations between the hostages and their captors. The guerrillas accused the Americans of imperialism, of butting into an internal conflict in ways that hurt poor campesinos, of being CIA agents, and of spying on their organization. Stansell, Gonsalves, and Howes vehemently denied the charges. In their opinion, their captors came to those conclusions because the guerrillas were brainwashed,

Jo Rosano, mother of kidnapped American Marc Gonsalves, with her husband, Mike, and journalist Jorge Enrique Botero at an August 2004 demonstration in Bogotá with the families of Colombian hostages. The demonstrators were calling for the government to negotiate for an exchange of prisoners and not attempt a military rescue. Photo: Claudia Rubio.

ignorant, and incapable of independent thought. What the hostages themselves believed was that without the billions of American dollars behind Plan Colombia, the drug traffickers and other criminals would continue to destabilize Colombia and the surrounding region. What the three men also believed, although there was no empirical data to support it, was that the work they were doing was impeding the flow of drugs from Colombia to the United States. And because they were working for the greatest country in the world, all three men were positive that the United States would take all military measures to free them. "By holding us, they [the FARC] were opening a Pandora's box," Howes told one of the high commanders they were introduced to on their march. "Instead of simply working indirectly against the FARC by interfering with their narco-trafficking, the U.S. could strike directly against them because they were holding Americans hostage."

But the U.S. government did not make any direct military moves to recover the hostages, nor were there any plans to do so. In fact, within days of the hostages' arrival in what they would call "Monkey Camp" (because of the monkeys, which would fling feces and urinate on the humans below), Secretary of State Colin Powell publicly admitted in a March 13 press conference that the State Department had no clue where the hostages were and no idea which FARC front was holding them. Powell did not offer any commitment on the part of the United States to engage in a mission to rescue the men or to negotiate for their release. However, he did take the opportunity to reassert the United States' goals in Colombia. "It's sad that [the kidnapping] happened," he said. "But it's a risk that we must run to defeat these narco-traffickers and help President Uribe. I am impressed by his total commitment to ridding Colombia of narco-terrorists and narco-traffickers and all the others who are trying to destroy Colombian democracy."

The families of Stansell, Gonsalves, and Howes were also under the mistaken impression that U.S. forces would attempt to rescue their loved ones. A week after the crash, President Bush had given the okay to send an additional 150 U.S. troops to Colombia to help with rescue efforts, but the rules of engagement still prevented Colonel Keen from taking charge of any rescue attempt, and U.S. troops played only limited advisory roles. "There was a lot of effort from the Colombians," says Keen. "They were doing the best they could do to try to locate the hostages." Keen said they were aided by U.S. military intelligence. However, the only other California Microwave Systems airplane was grounded while the cause of the first crash was under investigation. The United States did have satellite imagery, but it was mostly useless for reconnaissance because of the thick forest canopy. "We were using intelligence assets. But again, you can't take a pig's ear and make a silk purse out of it," says General Butler. Colombian troops were sent to interrogate local villagers and came up empty. "You must remember that many of the people in this part of Colombia were sympathizers or very friendly to the FARC. So we were not going to get an awful lot of information. Intelligence was very hard to come by."

El Caguán became hot with firefights between guerrillas and the military troops looking for the Americans. Complaints were filed by campesinos, who accused Colombian soldiers of harassing them to gain information. The allegations fueled resentment within the military ranks. "Colombians in the armed forces believe the rescue of our guys [the Americans] is not their problem," said one Colombian-American contractor who worked with Howes, Gonsalves, and Stansell. "They say, 'We have many of our guys [Colombians] there to die for these Americans, and where are the Americans while we are risking our lives?' "

The fact that there were hundreds, possibly thousands, of Colombian troops trying to rescue the Americans terrified Ingrid Betancourt's husband, Juan Carlos Lecompte. Lecompte knew it was possible that Betancourt was being held somewhere near the Americans, and he knew that an attempted military rescue would likely be a death sentence. If they weren't killed by cross fire, they would be executed by direct order from Marulanda, who demanded that hostages be killed at the first sign of a rescue attempt. Lecompte feared it would be an excruciating end to the nightmare that he and Betancourt's family had been living since her kidnapping a year earlier.

Initial reactions of shock and disbelief turned to anger for the families of Howes, Stansell, and Gonsalves as the days wore on and very little information came from the U.S. government or from Northrop Grumman. Two weeks after the crash, the State Department wrote identical letters to the wives of Gonsalves and Howes and to Stansell's fiancée, Malia Phillips. The letter to Shane Gonsalves read:

Dear Ms. Gonsalves:

On behalf of the U.S. Government, I would like to say how extremely sorry I am that your husband, Mark [sic] Gonsalves, was taken hostage in Colombia on February 13, 2003. I know this is a very stressful time for you and your family and I want you to know that our thoughts are with you. I promise we will do all we can to help you through this terrible time. . . .

The letter stated that the U.S. State Department would be the primary contact for the families until the men's release, but at the end of the first page, the letter gave little room for hope:

The United States views hostage taking as an act of terrorism. The official policy of the United States Government is to make no concessions to terrorists holding Americans hostage. The U.S. Government will not pay ransom, exchange prisoners, or change its policies. Let me assure you that the United States Government will continue to press the Government of Colombia to do all it can to effect the immediate release of your husband.

With each passing day, Shane Gonsalves became more and more aggravated and felt more and more alone. She found photos on her husband's laptop that made her suspicious of his fidelity. It seemed wrong to be angry with him while he was in such a terrible situation, but somehow, the anger almost helped her deal with the nightmare of everything that was going on. Northrop Grumman promised to send Gonsalves's paycheck to Shane, which was a great relief. With his six-figure salary, at least money would not be an issue. Gonsalves had been on the job in Colombia for only four months, and although he'd been told that the work was dangerous, the money had been too good to pass up. He'd enlisted in the air force right after high school and had struggled for years on military pay while supporting his wife, their eight-year-old daughter, Destiney, and Shane's two sons. His new salary had afforded him a small boat, a new motorcycle, and a large-screen television, but Gonsalves hated being away from his home in the Florida Keys. And according to Shane, the long separations had put a strain on their marriage.

In the stunning new Florida home where Thomas Howes had spent only twelve days before returning to Colombia to work, Peruvian-born Mariana Howes couldn't bear to tell her two boys that their father had been kidnapped; instead, she told them that he was on an extended work trip. The painful charade would continue for two torturous years. And in a small single-story house in southern Georgia, Keith Stansell's fiancée, Malia Phillips, first heard the news of the crash and was sure that Stansell was dead. Piecing together what little she'd been told, she tried to explain to Stansell's fourteen-year-old daughter and his ten-year-old son from his first marriage (whom she had been taking care of while Stansell was working out of the country) what was happening.

Just days after the crash, Phillips would be confounded by an article in *USA Today* about a woman named Patricia Medina, who claimed to be Stansell's girlfriend and to be pregnant with his twins. It was something that the Stansell family and Phillips did not want to believe was true. But it *was* true. Medina had been Stansell's constant companion in Colombia for the past ten months. The thirty-year-old flight attendant had fallen in love with him on an Avianca flight. She was working that day, and Stansell was a business-class passenger. On their second date, Medina went back to Stansell's apartment and, she says, "I never left until he was kidnapped." Although she wasn't sure of her future with the American, because Stansell had repeatedly told her that he did not want a commitment, Medina lived happily with Stansell in one of the most elegant condominiums in northern Bogotá. She knew that Stansell had been married previously and that after the divorce he had custody of his two children, which, he told her, was a huge responsibility. And even though Stansell revealed some details of his life to Medina—such as how he loved to hunt in Wyoming—she always felt that he did not like to talk about himself, and even less about his work. "He told me that he worked for Plan Colombia, but he never mentioned the name of the company where he worked. He only told me that he worked on the war against drugs," she says. When Stansell had meetings with his colleagues in the living room of the apartment, he made Medina stay in another room. Occasionally, she overheard the men talk about the inadequacy of the airplanes they used for work.

In November 2002, soon after Medina found out that she was pregnant with twins, she tried to muster the courage to tell Stansell. At the time, Medina remembers, Stansell was under a lot of stress because the CMS bosses were visiting Bogotá from the States. One night, as the two went to bed, she broke the news to him. "He turned out the light, and I said, 'I have to tell you something. I'm pregnant, and they're twins.' He was quiet for what seemed like an eternity. Then he turned on the light and began to pace across the room without saying anything. He said, What were we going to do? How was he going to tell his children? That he could not change their whole lives. That he had always taught them to be responsible. Later, he told me that it didn't matter, that my children would be taken care of but that he was not going to marry me. It was horrible. But in a certain way it also gave me peace, because he told me that the children would never lack for anything, not to worry about them, that he was a responsible person and that that was not going to change now."

But when Stansell returned from the United States in January 2003, Medina noted a marked change in his attitude toward her. He lavished her with loving attention, frequently asking how the twins were doing. Given his seeming change of heart, Medina was looking forward to the birth and having Stansell by her side. But Stansell may not have planned on being with Medina for the twins' birth. In early February, he flew back to Bogotá from Miami. Sitting next to him on the plane was a Colombian medical doctor who had treated the American contractors in Colombia. "Keith told me that he was about to quit working and leave Colombia," the doctor recalls. "That he wanted to be with his family in the States. That this would be his last trip." A week after the crash, Medina, four months pregnant, packed her things and left the apartment that she had shared with Stansell. Ralph Ponticelli, Stansell's best friend, who also worked for CMS, organized a barbecue and took up a collection from the other CMS employees to try to help Medina with the costs of her delivery. Ponticelli had been so wonderful to Medina during her pregnancy that she had hoped he would be like an uncle to the twins.

While Patricia Medina appeared in an interview for *USA Today* as Stansell's grieving, pregnant girlfriend, Malia Phillips and the rest of the hostages' family members were warned by the State Department that they should not, under any circumstances, speak to the media. A State Department counterterrorism official defended the decision: "When someone is taken hostage, it's not our intent to make them a celebrity. The more political celebrity status they have, the more it's likely they won't be released." Phillips continued to take care of Stansell's children and was the point person for communication from the U.S. government and Northrop Grumman. Several weeks after the kidnapping, the U.S. Embassy in Colombia called Phillips and asked her for a photo of Stansell and permission to use it on a flyer that would be distributed throughout the area where the guerrillas might be holding the hostages. When Phillips asked to see one of the flyers, the embassy sent her what they had printed—a three-by-six-inch piece of flimsy paper offering up to one million pesos ($345,000). "I was expecting a flyer with their pictures," says Phillips. Instead, the flyer was a sort of a "live the good life" offer for a campesino who could give information leading to a rescue. Rather than showing photos of Stansell, Gonsalves, and Howes, the flyers had grainy pictures of a horse, a jeep, and some cows. "I was none too pleased," says Phillips. "I was like, You've got to be kidding."

While Phillips continued to adhere to the State Department gag order, Jo Rosano, the mother of Marc Gonsalves, spoke to any media outlet that would cover the story. Rosano begged the FARC to release the hostages, and she blasted George W. Bush and Álvaro Uribe for refusing to do anything to facilitate her son's release. Although she took heat from Gonsalves's wife and his father (her ex-husband), as well as those at Northrop Grumman, the FBI, and the State Department, all of whom told her that she was doing more harm than good, Rosano would remain vocal throughout the entire ordeal of her son's kidnapping. Even though Gary Noesner, Northrop Grumman's security consultant, worried that her off-script rants might complicate the situation, the former FBI boss couldn't help but admire her, and he believed that her actions might have a positive impact on the case. "To some extent, she was keeping the situation in the spotlight," he says. But because Rosano was not considered "next of kin," Northrop Grumman and the U.S. agencies did not keep her as informed as they did Gonsalves's wife. "Jo's frustrations led her to be more vocally critical of the government," says Noesner, who believed that because there was no pressure at all from the other family members or the media, the government was basically allowed to ignore the hostage crisis. "So to some extent Jo's actions did do something; when she spoke out, the government had to pay attention."

Each week, Howes's and Gonsalves's wives and Stansell's fiancée got calls from the State Department. But each call was the same, and there was never anything new to report. Some family members began to wonder if the U.S. government was actually doing anything to get the hostages out. "Every time it's the same," says Shane Gonsalves, who was in regular contact with Mariana Howes and Malia Phillips. "You don't have nothing to tell me because you haven't done nothing. So I've already caught on to that. And that's bull. Hey, sorry your husband's there. My condolences there. Have a nice life." Lead FBI negotiator Chris Voss was not surprised by the families' bitter frustration. There were too many agencies involved. Most were not communicating or sharing information, and Voss likened the situation to "herding cats." Calls to the families came from State Department representatives, from the FBI, Control Risks, and Northrop Grumman, and often from multiple parties within each organization. "So that creates problems in the process," says Voss, "especially in a kidnapping whose scope was as huge as this one. Your family contact is going to call you up, angry because they heard something different than what *you* said from the other FBI person, and that just goes with the territory. You are going to become a punching bag at some point in the game."

What was worse than the seeming inaction and disorganization of the government agencies was the strong public statement by National Security Advisor Condoleezza Rice, which came shortly after the kidnapping and made the families believe that the situation was hopeless: "There will not be any negotiation in exchange for the hostages' freedom." It was an incredibly perturbing statement to Voss. "And how absurd is that, saying we don't negotiate with terrorists? The policy is *not* that we won't *negotiate* with terrorists; it's that we won't make *concessions* to terrorists," says Voss. "So first of all, you have to equate negotiation to communication. We got to the point where we were tired of saying, 'That's not the policy; *this* is the policy.' I can give it to you in black and white, and it's actually signed by the president [George W. Bush], who keeps saying publicly, 'We don't negotiate with terrorists.' He's the guy who personally signed the document [NSPD-12] that clearly says, 'We will communicate with anyone who's kidnapped an American.' "

The Bush administration's hard-line policy infuriated Gary Noesner, as well. The lifelong Republican despised the government's handling of the case. In addition to refusing to negotiate, the U.S. government seemed to be doing all it could to prevent Northrop Grumman from helping in any way. The company was originally told that any ransom paid would be considered support to a known terrorist organization. When it was apparent that there would not be a monetary demand, Northrop decided to put together some "humanitarian" packages for each hostage, containing some clothes, eyeglasses, reading material, and medications. The hope was to send these items in through an intermediary. "In the spirit of cooperation, Northrop Grumman advised the U.S. government of this and asked if there were any objections," says Noesner. (With between three and five billion dollars in annual contracts, Northrop Grumman could do little without the blessing of the government.) "Someone at DOJ came back and indicated that any such comfort items sent in to the FARC could actually be used by the FARC guys themselves, and therefore this could be a violation of the provision against providing material support to terrorism. As crazy and stupid as this argument sounds, it actually created quite a problem." Eventually, Noesner was able to leverage his FBI and State Department contacts to overrule the DOJ's objection, and Northrop Grumman was given permission to send in the items. "We later learned the items never made it in to the guys," Noesner says. "The items weren't diverted by the FARC; rather, the intermediary was told that the guerrillas wouldn't accept them."

The U.S. position not to negotiate with the FARC was echoed by

Colombian president Álvaro Uribe, and the only option either government would consider was a military rescue. "We're using intelligence,
we're using troops, we're using all the equipment and all the men that
we can provide to look for them, and to see if we can be able to rescue
them," said Colombian vice president Francisco Santos six months
after their capture. "Although it's a difficult operation, and we'd have to
take all the precautions so that they will be able to be rescued alive."
(Santos had been kidnapped by members of the Medellín cartel in 1990
and released through negotiations between the government and the
cartel.) In May 2003, Uribe got word from Colombian military intelligence agents that they had located a camp where another group of
political prisoners was being held. He approved a rescue operation.
Hearing approaching helicopters, the guerrillas shot all of the hostages
multiple times, including a well-loved governor and former cabinet
minister held captive for over a year. Army troops arriving on the scene
discovered three hostages in a bloody heap of corpses and found they
were still breathing. The camp had been swiftly abandoned, and no
guerrillas were found or captured. Even after the debacle, the U.S. government refused to contemplate negotiating with the FARC for the
release of Stansell, Gonsalves, and Howes and demanded that Colombian forces move forward with plans for a military rescue.

The case turned politically cold, and there seemed to be no hurry
or reason for Northrop Grumman to investigate the actual cause of the
Cessna crash. In fact, there was no mandate for military contractors to
report or investigate mishaps, even in the case of plane crashes or fatalities. However, because the intelligence equipment aboard the plane
belonged to the Department of Defense, the U.S. military would eventually require a crash investigation. Almost a month after the engine
was taken from the crash site to Bogotá, CMS site manager Steve
McCune requested that the National Transportation Safety Board
(NTSB) come and collect the destroyed engine. But NTSB officers
refused to go to Colombia to collect the wreckage because, they told
those at the airport, Colombia was "too dangerous." Finally, the engine
was shipped out on March 11, 2003, and taken to Patrick Air Force
Base, in Florida, where it was determined that there were internal
mechanical problems with the engine. The formal crash report, issued

later by the U.S. Navy, would offer more insight into the cause of the crash and the overall failure of the SRS mission:

> Evidence suggests that some or all of the aircrews who operated the mishap aircraft prior to the accident routinely did so while operating the aircraft engine beyond pilot operating handbook limitations suggested by the aircraft manufacturer. While extremely difficult to quantify the extent of such engine operation out of limits, the evidence and available data demonstrate a pattern of metallurgical distress caused by over temp condition in other engines of aircraft operated by the SRS contractor pilots.

According to the report, Northrop Grumman refused to give navy crash investigators information on how the SRS missions were handled, but the report concluded:

> The [SRS] contract failed to establish an adequate means to ensure quality control of the contractor's method of performance. Lessons learned from this mishap point toward a general failure of the contractor organization, apparently at all echelons, to establish internal standards and controls adequate to effectively manage all aspects of the SRS program within its contract mandate.

Toward the end of March 2003, the Colombian military still had not found any trace of the Americans. From Monkey Camp, Stansell, Gonsalves, and Howes were moved about half a mile away to a more permanent hostage compound that had been hastily constructed. The men were being held within the borders of the FARC's Eastern Bloc (in southern Colombia), the strongest military faction of the guerrillas commanded by Secretariat member Mono Jojoy. While most of the FARC high commanders dedicated a large part of their time to writing and reading, El Mono (a Colombian epithet used to refer to a person with light hair and skin color)—as everyone in the FARC called him—moved constantly throughout the jungle. He almost never slept in the same place and was always exploring ways to escape from the enemy. His troops admired him—many even revered him—but they also feared him. (The Colombian government and the media described him as the "military leader" of the FARC, but the FARC denied that there was any differentiation between military and political leaders.)

Mono Jojoy had been responsible for the FARC's most resounding military victories, including the massive attacks in the late 1990s, which left 250 soldiers dead and 500 as prisoners. On August 7, 2002, he planned and directed the mortar attack against the Casa de Nariño (the Presidential Palace) the day of Álvaro Uribe's presidential inauguration, and the prosecutor general accused him of carrying out the attack on the exclusive and elegant Bogotá club, El Nogal, which left thirty-five dead and hundreds injured. Mono Jojoy was also accustomed to dealing with the FARC's highest-profile hostages, and he was referred to as the "jailer" of the FARC. Already under his command were more than forty-five military and National Police officers and Colombian politicians, some of whom had been held for up to five years. He also held Ingrid Betancourt, whose yearlong captivity had turned her into an international celebrity and a tragic symbol of the dysfunctional nature of Colombia.

The Eastern Bloc's success had come with a price: Mono Jojoy and his men were bearing the brunt of Plan Colombia and a tremendously improved Colombian military. By 2002, thousands of Colombian troops surrounded many of Mono Jojoy's strategic positions. His troops were in constant battles with army forces. The high commander himself was a wanted man with a bounty on his head, and it was not only Colombian forces who were tracking him down; there were Americans looking for him, as well. After the crash of the Cessna, the guerrillas had intercepted the SRS mission orders that Marc Gonsalves had tried desperately to destroy. Their target that day had included intelligence on top FARC commanders.

In what they referred to as "New Camp," Gonsalves and Stansell were locked in six-foot-square wooden boxes, which the men thought must have been built originally as storage containers. Howes was given a larger bungalow, similar to the one the three of them had been in at Monkey Camp. The first night, when Howes heard the clank of chains as the guerrillas locked him inside, he was racked by terrible guilt that the other two men were in far worse conditions, and he suffered a debilitating breakdown. Stansell could not lie down in his cell, and Gonsalves got to a point where he couldn't even lift his head. But worse than the physical pain was the psychological isolation that the men felt because they had been forbidden to speak to one another. The captors were sure that if they could talk among themselves, the Americans could figure out where they were and formulate an escape plan. Three or four days into their stay at New Camp, Howes was emotionally falling apart and doubting his ability to live through their ordeal. It was then that Stansell dropped a note on the ground near him. Howes wrote, "I unfolded it and read 'We are not forgotten. People are looking for us. One day at a time. We will go home.' "

11

The Second Crash

Routine surveillance missions were briefly halted to wait for the results of an investigation into the February 13 crash, but many agencies depended on CMS's surveillance for their counternarcotics operations. Within four weeks, SOUTHCOM gave the go-ahead for the CMS pilots and crew to restart operations. They were to fly in the same model Cessna Caravan—the only remaining plane leased by CMS for the SRS contract—which had recently been in the United States for repairs. Not only were the contractors ordered to work the drug and guerrilla recon missions; they would also fly night missions to search for their missing friends.

Pilot Tommy Schmidt and assistant site manager Ralph Ponticelli—two of the remaining CMS employees—were close friends of Keith Stansell and Thomas Howes and were devastated by their capture. Both were ex-military men—Schmidt had flown night missions in Vietnam and was shot down and rescued five times. Ponticelli had been captured during the invasion of Panama and subsequently rescued by U.S. Special Forces. Although Schmidt had given notice just before the February 13 crash that he would be leaving the job, both he and Ponticelli lived by the motto Leave No Man Behind, and they felt compelled to remain in Colombia until their friends were released or rescued.

Employees of California Microwave Systems in 2002: pilot Thomas Howes (standing second from left) and systems analyst Keith Stansell (standing fifth from left), held hostage from February 13, 2003, to July 2, 2008; pilot Tommy Janis (standing seventh from left), killed by FARC guerrillas after the February 13, 2003, crash; assistant site manager Ralph Ponticelli (standing third from left) and pilot Tommy Schmidt (kneeling third from left), killed in the March 25, 2003, crash; site manager Lawrence "Steve" McCune (standing at far left). Photo: Government exhibit, U.S. v. Simón Trinidad, 04-232.

The SRS missions resumed on March 11, but there was ambiguity about what company the men were actually flying the missions for. This uncertainty was due to the fact that eleven days after the crash and kidnapping of Stansell, Howes, and Gonsalves, Northrop Grumman had shed the SRS contract, dissolved CMS, and handed all assets and personnel to a successor company called CIAO, Inc. The hastily formed company would essentially take over the contract, and the remaining CMS crew members in Bogotá were told that they would be transferred to the new corporation. "The name CIAO was thought up by [site manager] Steve McCune, who thought the acronym would be funny and [that he'd] finally be able to call himself a 'CIA operative.' To everyone else, he would say that the name was Italian for 'good-bye,' " said Sharon Schmidt in 2004, who was living with her husband, Tommy, in Bogotá. Sharon was incensed by McCune's foolhardy choice, especially since being thought of as a CIA operative in Colombia was a very dangerous thing. Tom Cash, a former regional DEA chief in Miami, agreed with Schmidt in an interview with the *Times-Picayune*. "Can you imagine any more absurd acronym in Colombia than to call something CIAO? Wouldn't that be a Kmart blue-light special, a luggage tag that says, 'Kidnap me'? If it were known they were working for the CIA or connected with it, it would be very dangerous for everyone involved." The California Microwave Systems owners and managers were shuffled around and some new names were added to formal documents, but the new company was essentially made up of all the same players.

At Ponticelli's apartment, the remaining crew held a small get-together that was sort of a memorial service for Tom Janis. Sharon Schmidt remembers that her husband and the other contractors discussed the possible change to the new company. "They had agreed that if this CIAO got approved, the single-engine plane was going to be based in Cartagena and only fly over the northern parts of Colombia, where they could make forced landings—that it wouldn't fly in the south anymore." According to Schmidt, CMS owners had been planning to replace the Cessnas with twin-engine King Caravans for the SRS program. "And they would just have to cancel the missions in the south until they got the twin-engine plane ready."

But the dual-engine plane did not arrive before Tommy Schmidt, Ralph Ponticelli, and the remaining crew members were ordered back to work. "Tommy felt that if they could find [Stansell, Gonsalves, and Howes], the Special Forces—the Delta Force that was down there—would go in and get them," says Sharon Schmidt. "Ralph was one of these cheerleader guys who says, 'Come on, guys. We've gotta go save 'em. It's gotta be us.' And I think Tommy just kind of got caught up in that. The U.S. Embassy was saying, 'Oh, they're here, they're there. Go. And if you can confirm it, we can send someone in'—which was all lies. They weren't going to send anybody in."

When the missions resumed, there were only two pilots in Colombia at the time, and Tommy Schmidt had to fly every mission. According to former CMS pilot Paul Hooper, Schmidt had always found it impossible to sleep during the day. Although Northrop Grumman denies that they were responsible for the CIAO employees, Patricia Tomaselli, Northrop Grumman's director of security, spoke to Ponticelli and expressed her concern about the night flights, which she considered too dangerous. (Ponticelli had been the assistant site manager at CMS at the point the company became CIAO, Inc.) The possibilities for successful night reconnaissance were dubious because although the infrared instruments could show a temperature differential and identify the presence of humans, it would be impossible to tell who they might be. Tomaselli said that Ponticelli seemed determined regardless of the fact that the effort would probably not be successful. "He told me, 'If they hear us above, at least they'll know that we haven't forgotten them.' "

The March 25 departure—the eleventh day in a row of flying the night missions—was scheduled for late afternoon. Ponticelli and Schmidt would fly with the newest CMS pilot, James "Butch" Oliver, who had been on the job for just two weeks. Oliver was a good friend of Tommy Janis and had told his father that one of the main reasons he took the job was to help find Stansell, Gonsalves, and Howes. Although Tommy was not superstitious, his wife says he felt an impending sense of doom about the entire operation. For her part, Sharon Schmidt wasn't too worried; she'd always considered her husband to be invincible. Schmidt had been shot at several times before in Colombia. Once, a bullet came through the floor and went right up in front of him, about six inches from his crotch; another bullet lodged in the armrest. "They take ground fire and they don't even know it, because with the roar of the engine, you don't even really hear it. So taking ground fire is just something that you hope doesn't hit anything critical."

Possibly because he was exhausted by the ceaseless schedule, Tommy Schmidt sat as copilot to the less experienced Oliver as they took off on March 25 from the Bogotá airport. Checking the instruments, Ponticelli noticed that something on the aircraft's transponder was not working. He likely wasn't particularly worried—small fixes to the planes were needed after many of the flights—he would report it to home base when they arrived in Larandia to refuel. Everything went as planned, and two and a half hours later, they were at the base. The sun dropped down behind the mountains just before they landed, and dusk quickly turned to darkness.

Soon after the plane arrived in Larandia, several Colombian witnesses heard a terrible argument break out among the Americans. None of the witnesses knew English and therefore they couldn't understand what the fight was about. At 7:00 p.m., with the Cessna fuel tanks at their capacity, Schmidt, Oliver, and Ponticelli readied for departure. Although the flight plan on file noted that there was a Colombian host-nation rider on board, there was no such person. The plane lifted into the darkness. Moonrise was a long way off, and cloudy skies hid the stars. To avoid potential gunfire from nearby FARC guerrillas and to clear the foothills, they were on a trajectory to climb to five thousand feet above the airport before heading out over the terrain. They should have been on the same flight path that Schmidt had taken nearly a hundred times before.

Ten minutes after takeoff, Colombian soldiers posted on a ridge heard the plane approaching. It was on a totally different trajectory than the one the Cessnas usually flew when leaving the airstrip. One soldier would report that it seemed from the irregular sound that something was wrong with the plane's engine. Then he heard the engine shut down, and the plane began to descend. Through the darkness came a loud crack as the plane's wing collided with a tree. The Cessna dipped sharply left and spun into a nosedive. Weighed down with fuel, heavy equipment, and the three crew members, the plane plunged three hundred feet into a gully. A deafening noise echoed through the rocky mountain slopes as the Cessna crashed nose-first into a shallow creek bed and erupted into a fireball. On the ridge, the soldiers watched, knowing there was nothing they could do. "It was a huge explosion," says one witness. "There were no indications that anyone had survived."

In California that evening, Sharon Schmidt saw news about the crash on the Internet. She spent the next few hours frantically searching for word of her husband. At 2:00 a.m. she read a report that said three Americans aboard the plane were dead. She called CMS headquarters in Bogotá, and Steve McCune told her that the Internet reports were false. "He told me, 'No, that's not true. That's not them. We haven't heard from them on the radio, but it's not crashed.' " McCune told Sharon Schmidt that he would call when he found out more, but she says, "He never called back to tell me that the plane had crashed. He *never* did. I got it all from the Internet. McCune was denying it, and he told me, 'No, don't come down here. No, there's no reason for you to come.' " Sharon would find out later, when she went to Colombia to investigate her husband's death, that two men armed with a letter signed by McCune had forced the assistant manager of La Fontana to open the Schmidts' apartment door. "They took everything from the apartment safe. They took our computer. They took all of our discs. They took all the pictures, which really pissed me off." Sharon never got any of the discs or the pictures back. "I got the computer back eventually. But just like Ralph's computer, the hard drive was gone." Sharon Schmidt was incensed. But a Colombian businessman who worked closely with the CMS crew defended McCune's actions as necessary to protect the deceased's privacy in the case of any extramarital relations that the men might have had. "Steve made sure that he did a sweep-up of the apartments to protect any harm to wives and families," he said.

The following morning, the Colombian soldiers who had witnessed the crash hiked down to secure the crash site. Later that day, McCune arrived with several others by helicopter to collect the remains of the men. The Cessna's aluminum fuselage was completely crushed by the impact and blackened by the fire. The bodies were charred trunks strapped into their seats. Tommy Schmidt had been decapitated. The back of Ponticelli's skull was missing. Former CMS pilot Phill Bragg (who suspects he was terminated by Northrop Grumman in December 2002 for throwing his support to Paul Hooper and Doug Cockes over their concerns about safety) was not surprised when he heard the news of the second crash. "I can only imagine how chaotic the atmosphere was down there after that first crash," says Bragg, who believes that the accident was due to pilot error. "It just didn't surprise any of us once we knew Tommy was down there with an inexperienced guy in the cockpit with him, and Ralph in the backseat just egging 'em on. It was just a recipe for disaster."

Sharon Schmidt found it impossible to believe the initial reports that the cause of the crash was solely due to collision with a tree. Although Oliver's remains were found in the left seat, she did not believe that her husband would have let Oliver fly unless Schmidt was completely unable to pilot the aircraft. The autopsy reports on the men were not released, but the Colombian pathologist found multiple bullets in the bodies of all three cadavers. The explanation was that the men's own weapons exploded in the fire; however, if a ballistics report was ever done, it was never released to the families. Sharon Schmidt was convinced that something happened to the engine, making it impossible for her husband to control the aircraft, and that they could have been taking fire from guerrillas, which would account for the bullets in the men's bodies.

Ralph Ponticelli's father, Louis, a retired aircraft mechanic, felt that there could have been damage to the engine before the flight, because the engine showed signs of erosion caused by water. "There was no rain the night of the crash; there was no rescue equipment to put a fire out with water. Where did the water come from?" he says. He also wondered whether the crew could have taken accidental fire from the Colombian military. "When I asked the State Department, 'Were they shot down?' They told me, 'Don't be ridiculous. No, there's no signs of bullets.' I said, 'Look, you jackasses, two-thirds of the aircraft was consumed by fire. How can you say without a reasonable doubt that they weren't shot down?'" Ponticelli said that the only way his son's skull could have been blown half off was "by getting hit by a pretty good-size bullet. There was only one heavy machine gun in that valley that night, and it belonged to the Colombian army. And seeing that there were no lights [on the plane], the Colombians get trigger-happy, and they will shoot anything at night. So there's a damn good possibility that this was friendly fire."

Albert Oliver, the father of Butch Oliver, felt that there was something even more sinister behind the bullets found in his son's remains. "First it was rumored that they had been shot down, but I knew that was a real long-range possibility," he says. "I really believe that the men [Ponticelli, Oliver, and Schmidt] were having some terrible disagreements when they were conducting the search down there. I firmly believe that if they were as mad at each other as they say they were—we heard tales that they were *really* going at it—there's a good possibility that one of them went berserk and shot my son ten minutes after he took off."

For the families, finding out exactly why the plane had crashed became all the more essential when they each opened identical letters from Northrop Grumman's insurance company. "I received a letter from the claims administrator for Gerber Life Insurance, telling me that Northrop had notified them that my husband had been 'terminated' and my claim for the personal accident insurance was therefore ineligible," says Sharon Schmidt. There would be no insurance or benefits for her and her son. It was the same news received by the families of Ralph Ponticelli and Butch Oliver: The families of the crew should expect nothing from the Northrop Grumman Corporation. The company claimed that Schmidt, Ponticelli, and Oliver were not employees of Northrop Grumman when they died. It stated that, instead, they worked for an unaffiliated company called CIAO, Inc. The families would not receive the $350,000 death insurance benefits that the men had under CMS because the policies had expired two days before the crash, and CIAO had not renewed the policies.

Sharon Schmidt was positive that her husband had refused to sign any paperwork related to transferring his contract from CMS and Northrop Grumman to CIAO. "The fact of the matter is that my husband never received a paycheck from anyone other than Northrop, and a contract between my husband and CIAO never existed," she says. When news reporters repeatedly called CIAO, Inc., for more information, they reached only voice mail. Calls were never returned, and the company's address led to an empty office space at a rural Maryland airport. Northrop Grumman also refused to comment on the crash.

Sharon Schmidt begged Senators John McCain and John Kerry to launch a congressional inquiry into the legality of how the company had handled the crashes and the company turnover. Schmidt said that she hoped such an investigation would also "help lead to a positive course of action to secure the release of Marc Gonsalves, Keith Stansell and Tom Howes. It would certainly show that Congress is more concerned than the current administration about the three hostages and their safe, expedient return." Neither war-hero senator (and in the case of McCain, a former prisoner released through a negotiated agreement between the United States and North Vietnam in 1973) pressed for an investigation or made any gesture to find a solution to the hostage crisis. Congresswoman Jan Schakowsky, an Illinois Democrat, who became involved after Schmidt contacted her, told *The New York Times*, "My complaint about use of private contractors is their ability to fly under the radar and avoid any accountability. Now we're finding out that because of their low profile, and so little scrutiny, they [corporations] are able to avoid liability or responsibility for these individuals." But the July 2003 crash report issued by the Department of the Navy would state that the absence of accountability to the U.S. government on the part of Northrop Grumman and CMS was precisely the idea behind having contractors handle the missions.

While Sharon Schmidt and the families of Butch Oliver and Ralph Ponticelli filed lawsuits against Northrop Grumman, the complex relationships among all of the contractors and subcontractors made it exceedingly difficult for the attorneys pursuing the cases. The SRS contract still remained with Lockheed Martin under a massive megacontract with the Communications and Electronics Command (CECOM) of the U.S. Army. So when Northrop Grumman chose to rid themselves of California Microwave Systems and CIAO was created, it was the responsibility of Lockheed Martin to request the switch from CECOM. The request was a formality that CECOM agreed to without objection. What likely seemed an abomination to the families of the deceased was actually perfectly legal.

While Northrop Grumman denied any responsibility for those killed in the second crash, the company continued to do everything they could for the families of Stansell, Gonsalves, and Howes. It was the U.S. government that garnered the ire of the hostages' loved ones. The State Department continued to call weekly, always stating that there was nothing new to report but claiming that everything possible was being done to find the men and secure their release. However, sources in Bogotá who worked closely with the American embassy never saw anything being done by the Americans in terms of rescuing the men, although U.S. dollars for Plan Colombia continued flow to antinarcotics missions. Plan Colombia was also funding Special Forces brigades to train Colombian troops in the town of Arauca (on the border with Venezuela), where they were tasked with guarding an Occidental Petroleum pipeline. Dozens of other American troops were training Colombians in counterguerrilla tactics across the country, but the rules of engagement continued to prohibit U.S. forces from entering combat or searching for the American hostages on the ground.

On July 4, 2003, more than four months after the crash, a letter arrived at the California Microwave Systems headquarters in Bogotá. Colleagues of the hostages felt that the letter was a testimony to how incredibly detached the U.S. military actually was from the case of the missing Americans. It was a birthday greeting to Thomas Howes from the head of the United States military group in Colombia:

Mary Ellen and I join your family and friends in wishing you a very happy birthday! We hope that there are many happy prosperous years to come. Thank you for all of your hard work and dedication to US Southern Command and US Military Group, Bogotá. Best wishes to you—I hope you enjoy your day!

P. K. Keen, Colonel, U.S. Army, Commanding.

12

Botero

Two and a half years before the Cessna crash and hostage taking of Stansell, Gonsalves, and Howes, forty-four-year-old journalist Jorge Enrique Botero emerged from the jungle of southern Colombia with video interviews of Colombian army soldiers and National Policemen who had been held hostage for as long as three years by the FARC. The shocking images created a firestorm and became the catalyst for a massive prisoner exchange between Pastrana's government and the guerrillas. Botero was very proud of the work he had accomplished with this story, but the images of those he had recorded would haunt him so intensely that he grew to believe that he would never be released from the grip of the story of the *secuestrados* (hostages) until all of the captives were free.

For Botero, the incredible suffering of the hostages and their families was just another in a long list of his country's human injustices that had tormented him throughout his life and career. Born in 1956, Botero lived with his family in the north of Bogotá—a city divided between the poor south and the rich north. It was a world of excess, with large American-style homes full of housekeepers, exclusive golf and tennis clubs, and expensive schools. Nearly every family in the wealthy area of Bogotá left the bustling city each weekend for fincas, sprawling recreational properties, which ranch hands and caretakers ran so that well-to-do owners could enjoy the environmental and social riches of their beautiful country.

At home, the only son in a family of six children, Jorge Enrique was constantly arguing with his conservative father. "I remember those long debates he had with our father about politics and about human rights and things like that," says Botero's youngest sister, Angela. "Our father was politically very right—the son of a minister of public works under President Mariano Ospina in 1948—and very traditional. That's why sometimes Jorge Enrique and my father had big differences about how they saw life and how they saw politics and economics and even literature. They had very opposite views." Jorge Enrique was tremendously spoiled by his mother, his five sisters, and his two grandmothers, and he reveled in the attention. Perhaps because of his charm and charisma, which were evident at an early age, Jorge Enrique's conservative mother became swayed by her son's passion. "She always listened to

Journalist Jorge Enrique Botero (right) covering a conflict for the news program 24 Horas *in 1995. More than 100,000 coca growers were marching to protest fumigation and were stopped by Colombian troops with bullets and tear gas. Photo: Felipe Caicedo.*

him very carefully," recalls Angela. "And I think she has been very open-minded. She was raised by a very traditional family, but she started changing the way she saw things."

In college in 1975, Botero joined the Juventud Comunista. "That was a very important political party during that time. And he was really involved," says Angela. In Colombia, the 1970s were a time of enormous student agitation, and as the president of the student council, Botero led several strikes and street marches, which almost always ended in confrontations with the police. "At the time I entered the university," Botero says, "I wasn't only ready but anxious to be part of the student groups that fought alongside the workers, the farmers, and, many times, the guerrillas, to change our country." The students demanded better salaries for workers, a better educational system in Colombia, and social programs for the poor. They punctuated their cries with violence, throwing rocks at police barricades. In 1978, during a national day of protest against the government, Botero was detained by the National Police. At the time, the city was under martial law. "The police could take you, bring you to prison, and the same police could condemn you," Botero recalls. "There weren't judges or anything." Botero's family was devastated when they learned of his arrest, but not surprised. "I think my parents already understood that it was going to be a ride for the rest of his existence," says Angela. "It was tough for everybody, but it was his decision. And he had been doing pretty much what he believed in." After several days of physical abuse and threats (at one point a gun was put to his head), a police captain sentenced Botero to six months in jail.

Along with other student protesters who had been jailed with him, Botero formulated a plan to survive the hard conditions of the Colombian prisons, and at the same time, he set out to do political work with the inmates. "So taking advantage of the fact that we had managed to get authorization to have a television, we organized a study group with the inmates. They attended our conversations about the social and political situation of the country, and—in exchange—we let them watch the World Cup soccer matches, which were played in Argentina that year."

Across the compound in the seven female quarters of the jail was

Danelli Salas. At twenty-eight, she was five years Botero's senior and a student leader of the Juventud Comunista. "At the time, in the mid-1970s in Bogotá, there were many strikes, many work stoppages. The people in the street were shooting and throwing rocks and everything. And that's where I met Danelli. We were young and totally intoxicated with revolutionary ideas and socialism," he says. Salas was bright, lively, and constantly upbeat—and the single mother of a five-year-old son. Her path to the student revolts was far different from Botero's; she came from a very poor family in Cali, one of seven children of a *zapatero*, a shoemaker.

Botero and Salas were released on June 24, 1978. Botero was a changed man. The 180 days that the aspiring journalist spent in the Bogotá District Jail marked a kind of dividing line between what he had been until then—a rich boy who ventured to explore the world of rebellion—and what he would become afterward, a journalist obsessed with finding the humanity beneath his country's endless violence. Botero and Salas rented a small apartment in the south of the city, and in 1979, Salas gave birth to their first child, Alejandro. A year later, their daughter, Juliana, was born. Botero's father paid for his tuition at the university while Botero studied and supported his new family by writing for a Communist newspaper. In 1980, the couple separated, and for all of his liberal views, Botero would blame class difference for the demise of their relationship.

Salas was becoming more and more fanatical in her political beliefs, and Botero began to worry that she might be involved in a violent urban guerrilla movement called Ricardo Franco. While Botero was walking with three-year-old Alejandro, the boy pointed to a soldier with a machine gun. "He said, 'Look, Papi, my mama has those in her house.'" Several weeks later, Alejandro had an accident when he was in Salas's care: he was burned over his entire back from boiling water. The three-year-old spent two months in the hospital. "Then I asked her if she would give me the kids, and she accepted because she knew that she couldn't take care of them. I also believe at that time she knew that she was in danger—extreme danger," Botero says.

Salas left Bogotá for Medellín, but she would return every three months. Botero would take the children to a meeting spot so that she could spend a weekend with them. "I never asked her anything, because I didn't want to know what she was doing. I already had the kids. I took them to school every day. I was their father and their mother," he says. Botero felt that he knew little about the woman whom he'd been with for three years, and she was becoming more and more of a mystery to him. One day in 1985, Salas asked Botero to bring the children to her. Botero waited with Alejandro and Juliana. "One hour, two hours, I waited. I waited and waited. I thought that she would call. But days went by, weeks, months, and she never appeared. We went to the places she'd been and asked her friends and people at the university when they'd last seen her. Finally, we filed a missing person's report with the police. One night I was in my house and the police called me: 'Mr. Botero, there's a woman's body at the morgue.' Then I went, half-asleep, drove there, went and looked at the body. They lifted the sheet. I said, 'This is not her,' and they covered it again. And for an entire year I did this, looking at cadavers. I think that was the worst year of my life. Because, you know, you're in the house and then, 'Mr. Botero, we found a dead body.' And me: Son of a bitch, please don't let it be her. Please don't let it be her." Botero spent the entire year telling Alejandro and Juliana that Salas was on a trip, that she would come back soon. "I was inventing things, and that was unbearable for the kids. They were asking every day, 'Where is my mama? Where is my mama?' "

Almost a year after Salas's disappearance, her sister came to speak with Botero. She and her siblings had been searching for Salas as well. "She had a photo from an old newspaper, one of those ripped, crumpled newspaper pages from a tabloid that commonly showed graphic photos of massacres—three, five, ten people killed in the same event. The photo was of some dead people tossed among piles of garbage. Salas's sister pointed to one woman whose face stood out and asked me, 'Do you think this is Danelli?' I looked at the photo. It was a very blurry photo. But for me, it *was* her." Salas's sister did not want to believe it was true. "She said to me, 'No, it's not her. It's not her.' Denying it, trying to deny it. But when I saw it, I saw an expression on the face of that dead woman that was very much Danelli."

During Botero's adjustment to life as a single father, he experienced his first direct contact with war when he traveled to the city of Urrao, in northwestern Colombia. The town was under attack by two guerrilla factions, and the novice war journalist was intoxicated by the mélange of life and death playing out in the streets. "That first trip to the world of the guerrillas had *everything*: night marches through the mountains, camping, and ten hours straight of firefights in the streets of the town. There were also wounded, airplanes firing bursts onto the town's streets, chaos, panic, autographs of the good-looking guerrillas for the young girls of the town, and hurried fleeing of the insurgents, who were not able to complete their objective of taking over Urrao."

In those years, Botero also watched the metamorphosis of Bogotá; an uncontrollable wave of Caribbean sounds and flavor sprinkled his gray city with colors. "Bars and salsa and bolero clubs opened, many full of the unmistakable air of the rebellion, of secrecy and conspiracy. It was not strange to see the leaders of the urban commandos of the M-19 [Movimiento 19 de Abril], the FARC, or the ELN enjoying the nightlife. I frequented these places and it allowed me to stay up-to-date on the subjects of the war, as well as to maintain contact with the sources."

At the end of 1986, thirty-year-old Botero was offered a job with a major Cuban media organization called Prensa Latina at the company's headquarters in Havana. "I decided to go with the kids, because it had already been a year, and Danelli hadn't appeared. So I knew that she was dead." Botero was almost certain that the Colombian military had "disappeared" Salas. The term *desaparecido* is a common one used throughout Colombia and the rest of Latin America. It is a fate that affects many families when a loved one—sometimes someone connected to a subversive movement, sometimes someone completely innocent but suspected of subversive activity—disappears without a trace. Occasionally, bodies are discovered in back alleys or shallow graves, and the culprits are assumed to be military or paramilitary forces. But most often, the victim is never seen or heard from again. The anguish of having a loved one disappear is similarly excruciating to what a family experiences in a kidnapping situation. However, there is never an end or any answer to fill the emptiness.

Once in Cuba it was the five-odd interviews Botero landed with the country's charismatic dictator that left him with his most lasting impression of the island. "Before I went to Cuba, Fidel Castro was almost like an idol to me, someone I admired and very much respected. What I'd most wanted when I came to Cuba was to meet him, to see him in person. But when I arrived, it immediately felt like I wasn't in Cuba. It was the land of Fidel Castro. Turn on the TV, there was Castro; on the roads on giant billboards, Castro; everywhere, Castro. I felt like it was a cult of personality. The impression I had was that Castro was almost like something religious, sacred. The idea of Castro as the supreme leader was something unquestionable. For the majority of the islanders, Castro's word was the last word—the only word."

The dictator made constant public appearances, and Botero was always sent to cover them. Arriving three hours early, he would be corralled with dozens of other reporters and cameramen. On each occasion, an impressive array of security surrounded Castro, who was illuminated by massive spotlights, giving the events a cinematic flair. "In the midst of the excitement, I tried to make myself noticed, going around the security ring that surrounded Castro. When I was able to catch Castro's eye, I showed him my recorder and made hand signals like I wanted to ask some questions." When Botero managed to score an interview, he experienced the double sensation of having achieved a journalistic trophy and of having blown an exceptional opportunity. "In the midst of the bright lights, Fidel seemed to grow in stature, and his towering figure intimidated me. To top it off, he had the habit of constantly tapping his fingertips on the shoulder of the person he was speaking to—in this case, me—which rattled me completely." Each time he interviewed Castro, Botero would ask a question, and the Cuban president would launch into a monologue, which could last up to twenty minutes. Then the interview was over.

What Botero encountered during those short meetings wasn't the courageous revolutionary he had idolized during his college years. Botero saw Castro as arrogant, with a stifling air of superiority. In addition to his dislike for the Cuban president's character, Botero was left cold by Castro's policy toward Colombia. "I never liked the way that Fidel handled his relationship with Colombia. To me, it didn't seem right. I think he played a game so that he could have good relations with the government of Colombia, even if the government was far right, even if the government was persecuting the people." Botero also found it interesting that even though those in the FARC worshipped Castro—feeling an intense brotherhood with Cubans, whom they believed had achieved the perfect society—Castro had little interest in the guerrillas.

Not everyone on the island was a believer in Castro. In the Prensa Latina office where Botero worked with seventy other journalists, "there was a lot of sarcasm in the circle of friends that I hung out with about Castro. They were always making fun of him." The company was pleased with Botero's work. But for Botero, "the effects of a closed political system were felt strongly in the exercise of journalism. We had to self-censor. We knew that there were prohibited topics, and people we could never write about. At the time, Celia Cruz was the biggest singer in all of Latin America. But because she was a Cuban dissident, to Prensa Latina, she didn't exist. Sometimes I felt that I was creating propaganda, not journalism, so I started to have a lot of problems with my bosses." In 1991, after Botero had spent four years on the island, the Soviet Union collapsed. Cuba was left adrift, without allies and without foreign aid. One of the first decisions that was made by the Cuban government was to expel foreign journalists. Botero returned to Bogotá with his family and began to work in television news. Compared with a newsroom, the pace of the television studio was dizzying. And it was during Colombia's greatest political corruption scandal that Botero would make a name for himself as a journalist and begin a long-standing antagonistic relationship with many of his country's political elites.

Shortly after the presidential election in 1994, the first signs began to appear that the Cali cartel had financed the campaign of Ernesto Samper, the Liberal party candidate, who had won the election. After seven months, with the administration under a constant barrage of accusations, on Monday, July 31, 1995, the minister of defense and the minister of the interior held a tumultuous press conference. Botero inscribed his name on the long list of reporters who wanted to ask questions. An inside source had tipped him off; Samper's campaign treasurer, Santiago Medina (who had been indicted and arrested the week before), admitted to prosecutors that the Cali cartel had donated millions of dollars to Samper's campaign. But Medina's recorded testimony had been stolen over the weekend. In the press conference, the minister of defense quoted portions of Medina's testimony, and accused him of lying. Botero took the microphone. He knew that no one outside of the prosecutor's office should have seen Medina's testimony. "I asked the minister of defense, 'How is it possible that you are revealing the content of statements that are secret?' " Ingrid Betancourt remembers the question igniting a firestorm. It was "an unprecedented television moment," Betancourt wrote in her memoir, *Until Death Do Us Part: My Struggle to Reclaim Colombia.* "Naturally, they can't admit that they've stolen the investigative file over the weekend." The minister of the interior hesitated and then mumbled that an anonymous source had brought the file to the Interior Ministry. Those close to Samper ducked or ran for cover. The minister of the interior was forced to resign two days later. A handful of others, led by first-time congresswoman Betancourt, doggedly began to pursue Samper's impeachment.

By the time Betancourt took the lead to bring down Samper, the thirty-four-year-old had already gained attention for her nontraditional campaign style. In her congressional race, Betancourt handed out condoms in the streets of Bogotá, promising to "protect" Colombian politics against corruption. She was attractive and determined. As a congresswoman, she dressed in short skirts, wore large costume jewelry, and played expertly to the media. On the campaign trail, she dressed down and traveled through rural Colombia in traditional colorful "Chiva" buses. But it was the impeachment trial against Samper that launched her definitively into fame and gave her national notoriety.

In the many months that Botero reported on the downfall of Samper, he became well acquainted with Betancourt, whom he would later spend more than six years trying to find in captivity. At the time, Botero, by now a well-known television anchor, was working for an evening newscast called *24 Horas,* on assignment to cover the impeachment trial. "Around six p.m. every day, we would set up a small television set, with the cameras, lights. Ingrid would arrive each day at that time because she knew that the media would all be there, and that she would be on every channel's evening news." Botero interviewed her on many occasions. "At times I found her charming and genuine. She was very clever. Other times she seemed like a typical duplicitous Colombian politician."

Botero felt that Betancourt took advantage of the widespread antipathy and mistrust that many Colombians felt for their political leaders by publicly and continually calling for transparency in the government. Traditional politicians, who saw her as a threat, called her a rich little girl—more French than Colombian—and an upstart in politics. In stand-up interviews in the congressional hallway, Betancourt told Botero and other reporters that she was convinced Samper was guilty, and she forcefully called for his resignation. When only close allies of Samper were appointed to a committee to decide whether to convict him, Betancourt went on a hunger strike. The media covered her hunger strike every day. Then an ambulance took her to the hospital, and television cameras followed her like a celebrity. The Colombian public, fed up with the broken political system, fell in love with Betancourt, and she quickly became a rising star—a symbol of opposition to the entrenched Colombian government and to its long-standing acceptance of corruption.

On June 11, 1996, Betancourt appeared in front of the Colombian Congress to detail the evidence of Samper's links to the drug cartel and to convince her fellow representatives and the millions of Colombians watching her on television of Samper's guilt. Her testimony was brilliant. It lasted more than an hour, was well documented, and was rated by pundits as the best of the more than one hundred speeches heard during the trial. In the end, Samper was acquitted. Betancourt was crushed by Samper's acquittal, but all of her work had paid off politically. Afterward, she was considered one of most promising figures in Colombian politics.

For his coverage of the trial, Botero achieved a sort of celebrity, something not missed by those in the media business. "Job offers rained on me, and my editors pretty much let me do any story that I wanted," he says. What he wanted was to cover his country's civil war. As a teenager in the early seventies, Botero had followed news stories about the guerrillas. At the time, the FARC was still a small army that occasionally achieved high visibility by attacking the military in remote mountain areas. They also took towns, killed police, robbed banks, and gathered the campesinos together and gave revolutionary speeches. "The guerrillas were admired by young leftist university students, including me," says Botero. When Botero finished college and started working in the media, he heard stories of former friends who had joined the guerrillas. "I'd inquire about an old friend, and the response was, 'He went to the mountains.' One particular friend from Botero's days with the Juventud Comunista was Guillermo León Sáenz, a chain-smoking radical, a womanizing and gregarious revolutionary leader who was greatly admired by all of the younger students and who had studied anthropology at the National University in Bogotá. Together with three other Juventud Comunista comrades, Botero and Sáenz marched in the streets of Bogotá, stopping traffic and yelling revolutionary slogans. They played all-night poker games, drank in excess, and expounded political ideology. In the early 1980s, Sáenz—who was eight years Botero's senior—became FARC soldier Alfonso Cano. Over the years, the highly educated Cano spent a great deal of time with Manuel Marulanda, and the upbeat conversationalist and dedicated revolutionary deeply ingratiated himself with the commander in chief.

Aside from a brief fantasy he'd had as a high school student, Botero had never considered joining the guerrillas. "After graduating from the university, I was already a father. I'd left my political life with the Juventud Comunista and gone into journalism, which I liked a lot." Even though many of Botero's friends had been killed or had joined guerrilla movements, his country's civil war had always seemed very far away— until the early 1990s, when he began to hear stories from deep within the jungle and from the most remote mountain regions. "The tales were very intriguing, very journalistic. They were stories that always navigated between fiction and reality in the vein of magic realism."

Getting an interview with the guerrillas would be somewhat difficult because the FARC had become a very reclusive organization. By 1997, Marulanda and other leaders of the Secretariat were still in the process of rebuilding after the massacres of the Unión Patriótica. They almost never spoke publicly and rarely gave interviews to the media. But because of their twenty-year history, Botero wasn't surprised when

Cano—whose intense dedication to the movement had earned him a place in the Secretariat—agreed to an interview. Cano was known to be the FARC's great ideologue, but it was still a shock to Botero when he came face-to-face with his former friend in May 1997: Cano had become a deeply reflective revolutionary and seemed to belong to a period three decades earlier.

In the videotaped interview, Cano expounded on the FARC's struggle against state-sponsored terrorism. He said that the FARC was growing in numbers of troops, just like other revolutionary groups around the world. He cited conflicts in Mexico, Peru, the Philippines, and the Congo, and insisted that the phenomenon of armed insurgencies was global. Cano chastised what he called a "farce" of democracy in Colombia. "If anything was proven in the last four years [during the scandal-ridden Samper administration], it is that the elections in this country are not democratic. They are corrupt; they are full of tricks, of deceptions, of a deep disregard for what the people express, how the country should be, who should govern, et cetera." He also told Botero that only if the FARC came to power would the violence in Colombia come to an end.

For mainstream Colombians, who wanted to believe that the guerrillas no longer had the idea of taking over the country, the Cano interview was an unwelcome wake-up call. The interview was aired in its entirety, and Botero took a lot of heat from the government for giving Cano such a forum. At the end of the 1990s, Botero took the job of director of news-magazine programs for one of Colombia's largest networks, Caracol. He covered many stories and proposed dozens of others to the network producers, but no news story enticed him more than one that had simply disappeared from the public consciousness—that of the nearly five hundred kidnapped soldiers who had been captured in 1997 and 1998 when the FARC overtook several military bases.

"Pastrana had recently given the FARC the DMZ, and I went to El Caguán because I wanted to do a large report about the military people whom the FARC held in captivity." Botero traveled without his camera because he was working on preproduction for his story—securing locations and getting authorization for interviews and access. He arrived in Los Pozos (a three-hour trip from San Vicente del Caguán), where the dialogues between the government and the FARC were being held. The camp was only eighteen miles away, but the jungle roads were ridiculously difficult to travel, especially during the rainy season. "I was talking with various leaders and commanders of the FARC about my idea to do this report, and a car passed by with a man who caught my attention because of the way he acted, the elegance of his uniform. So one of the guerrilla commanders who was there said, 'Look, comrade Simón, this is the journalist Jorge Enrique Botero.' " Trinidad's car stopped, and he got out. "He said, 'It's a pleasure to meet you. I have heard a lot about you.' And of course, everyone in Colombia knew the story of the banker turned guerrilla, so I said, 'No. The pleasure is mine because I have heard a lot about you.' " Trinidad, who was with his companion, Lucero, invited Botero to spend the night at their camp.

"I was happy that I'd brought a bottle of Old Parr whiskey," says Botero, who was thrilled to get such great access to the senior guerrilla. The camp, which belonged to Secretariat member and senior negotiator Raúl Reyes, was two hours away by car. Several other members of the FARC negotiation team were also there. "We were talking and drinking whiskey almost until two a.m. I had many questions because I had heard many things about Trinidad, about how he was a banker, about his past as a member of the social elite of Valledupar, that he had studied in Bogotá, all of that. We talked a lot about Bogotá in the seventies, when he was a young student. We knew the same places, and many of the people he mentioned were also friends of mine. It was a very interesting night because he was the first guerrilla whom I met who had a social upbringing similar to mine." The two men discussed cinema, literature, women, and soccer. Botero found Trinidad eloquent, with a keen sense of humor, but also very determined politically. "When we talked about politics, he adopted an uncompromising attitude. He referred to 'the oligarchy' with contempt and hatred and defended the most radical positions within the FARC. The whole night he kept insisting that the FARC would never have to turn over their weapons, that they would never put them down. But at the same time, he seemed to be, from the human point of view, a happy man—not a guy who was sad with life or unhappily resigned to the fact that he was a guerrilla. He also seemed like a man completely in love. Lucero was always at his side. He always held her hand. She was always enjoying his jokes. It was as if they were almost one single person."

The following day, Trinidad drove Botero back to Los Pozos, where he would meet the guerrilla commander Mono Jojoy to ask for authorization to report on the military hostages.

Several weeks later, Botero received word that Mono Jojoy would allow him access with his cameras. He would travel by car on remote muddy roads and by river and by foot for sixteen days into the jungle until he reached the hostage camp. What he encountered when he arrived was something he couldn't have imagined. "I had never seen so much sadness in one place. Men, soldiers trained in rigid military discipline, cried like children in front of my eyes. They sobbed, begged that I would help them get out of there." The prison was deep within the jungle, where the guerrillas had constructed camps surrounded by barbed wire. "Some were walking like zombies, ignoring reality; others clung fanatically to prayer, raised their arms to heaven, and asked for clemency, compassion, freedom." From what Botero could see, the hostages were not subjected to torture and were in decent physical condition. "But their spirits had collapsed. Their souls were empty." Botero thought the camp looked similar to images he'd seen of Jews held in Nazi concentration camps. "When I saw what it was like, I thought, This war is incredibly cruel. I also thought that no one in the world had any idea what these men were suffering, and that maybe if they did, something could change." Although Botero had no idea if anything he could do would actually help, he says, "I promised that I would not rest for one minute until they were free."

With more than ten hours of recorded videotape, Botero returned to Bogotá and locked himself inside a Caracol office for over fifty hours to edit his story. When he finished, his bosses gave a copy of the final program to the government's peace commissioner, who had requested to see it after the station had run commercials for the upcoming show that included shocking images of the hostages. The following day, the channel received a letter from the National Television Commission demanding the story not be broadcast because it could "seriously hurt the feelings of large segments of television viewers, such as children," and that "this sort of broadcast could turn out to be counterproductive" in regard to the peace talks. Caracol agreed to scrap the program. A furious Botero went public, admonishing the government's and Caracol's censorship. He was fired the next day. But clips of his disturbing images had already reached the masses in the promotional spots.

The public outcry over the scenes of men behind barbed-wire fences and the heartbreaking messages from the captives to their families became the catalyst for the Colombian government finally to take action. The result was a successful negotiation between the FARC and President Andrés Pastrana's government less than a year later to exchange some three hundred hostages. Amid great fanfare, Pastrana released dozens of FARC guerrillas from Colombian prisons. But the FARC Secretariat freed only the rank-and-file soldiers and continued to hold higher-ranking military and members of the National Police. The family members of those released were elated. But it became painfully clear that the FARC had no plans to do away with the practice of kidnapping. That same day, FARC commander Mono Jojoy made a startling statement: "We are going to grab people from the Senate, from Congress, judges and ministers, from all the three powers [of the Colombian government], and we'll see how they squeal." Although much of the country supported the exchange, many others were furious and thought Botero had crossed a line. The journalist began to receive death threats by mail soon after some of his video footage aired: "Shut your mouth, motherfucker. We're coming to get you. You have five days to get lost."

"The people who threatened me never identified themselves," Botero says. "But it was clear that the threats came from the ultra-Right, since in the letters they sent to me they accused me of being 'a journalist of the guerrillas,' 'guerrilla disguised as a journalist,' and so on. At that time, those who were threatening or murdering people were the paramilitary groups, and often special groups from the army or the police." The Center to Protect Journalists reported, "Sometimes, the caller played a recording of Botero's private phone conversations from a few minutes earlier, revealing that the reporter's phone was being tapped." In January 2001, a hand-delivered note appeared at his home with the message "We offer our condolences to the Botero family for the death of Jorge Enrique Botero." The false condolence letter was a standard death threat in Colombia. Botero sent his family to a safe house in Cuba and went into hiding for two months.

Even though the threats resumed when he returned, Botero was content. He believed that his work had been the impetus for freeing the hundreds of captive soldiers. On the topic of hostages in Colombia, Botero became a well-known expert. Not only had he been the only journalist to venture into the jungle to record the conditions of captivity but he had presented the country with the drama of the families, their desperation, their anguish, and their struggle to recover their loved ones. There were more than a few who accused him of exploiting the pain of others for money, while others in the Colombian government and military pointed to him as a puppet used by Marulanda to apply pressure for an exchange of prisoners. "I wasn't surprised," says Botero. "I expected it. It's a tactic of the government and the official press outlets to discredit or delegitimize independent journalists. I didn't give a shit. And I did not feel bad. To the contrary, it confirmed that I was doing my job."

13

Proof of Life

On April 1, 2003, dramatic images of Pfc. Jessica Lynch exploded in the American news media. The story was indeed incredible: the petite nineteen-year-old Lynch wounded and fighting off her Iraqi captors; a horrifying eight days in captivity; and the Hollywood blockbuster rescue by a joint unit of Delta Forces, U.S. Army Special Forces, and U.S. Navy SEALs. The fascinating tale inspired patriotic fervor in a country not fully convinced of the necessity of the Iraq war. The story was later proved to be highly embellished, and many, including Lynch, accused the Pentagon of manufacturing a propaganda campaign to rally support for the invasion. There was no benefit to the U.S. government to publicize the plight of Thomas Howes, Marc Gonsalves, and Keith Stansell, and few people in the United States even knew there *were* American hostages in Colombia. For the first six months after the crash, the U.S. government could not confirm if the men were even alive. The Colombians were still tasked with looking for the American hostages, but the trail was cold, and there were no reported sightings and no new intelligence. There were also no American military forces put on the ground to find them.

While the American media mostly ignored the story of the American hostages, Jorge Enrique Botero was conducting a relentless and cal-

Americans Keith Stansell, Marc Gonsalves, and Thomas Howes in an interview with journalist Jorge Enrique Botero while in captivity, July 25, 2003. Photo: Jorge Enrique Botero.

culated campaign to get back into the jungle. He fervently believed that good fortune came to those who had patience. And if anyone had the patience to wait for the FARC (with all their frustrating pragmatism and guerrilla bureaucracy) to grant him an interview with Ingrid Betancourt and the three Americans, he did. After being fired from the network, Botero had formed his own company with the goal of surviving as an independent journalist, and an interview with Betancourt would be the journalistic coup of his career. Ingrid Betancourt's case had been front-page news all over Europe since her kidnapping, and a video interview of Betancourt and Clara Rojas would not only prove they were still alive—something that no one was sure of—but also make headlines around the world. And maybe, Botero hoped, it would cause the Colombian government to do something to free the hostages.

In June 2003, Botero finally learned from his contact that he would have access to the camps where thirty-five Colombian military officials, members of the National Police, and politicians were being held. He was not told whether he would be able to interview Betancourt or the three Americans. Many of the hostages he would see were part of the same group he had reported on in 2001 and those who had been held back during the prisoner exchange with Pastrana's government. Botero knew how hard the conditions were in the jungle, and he wondered how the hostages, whom he now considered friends, were faring. In several different packs he gathered the things he would need for his journey: a couple of shirts, a pair of jeans, a lot of underwear, and all the tapes he could fit. He also packed his green book for taking notes, pens of different colors, the audio recorder, batteries, and, above all else, his camera, a bright, flashy Canon XL1—a machine difficult to take into the jungle because of the humidity, but ideal for ensuring a quality sufficient for television broadcast. In his backpack he put videos that he had shot over the past few months of the hostages' relatives sending messages to the captives. If he had the chance, he would show the videos to the hostages and take the opportunity to record them watching, creating a type of virtual meeting between family members who had not been able to speak for up to six years. He also carried magazines in which the hostages were mentioned, books to soothe the boredom and raise their morale, plenty of cigarettes, candy, chocolates, and real-world essentials: toothpaste, disposable razors, sanitary napkins, shampoo. In a moment of wishful thinking that he might be able to interview the Americans, he added a John Grisham book in English that he'd found in a bookstore and two copies of *Newsweek* and *The Miami Herald* so that the men could have some news from the United States. The prospect of seeing the Americans was what truly excited him most, but he was nervous and angry with himself for never having learned English.

Botero's motivation was twofold. He was sure that if the U.S. government saw an interview with its three kidnapped citizens direct from their jungle prison camp, something would definitely have to be done to help get them released. Perhaps President Bush would even pressure Uribe's government to make an exchange of prisoners so that the Americans could be freed, which would help liberate Ingrid Betancourt and all of the others, too. It would also be the first time in his career that his coverage of the Colombian civil war would reach the United States.

To learn more about the Americans, Botero searched the Internet for stories in the U.S. press. He found very few. But there was one extensive article on MSNBC.com about the crash, and it included quotes from Jo Rosano, the mother of Marc Gonsalves. There weren't any interviews with other family members, and Botero couldn't understand why. Because Botero was sure that he would be the only civilian the men had seen since their kidnapping, he wanted to take something into the jungle that would help gain their trust and give the men some solace. He contacted two colleagues in the United States and asked them to record an interview with Rosano—specifically, to record a message from Rosano to her son. In her Connecticut home, Rosano was nervous and suspicious, but she agreed to the interview. Against a backdrop of flickering candles and dozens of sympathy cards, she cried as she spoke:

> Marc, I just want to tell you that I love you very much. I think about you day and night. I hope you come home soon, safe and alive and also your two colleagues. There's hundreds of people praying for you. And I just need you to come home because I miss you so much. And I worry about you. Please stay strong. You'll be home soon. I love you.

Botero downloaded the video file from the Internet, packed it along with the messages from the other families, and set off to find his contact. The trip was perilous. For the first three days, he traveled alone, catching a ride when he could along the country's paved roads. At each of the seven military checkpoints, he convinced the soldiers who tried to stop him that he was making a documentary about "the reality of the battlefields." Then he crossed the boundary that took him to the "other" Colombia—the former DMZ, where the FARC was still the law of the land—and met his two guerrilla guides. Along the way, he took copious notes in his journal, describing the sounds, smells, and mysteries of the jungle, telling about walking on trails and navigating rivers, traveling in boats and on mules and on foot over impossible routes through endless green.

It was the middle of July, one of the rainiest months in the Amazon.

At night, Botero and his guides suffered under heavy downpours. Each morning, the jungle was bathed by fog, which only lifted at midday, when humidity took hold of everything. The guerrillas told Botero that they preferred the apocalyptic rains to the dry months, when water was scarce and the enemy was freer to move about. But the season brought many difficulties as well, they said. Moving through the jungle was more difficult, clothing never dried, illnesses increased, and food got wet and rotted. The hours standing guard in the rain seemed eternal, and a collective melancholy took root in the rustic housings that the guerrillas continued constructing and dismantling throughout their nomadic travels.

Botero appreciated that his guides helped carry his gear, but he cursed them when they dropped his pack and broke his provision of J&B scotch. As they continued past village after village, each more isolated and impoverished than the last, Botero felt like a visitor to a war that interested no one. Many Colombians, especially those from the cities, seemed accustomed and resigned to listen, read, and watch the news of the deaths, explosions, and pain and suffering of thousands of families in the remote areas where the battles occurred. Even as four million internally displaced people arrived in Bogotá and other big cities to escape the endless violence in desperately poor settlements, life seemed to proceed normally. News of the war was mixed with that of corruption scandals and soccer goals and beauty queens, and somehow became a part of everyday life. Many times, Botero felt that people watched the news of the dead, wounded, and displaced as if it were one more soap opera of the many that aired on Colombian television. It was a world that Botero found difficult to explain when talking with colleagues or with politicians from other countries. The only reason he could think of as to why there was so much indifference toward his country's suffering was that perhaps people in other countries had become bored hearing the same news from Colombia: murders, bombs, kidnappings, drug traffickers, guerrillas, paramilitaries.

In the afternoon of the fifteenth day of his trip, Botero sat on the edge of a makeshift bed of planks, checking his equipment and writing in his notebook, when a young guerrilla named Nancy suddenly appeared. At first, Botero did not hear the great news that she brought because her fresh scent and wide, flirtatious smile overwhelmed him. "You have been given permission to interview the gringos," she told him.

It had been five months since the three Americans had been kidnapped, and during their captivity, they had not spoken to anyone other than their captors. While many of the other political hostages were kept together in a large prison camp, the extremely valuable nature of the Americans caused the guerrillas to keep them far away from all other captives. They had no access to radio broadcasts or newspapers, and they were desperate to find out what was going on in the outside world, especially what was being done on their behalf. At New Camp, where the three men slept in separate quarters, they were still forbidden to speak to one another, but despite the unbearable loneliness, the men had found ways to cope. Thomas Howes used pages from his notebook to make a full deck of cards, but because he was still not allowed to speak to anyone, the only game he played was solitaire. Marc Gonsalves drew a picture of his house, the layout of each room, in a small notebook that the guerrillas had given him. Every morning, he would open his journal to page 13 and say "good morning" to his family.

Howes, Stansell, and Gonsalves still had no idea what their future held, but there seemed to be very little urgency for the guerrillas to do anything with them. Howes, whose Spanish was better than that of the others, asked a guard what they were being held for and what the possibility was for their release. He didn't quite understand the soldier's answer, but he gleaned that the three of them were being offered as an exchange for FARC prisoners in Colombian jails. To the three men, it actually seemed promising. Stansell was a former marine and considered himself an intensely patriotic American. He was sure that the United States was doing everything it could to ensure their release. One day in mid-July, the captors came to the men and gave them soap, razors, toothpaste, and toothbrushes and told them they would be moving out. They traveled on motorized aluminum canoes down shallow rivers full of debris. But being out of the jungle was a welcome relief. "With blue sky above us, and even bluer skies on the horizon, the boat trip felt a little bit like a vacation," wrote Stansell. Because they were traveling by day—which was unusual, since mostly they had been moved during the night—the men were hopeful that the FARC had made a deal with the Colombian government and they were going to be released. On July 23, the guerrillas told the Americans that the following day they would be interviewed by an international journalist—that the world would be able to see just how decent the FARC were. Then they asked the men for their clothing sizes in order to "look good for your visitors." All three received haircuts and were given the chance to bathe in clean water for the first time. The three began to speculate wildly on who might be coming. Stansell thought that maybe it would be Christiane Amanpour, the venerable CNN reporter, who, he knew, was famous for getting into difficult spots and covering conflict zones. Stansell also thought that the interview was for proof of life, probably demanded by someone in Washington, D.C., who was working on their release. As they mulled over the possibilities, the men began to wonder whom else they might meet besides the journalist. Would they see the U.S. ambassador to Colombia, Anne Patterson? Someone from the State Department or from Northrop Grumman? Possibly a Colombian minister of justice or minister of the interior? Their minds raced as the guerrillas brought them to a small camp with a wooden structure, where they were told they would spend the night.

Nearby in the jungle, Botero slept restlessly. His body ached from the many days on the trail, and he was nervous about the interview and his poor English. He was told he would have a translator, a guerrilla who spoke English, but he never fully trusted anyone to translate his interviews. When the clock struck 4:00 a.m., a guerrilla shone a flashlight into his face and told him to get up. With two guerrillas in front and two guerrillas behind him, Botero was guided through the dark. "When the sun rose, we arrived at a kind of oasis, where the vegetation was not as thick and an abundant spring formed a pool surrounded by delicate white sand," Botero recalls. After breakfast, around 10:00 a.m., Mono Jojoy arrived in the camp. Botero, Mono Jojoy, and several other guerrillas climbed a small hill. On the hill's summit was a little cabin with two rooms and a small porch. With each footstep, Botero felt the growing tension as he moved toward the structure. Botero was filming as he stepped onto the porch, ready to record the first moment he would meet the Americans.

Gonsalves, Howes, and Stansell seemed surprised and nervous when they were introduced to Mono Jojoy, whom they had met only once before, in the initial weeks of their captivity. Mono Jojoy then introduced them to a thin Colombian journalist wearing a backward baseball cap that read WORLD'S GREATEST GRANDPA, and he told the hostages that they would be able to record messages to their families. The hostages were immediately deflated. Botero was obviously a Colombian, not the international journalist they had been promised. He had no production crew with him, no obvious credentials, only two small cameras and a backpack. They were even more stunned by Botero's first words, which he directed to Gonsalves. "Marc," Botero said in a sentence he had memorized in English, "I have a message from your mother."

"I wasn't sure what to expect from the proof of life, but when Botero uttered those words, I realized just how hard this was going to be," recalls Gonsalves. "After telling me that he had a message from my mother, Botero immediately turned his back on me and stepped to the other side of the table. I was stunned by what he had said, and I couldn't figure out why he hadn't given me the message. The last thing I expected out of the POL [proof of life] was to hear from anyone in my family."

Botero filmed as Mono Jojoy sat at a long table across from the hostages and began to speak. A European-looking female guerrilla, who spoke perfect English with an accent that the hostages couldn't place, translated for the commander. Mono Jojoy accused the three of being spies for the U.S. government and of violating the sovereign airspace of the FARC. He informed the men that they were being held as prisoners of war until there was a prisoner exchange, what he called a "humanitarian exchange." When Stansell was given a chance to speak, he asked Mono Jojoy, "If Colombian president Uribe refuses to negotiate, if he doesn't go along with the idea of a prisoner exchange, then we could be here for five or ten years?" Mono Jojoy seemed certain that an exchange would take place eventually. "One day these negotiations will be here, but we don't know when." After they met with Mono Jojoy, the men walked out to the porch and were joined by the translator. Gonsalves took the opportunity to ask a question that they all were desperate to know the answer to: "Do you think we're going to live through this?" The young woman replied that it would depend on what the

Colombian government did. At that moment, she told them, the army was training troops to rescue the political hostages. "Rescue comes," she said icily, "we kill everybody."

When the interview with Botero began, the Americans were instantly suspicious. "We didn't know Botero at all, but the fact that he was allowed into the FARC camp and his chummy demeanor didn't sit well with us," wrote Stansell. "We knew in some ways we were being used by him," wrote Gonsalves, "but we also wanted to let our families know that we were okay—even if he wasn't from the States or from CNN." Botero had not been given any restrictions on what he could ask the Americans, and he had more than a dozen questions that he wanted all three of them to have a chance to answer. For two hours, he filmed as the men were questioned about what they were doing in Colombia, what they thought of the country, and what their opinion was of the war on drugs. With the camera lens fogging up in the humid-ity, Botero turned it off while the guerrillas turned on a fan, which he hoped would help fix the problem. During the break, Botero gave the men the newspapers he'd brought with him and two printed Internet pages of articles about the murder of Tommy Janis and Sgt. Luis Alcides Cruz and the crash that had killed Ralph Ponticelli, Butch Oliver, and Tommy Schmidt. The news was too much for Howes to bear. "Botero must have planned all these revelations in order to elicit some emotion from us, and he succeeded," wrote Gonsalves. "Tom was so upset about Ralph's death that he grabbed the copy of the day's *Miami Herald* they had intended to use in the [proof of life] to shield his face from the camera." (Gonsalves erroneously assumed that the news-paper Botero had brought for them to read was a tool the captors would use to prove the date of the video.) Gonsalves, who was also in tears, was incensed that Botero had turned the camera on again.

The men were also stunned when they read that their SOUTHCOM Reconnaissance Systems contract had been transferred by Northrop Grumman to a company called CIAO, and they were very worried that Northrop Grumman had abandoned them and their fami-lies. They also had to deal with the fact that the guerrillas thought they all worked for the CIA. "None of us had ever heard of [CIAO], but we were incredulous that someone who was contracted to do intelligence operations would call themselves CIAO," wrote Gonsalves. When Botero asked the men to comment on an article he'd brought with him about the war on drugs, Gonsalves spoke somberly to the camera: "There is a toll here," he said. "We're victims of the toll of the drug war in Colombia. There's other ways I think that are safer that we can tighten up our border control, educate U.S. citizens because there's a demand for this cocaine product, and if we can kill the demand, then we won't have a problem anymore."

Gonsalves wrote that when Botero played the message from his mother, "I was determined not to become a part of Botero's propaganda scheme. Despite how I was feeling about hearing a voice from home, I told myself I wasn't going to cry when I watched the message. I hated that this journalist was manipulating us, but I tried to remember something Keith had said to us earlier, before we'd even gone on camera. We knew that our families might see this video, and we did our best to put a positive spin on everything. At every opportunity, we told them that we were well; we were healthy; we were being treated humanely. None of it was true. But it was what we needed to tell our families." Howes was also suspicious of Botero's motives, but he desperately hoped the proofs of life would make it to his family. "Botero had told us that two journalists in Los Angeles were working to track down our families so that they could be provided with our messages," Howes wrote, "but that wasn't the most precise answer to our questions about how the video would be used. Maybe they wanted to do the proof of life just to calm us all down, to make us think that our release was near. We all knew that happy prisoners were easier to control."

It took eleven days for Botero to get out of the jungle and back to Bogotá with his videotapes. He was completely unaware of the disdain that the Americans had for him and felt relieved that they had appeared to be in good physical condition. In addition to Stansell, Gonsalves, and Howes, he'd interviewed many of the other political prisoners in a camp that was several days' travel from where the Americans were being held. He knew that the families of those hostages would be ecstatic to see that their loved ones were alive. Whenever Botero had gone to the jungle and emerged with videos of hostages, he always made sure that families got to see the messages first, before they were ever released to the media. This way, they would have time to deal peacefully with the pain and absorb the weight of their loved ones' messages. Sometimes Botero would watch the videos with them. Sometimes he preferred to give the tapes to the families to avoid having to watch the suffering. The families always wanted to know more: "How are they really doing? What else did they say? Are they sick or well? What are they eating? How are they being treated?" For the families of the Colombian hostages, Botero's videos were often their only ray of hope after years of silence.

After making sure the families of Stansell, Gonsalves, and Howes were given the opportunity to see the messages that the men had recorded, Botero agreed to give the video to the U.S. government. Facilitating the handover was Gary Noesner, who invited his former colleague FBI agent Chris Voss, a State Department counterterrorism official working on the case, and Northrop Grumman's vice president, Lloyd Carpenter, who was deeply concerned for the men's welfare, to view the proofs of life. While the agents on the case were glad to have the information and to see that the men were alive, there was little action they could take, given the Bush administration's refusal to engage the guerrillas in any way beyond backing what Uribe decided to do.

While Stansell, Gonsalves, and Howes would be terrified for the rest of their captivity of being executed during a rescue attempt and bristle whenever they heard the sound of helicopters, they had learned one positive piece of news in the days before the proofs of life. "The news leaked out to us that Colin Powell, the God-bless-him-four-star-general secretary of state of the United States of America, had just been in Colombia on our behalf. We were completely jacked up to hear that," wrote Stansell. It was a hope that the Americans would continue to hold on to throughout their captivity. However, Powell had not been in Colombia since the men's capture. A month earlier, he'd traveled to Santiago, Chile, to garner support for the U.S. government's policy against Cuba for its "appalling repression of human rights and civil liberties." About Colombia, Powell praised "Uribe's efforts in Colombia to bring peace and security to that troubled country which is under assault from narco-traffickers and terrorists." But about Stansell, Gonsalves, and Howes, the United States secretary of state was silent.

14

Capture and Extradition

For a few days in October 2003, after Botero's footage of the three American hostages appeared in the United States on CBS's *60 Minutes II*, the case was prominent news. At the time, Patricia Medina was working full-time to support her and Stansell's four-month-old twins and living with her mother, sister, and brother, who helped care for the babies. Northrop Grumman and Stansell's family in the United States did not recognize the twins as Stansell's, and therefore, Medina received no financial support. To try to get some kind of help, Medina went to the U.S. Embassy, where agents informed her that she couldn't file any type of paperwork on the boys until she could prove paternity—and to prove paternity, she would need the father's DNA. (Years later, when she learned that the embassy had a sample of Stansell's DNA from his older children, Medina was told that it could not be released to her because she was not Stansell's next of kin.) As difficult as things had been for Medina, she still hung on to the hope that Stansell would be released, and that he would want to have a relationship with her sons. So when Medina heard that there was proof that Stansell was alive, she felt immensely relieved. But her relief was short-lived. Stansell's message to the world would be like a knife to her heart:

I one hundred percent miss my family. I have . . . I'm kind of a hard-ass, I apologize. But in my life the two things that really hit me in my heart are my children and my fiancée. And when I feel like sometimes not going on, I think in my mind of my 11-year-old son—and I'm sorry, Kyle, for missing your birthday—and my 14-year-old daughter, Lauren, and my fiancée, Malia. What would they want me to do? And I think most what they would want me to do is to come home. My mother died when I was 14, and she left myself and my brother and my father. And if I die now, the exact same thing is happening to my children, and that's a very hard weight for me to carry. So what I miss most is my immediate family, and my father and my brother, I love them.

For Medina, the proof-of-life video that blasted across Colombian and U.S. television was the painful explanation of why Stansell had

Ecuadorian policemen guard FARC commander Simón Trinidad the day after his January 2, 2004, capture in Quito, Ecuador. Photo: Jorge Vinueza/AFP/Getty Images.

never wanted a commitment with her—he had a fiancée in the United States. The fact that he didn't even mention her or their two boys in the video was unbearable as well. "Hearing him speak in this video, I felt like it was another Keith. It was not the same man that I lived with for more than ten months," she says. Still, Medina could not give up hope that things would be different when Stansell returned. And even though Stansell said in the footage that he did not have access to a radio, she began to send messages through a radio program set up specifically to broadcast to hostages, *Las Voces del Secuestro* (The Voices of Kidnapping), giving Stansell updates on her life and the life of their twins, never mentioning her heartbreak over his other life.

In addition to Stansell's message to his family in the United States, he also made an impassioned plea to the U.S. government, which aired in the *60 Minutes II* segment:

> I love the U.S. I think it's the greatest country in the world, and I'm a proud American. And if I die here, I die here. I believe that we have the force to come kill everybody that's holding us, but in that rescue attempt, we're going to die also. I know some people don't like me to say that, that's probably not what they want to hear. But please kids, anybody here, listen to your . . . to the words out of my mouth. A rescue attempt for us is very serious. This isn't a movie, and I do not believe we will live. I pray for a diplomatic solution.

The Bush administration responded to the media coverage of the hostages by offering a five-million-dollar reward for information leading to the rescue and the safe return of the men. There was no mention of the possibility of negotiating for their freedom. In Colombia, a contractor who tried dialing the number to see if it was a legitimate offer says that there was no answer. The following week, a State Department spokesman announced that the "campaign" for the reward was still being developed. The mood of those working out of the American embassy in Colombia was somber. According to a Colombian-American contractor who worked closely with the embassy as well as with many of the U.S. contractors, "If you ask any pilot, any contractor, even anyone in the military, 'Do you think the U.S. would do anything different to rescue you?' the answer is *no*. Before this crash, they totally thought that the U.S. would come get them. Now, no one does."

With the war in Iraq filling the airwaves, the plight of the American hostages quickly disappeared from the news and no further word came from the Bush administration on the situation. So in December 2003, Manuel Marulanda met with some of his commanders, desperate for a way to jump-start the faltering hostage negotiations. Initially, the FARC Secretariat had been sure that the American government wouldn't let their "spies" rot in the Colombian jungle. Their thought was that President Álvaro Uribe followed President Bush like a dog. The United States would want its men out, and Bush would command Uribe to make an exchange of prisoners. Not only did this strategy fall flat, but the only solution the U.S. government and Uribe continued to pursue was a military rescue by Colombian troops. This was a constant threat and a potentially deadly maneuver for both sides. The miracle gift of the "gringos who fell from the sky" was not the ultimate catalyst for the exchange that Marulanda had hoped for.

With the case totally stymied, Gary Noesner kept trying to get a meeting with Jorge Enrique Botero, who was still the only civilian who had seen the hostages in captivity. "We keep trying to open a humanitarian link," Noesner said in January 2004, "but nothing is working. Plus, the FARC leadership is all in hiding now based on the recent successful military operations against them." But for Botero, the story had also grown completely cold. The guerrillas seemed uninterested in letting him anywhere near the hostages, and all of the sources who had connected him to the FARC had disappeared.

As time wore on, there was still almost no media coverage. The occasional comments from lawmakers in Washington got little press and did almost nothing to move the case along. In early 2004, Senator Patrick Leahy, the ranking Democrat overseeing appropriations for U.S. activities in Colombia, commented, "It is very disheartening that we appear to be no closer to seeing the release of these American captives captured more than a year ago. . . . Also troubling is that no one has been held accountable, nor have adequate changes been made in a poorly conceived program with lax oversight. Using contractors as 'private soldiers' in combat zones, without the backup we would provide our armed forces, is fraught with dangers." Five months later, in June 2004, Noesner would encapsulate the continuing lack of progress:

There is absolutely nothing happening on the case. There has been no confirmed proof of life since Botero's videotape came out—zip. It's been very frustrating for the families but they seem to be holding on. The ongoing military campaign has the FARC on the run and showing little interest in talking about our three guys. As far as we know, they are alive and well, but nothing positive has been received despite our continual efforts to obtain verification of same. Talks of the humanitarian exchange ebb and flow, but nothing is certain as to whether or not that has any realistic chance of moving forward. Both sides, the Government and FARC, remain far apart on the issue. Northrop Grumman's Crisis Management Team continues to meet weekly with [Control Risks] involvement. They continue to support the families both financially and morally, but aren't able to give them what they want most, the safe release of their loved ones. The U.S. Government's attention is completely Iraq focused at the moment and Colombia has fallen off their radar screen. I see no attempts to explore other options by the government.

On the FARC side, there was great frustration as well. To try to push for movement toward negotiations, at the end of 2003, Secretariat member Raúl Reyes called upon Simón Trinidad—who during the years in the DMZ had earned himself a trusted place in the top FARC ranks—and ordered him to neighboring Ecuador. Trinidad was told to contact officials from the United Nations and European countries whom he'd met during the dialogues between the Colombian government and the FARC. His specific task was to contact James LeMoyne, a former El Salvador bureau chief for *The New York Times* who had been a United Nations special advisor to the 2001 talks. Trinidad was also instructed to make contact with Fabrice Delloye, the French ex-husband of Ingrid Betancourt. Delloye had been very active in trying to persuade the French government to help secure Betancourt's release and was now working for the French government in Ecuador.

For Trinidad, the chance to be actively involved in some high-level negotiations once again was likely a welcome relief from the nearly two years he'd spent in the Amazon since the end of the demilitarized zone (some would say that Reyes hated Trinidad for upstaging him during the dialogues and had sent him to Ecuador to get him out of the picture). Jorge Enrique Botero had last seen Trinidad in February 2002, the day the peace dialogues collapsed and Pastrana called the military into El Caguán. "That morning, I was in a town called La Tunia and Trinidad passed through, driving a truck crowded with guerrillas. At his side, as always, was Lucero. I asked Trinidad what the future would hold. What was in store for him and for the FARC?" He told Botero, "This area has historically been ours and will continue to be ours, with or without a DMZ." The guerrillas' plan, explained Trinidad, was to retreat deep into the jungle, where the FARC had managed to create another world with roads, camps, trenches, supply routes, escape routes, hospitals, radio stations, training camps, and political training schools.

"After that, the jungle swallowed Trinidad," says Botero. "When I traveled in 2003 to interview the three gringos, I passed through several camps. In all of them, I asked about Simón, but nobody knew anything, or perhaps they were unwilling to say anything." Later, Botero would learn that Trinidad had been assigned to teach basic politics to new recruits. "My opinion is that it was a particularly desperate time for Trinidad, that the commander experienced something like fading celebrity. There was no longer a demilitarized zone. There were no cameras. He no longer appeared in the newspapers. He could no longer meet his old friends. In addition, he had become trapped in the jungle at the south of the country, unable to return to his Atlantic coast region and his post as second in command of the Forty-first Front. So teaching basic politics to dozens of young people who entered the FARC would not have been very attractive to him."

In late December, Trinidad and Lucero traveled to Ecuador and began to work on getting fake passports, in the hope that they could travel to a third country, possibly France, where Trinidad could represent the FARC in hostage negotiations. The couple was put up in the house of a family that worked for the FARC. To the guerrilla commander, the house seemed unsafe from the beginning. "Simón told me, 'If we come out of here alive, it will be a miracle,' " says Lucero. Shortly after they arrived, the couple's eleven-year-old daughter, Alix Farela, joined them from her grandmother's house. Trinidad and Lucero spent Christmas with their daughter, enjoying Quito. Perhaps it was the season, or being in a peaceful country, or the joy of being together as a family that made the two seasoned guerrilla fighters drop their guard. They had no idea that nearly every minute they were being watched. A Colombian secret police command had been dispatched to Quito, having been alerted to the presence of an important FARC commander in the Ecuadorian capital.

According to Lucero, on the evening of December 29, she and her daughter left the house to buy some bread for the following day. At the last minute, Trinidad decided to accompany them. The three were walking casually, when dozens of heavily armed men ambushed the family. They threw Trinidad up against a wall, handcuffed him, and pushed him into a waiting car. Lucero and the child were forced into another vehicle. Minutes later, they were in an Ecuadorian military garrison, Trinidad in one cell and his wife and child in an adjoining one. "It was a hellish night," says Lucero. "They interrogated us the whole time. Sometimes, someone friendly came and told me that if I collaborated with them, they could help us. Then ten minutes later, very aggressive men came. They threatened us and said that they could kill us and no one would ever know, that they were going to torture us so that we would talk." Lucero's daughter began to scream and howl uncontrollably. "I went near her to calm her, but she spoke into my ear to calm *me* down. She said that she did all of this so that they wouldn't hurt her father." (A Colombian police commander would later offer a conflicting story of Trinidad's capture to Reuters, saying that Trinidad was captured alone while visiting a health clinic. Lucero adamantly denies the report.)

In Trinidad's holding cell, the guerrilla commander told his interrogators that he and his family were in possession of false identity documents, and he immediately asked that they charge him with the crime of having counterfeit papers. Trinidad knew that the sentence for the offense was very light and that he would be released on bond. He also asked the Ecuadorian authorities for political asylum, but the Colombian government was calling for his immediate extradition. In the morning, police guards took Trinidad from his cell and allowed him to briefly say good-bye to his family. The three hugged, and he repeated to Lucero various times that she would have to continue in the fight that they both so believed in. "You already know what you have to do," he told her.

Trinidad was flown to Bogotá, while Lucero and their daughter were set free. "I was released because they wanted to present the image that they had captured a dangerous terrorist, and he couldn't be seen on television with his wife and child," Lucero says. The Colombian television stations interrupted their regular broadcasts to fill the screen with special news updates: The image of Trinidad handcuffed, guarded up to his ears by dozens of armed police, went around the world. In the Casa de Nariño, the presidential palace in Bogotá, Álvaro Uribe's first substantial victory in his war against the FARC was celebrated exuberantly. Trinidad was the highest-ranking guerrilla ever captured.

As he was transported from the helicopter and taken by car to Cómbita prison outside of Bogotá, Simón Trinidad cheered to the television cameras for Simón Bolívar and for FARC commander in chief Manuel Marulanda. After he was placed in solitary confinement, his only friendly visitors were his lawyer and, once, his mother. (After her visit, his mother received death threats from sources she believed to be close to the government, so she decided to leave the country.) Trinidad did have other "visitors": a pale parade of U.S. government agents passed through his cell. Some of the gringos acted friendly; some were threatening. All of them asked him to collaborate, to give them information about the FARC, and to tell them where the American hostages were being held. If Trinidad knew, he did not tell them. (Eight months earlier, on April 27, 2003, the FARC had released a communiqué, in which it named Trinidad as a FARC representative to negotiate for the Americans and other political prisoners. The memo put Trinidad high on the radar of U.S. intelligence.)

Shortly after his capture, the call to extradite Trinidad to the

United States came as a joint effort by the FBI, the Department of Justice, and the State Department. Whether his extradition would hurt the situation of the American hostages "was toiled over on an interagency basis, *a lot,*" said a State Department counterterrorism official who was involved in the case. "The bottom line was: Will we further endanger the hostages beyond the danger they're in now by bringing Trinidad up here and trying him? There was some spirited conversation, but it was decided that, based on the FARC's previous activities, we could [extradite Trinidad] without endangering the hostages. Anyway, the likelihood of them ever letting these guys out, we knew, was between zero and zero point one percent." The official said that he and his counterterrorism colleagues believed that the FARC were already angry with the United States for helping fund the Colombian army, which was bombing the guerrilla camps. "It's probably not much of a stretch to say that indicting one guy [Simón Trinidad] who's been out of circulation for a while is not going to further tick them off."

On December 31, 2004, Trinidad's nightmare of being exiled from his country became a reality. From the window of a U.S. government Gulfstream jet, as the clock struck midnight and the new year began, the guerrilla commander gazed out at the lights of Bogotá. Alejandro Barbeito was one of the FBI agents on board the plane. He had been on the hostage case since the beginning, when he collected Tommy Janis's body from the crash site. On the airplane, Trinidad talked openly with Barbeito about his life in the FARC and his reasons for traveling to Ecuador. He also told Barbeito that he did not believe in the policy of kidnapping because it was difficult and costly to the guerrillas. He also tried to give Barbeito advice on dealing with the hostage situation. "He said, 'Why doesn't the U.S. government establish official contact with the FARC?' " says Barbeito. "And I explained to him that, no, I was not allowed to do that because the FARC is a designated terrorist organization. And then that's when he suggested that we do things—and he said, '*por debajo de la mesa*'—'under the table,' which means, *unofficially.*" Barbeito asked Trinidad if he could be of any assistance in that regard. "I was hoping that he would cooperate with us, given his status in the FARC and his being named as the FARC negotiator involving our three hostages."

One month after Trinidad's celebrated arrest, in February 2004, another FARC member would become an actor in the international hostage drama. While traveling to a meeting with other FARC commanders, Sonia (the commander who controlled the river outpost Peñas Coloradas) and two fellow guerrillas, Juancho and Pantera, decided to spend the night at her brother's farm. There wasn't even the slightest indication of Colombian military in the zone, so they decided that no one needed to stand guard. Sonia went to bed in her underwear, left her weapon tossed on the floor, and fell into a deep sleep. Her comrades slept in various areas of the house. About three in the morning, a terrible roar reverberated through the house. Sonia knew immediately that it was a helicopter. She peeked through a crack in the curtain at enormous rotors practically grazing the house. Soldiers descended from a rope ladder like spiders. Sonia dressed in an instant and grabbed her weapon, her radio, and a book full of details of her business dealings in Peñas Coloradas. In complete darkness, the three guerrillas moved like shadows, trying to find an escape route. If they were able to head for the mountains, Sonia knew, they could escape. But their only exit was blocked by a chicken coop, so the three hid in the bathroom and made a pact to escape or die. Sonia quickly shoved her book into a space in the ceiling. As the soldiers entered the house, Sonia whispered that they should fire shots as they exited and search for a way to escape. When the commandos were less than three feet away, Juancho jumped out, with his pistol ready to fire, but before he could, he was hit by a direct shot to his face and fell dead. The tip of Sonia's rifle reflected a bit of light and a soldier pushed his hand into the bathroom and grabbed the AK-47 by the barrel.

"He told me to let go of it," Sonia says. "They threw me down on the floor and a soldier put his foot on my neck." When she saw them stepping on her comrade Pantera, who had been taken down and handcuffed, she protested. "I told them, 'You already have him under control. Take your foot off his neck.'" Sonia prayed that the soldiers tearing the house apart would not find the book she'd hidden in the bathroom ceiling, which would implicate her and many other FARC members. After searching the house for two hours, the commandos loaded Sonia, Pantera, and Juancho's corpse into the helicopter. Then they grabbed Sonia's brother and sister-in-law, the farm's cook and her two-month-old baby, and a sick woman who had been staying in the house and forced them into the helicopter as well. They also confiscated several kilos of cocaine paste and 27 million pesos (approximately ten thousand dollars) that belonged to Sonia's brother, a midlevel drug runner. The group arrived at the military base in Larandia blindfolded and handcuffed and then were taken to a large office where, she says, "some agents harassed us with obscene gestures with their fingers. They called me by my name, and they were celebrating the success of their operation, which included the infiltration of satellite telephones into our ranks."

Sonia was then transferred to the U.S. Embassy in Bogotá for further questioning, specifically about the three kidnapped Americans: Where were they being held? Who had them? Who kidnapped them? But Sonia had had nothing to do with the kidnapping and could tell them nothing. The U.S. agents also drilled her about the guerrilla organization and asked her for the names of the FARC Secretariat. "They told me that I should collaborate, should talk. They offered to bring my child and family to the United States in exchange for providing information. Otherwise, I would be extradited, locked in a dark room, and I would have to spend many years without seeing my family. They tried to pressure me by saying that the Secretariat was going to have me killed because I knew so much." Sonia was transferred to a women's prison in Bogotá. The guards at the Buen Pastor jail had rarely seen a prisoner like her; she acted almost like a rabid animal when they approached her cell. After a brief trial, a judge sentenced Sonia to fifty-six months in prison. The conviction was for "rebellion." What was much worse than the relatively light sentence was that Sonia awaited extradition to the United States on charges of narco-trafficking. "The biggest narco-traffickers are strolling around the streets, sitting in the Congress of the Colombian Republic and in high positions of power," Sonia told a reporter after hearing of her pending extradition. "My only crime is to have rebelled against the violent, anti-democratic, and inhumane State."

After several months in solitary confinement, she was abruptly taken from her cell. "When they woke me up, it was barely dawn. They told me to pack some clothes and they put me into a military vehicle. The guard who took me said, 'This is for your security, *mamita*.' " When they forced her onto an airplane, Sonia had no idea where they were taking her. But on the trip, she looked out the window and saw a large expanse of deep blue water, which she assumed was the ocean. The plane landed after an hour, and Sonia recognized she was at the Juanchaco military base on Colombia's Pacific coast. She'd seen the area on television in 1994 when the then president, César Gaviria, had invited U.S. forces to build a school for antinarcotics training on the military base without seeking the approval of the Colombian Congress. The move had caused a public outcry, and the court ruled that allowing American troops to enter Colombia without congressional approval was unconstitutional. An angry Gaviria told the media, "I am surprised that Colombians demand more international cooperation in the fight against drugs and then criticize such operations." At the same time, American and Colombian officials admitted only that the work on the base was an "army exercise," and denied that the operation involved antinarcotics activities.

From Juanchaco, Sonia was forced into a helicopter and delivered to what she believes was a U.S. Navy frigate. "On the frigate, I spent more than twenty horrible days, vomiting everything I ate, with an eternal dizziness." But there was something that gave the untraveled guerrilla a sizable amount of pride as well. Two years later, from her jail cell in Washington, D.C., she would brag to Jorge Enrique Botero, "I had the good fortune to see the ocean. What do you think of that, journalist?"

At Control Risks, just a few miles from the D.C. Jail, Gary Noesner was incensed by the charade that had brought Trinidad to the United States, and he felt that his former colleagues at the FBI were totally mishandling the case. "The strategic incompetence of extraditing Trinidad in the middle of what was going on with the Americans ran smack in the face of all these government people who stand in front of the families and say, 'The freedom of your guys is the most important thing in the world to us.' That was pure crap, and their actions certainly didn't support their words." Noesner believed that Trinidad's extradition would be a nail in the coffin for the three Americans. Months before, he'd helped Northrop Grumman craft a letter to the Department of Justice, begging that they not make such a grave mistake. Noesner believed that the FARC would demand Trinidad's return in exchange for the Americans, and he was sure that the U.S. government would never let that happen. Two months after Trinidad landed on U.S. soil, Sonia was also in the D.C. Jail, and Noesner's prediction had come true. The FARC demanded that, as a condition to release the "exchangeables" (which included Stansell, Gonsalves, and Howes), all incarcerated FARC members must be freed, including Sonia and Trinidad. It was all becoming an inconceivable mess.

FBI negotiator Chris Voss would disagree with his former mentor about extraditing Trinidad. "That was one of the things that I actually thought was a smart move. Your adversary has to respect you. The FARC is not going to deal with anyone who they think is weak," he says. After nearly two years had passed, Voss was not afraid that the FARC would kill the Americans, because they considered them to be so valuable. However, he was still gravely concerned for their safety. "We completely changed our threat assessment to include *all* peril that they faced. And the real threat to these guys was from disease and dying in the jungle. And absent the change in the [U.S.] government's approach, the risk that these guys would end up dying in the jungle was very high."

While the former FBI colleagues did not see eye-to-eye on the subject of Trinidad, Voss completely agreed with Noesner's take on the FARC as "an organization that never missed an opportunity to miss an opportunity." Days prior to Trinidad's scheduled departure for the United States, Álvaro Uribe had offered to cancel his extradition if the three Americans were released, but the FARC did nothing. "Imagine the world's response if the FARC's response to the extradition and prosecution of Trinidad and Sonia was to hold a very public humanitarian, spontaneous, unconditional release of one of the American hostages," Voss says. "How much pressure would there have been? It would have embarrassed the U.S. government and the Colombian government. Nobody would have known what to do with that." However, it would be another two years after Trinidad's extradition before the guerrillas would consider the idea of releasing one of the hostages in the hope of just the reaction that Voss was predicting.

15

The Jungle

By mid-2004, a year had passed since Botero's interview with the three Americans, and the fact that they were still stuck in the jungle along with forty-seven other political prisoners continued to haunt him. Many times he awoke terrified and sweating, recalling the beige shawl that captive congresswoman Consuelo González de Perdomo had given him to take to her daughters; the desperate letters from Gloria Polanco, a woman who had been kidnapped with her two teenage sons and then separated from them while in captivity; the perpetual smile of Alan Jara, the former governor of Meta, who taught Russian and English to his companions in captivity. "The images of Marc, Keith, and Tom appeared to me at all hours of the day, becoming a kind of torture. Almost no one was interested in the case of the hostages. My stories were broadcast on television and radio and published in newspapers or magazines. But the following day, other news buried them and everything returned as it was before: into oblivion."

The only interest in the hostage situation came from Canada and several European countries, including France, Belgium, Spain, and the Netherlands, where private citizens formed Ingrid Betancourt support committees and various lawmakers made public calls for the FARC to release the hostages. Support came most strongly from the French gov-

Jorge Enrique Botero reporting on the Colombian military and National Police hostages being held by the FARC in 1999. The documentary he made for the news station Canal Caracol was eventually censored at the request of the Colombian government. It was the first time the FARC allowed a journalist into the hostage camps. Photo: Jorge Enrique Botero.

ernment and President Jacques Chirac, who, because of a groundswell of public pressure to free Betancourt, pushed Uribe's government to make an exchange happen. Chirac even offered to allow FARC guerrillas released from prison to emigrate to France. Uribe denied Chirac's requests, and diplomatic ties between France and Colombia were severely strained when French foreign minister Dominique de Villepin tried to coordinate the release of Betancourt without the authorization of the Colombian government.

The debacle happened in July 2003. Betancourt's mother received a message from President Uribe: A FARC informant had reported that Betancourt was very ill, and that the guerrillas would release her near the border with Brazil. Betancourt's sister, Astrid, got the message to longtime friend Villepin, who had been one of Betancourt's professors when she was attending college in France. And with intense pressure from Betancourt's mother and sister, Villepin dispatched French commandos and medical staff in a Hercules C-130 hospital plane to an airport in the Brazilian city of Manaus, near the border with Colombia. After landing, the French team hired a Brazilian pilot and small plane to take them to a landing strip near the given coordinates. The pilot had no idea what the French were up to in the well-known drug-trafficking area. Frightened for his safety, he contacted Brazilian police, exposing the mission and causing an international incident.

All the while, Betancourt's husband, Juan Carlos Lecompte, along with a rural priest who had been told by the FARC informant to act as an intermediary, waited for Betancourt in the pueblo of San Antonio de Isa, Brazil. During the night, Lecompte slept in a stifling windowless room at a run-down pension. During the day, he and the priest sat on a large floating pier on the Putumayo River, watching boats pass by and waiting for Betancourt to be delivered. "The priest kept saying that I had to have faith," Lecompte told a reporter, but he was beyond praying. After more than a week of waiting, he saw a newscast about the unannounced French military aircraft in Brazil. After seeing Brazilian air force planes fly overhead and drop soldiers into the surrounding jungle near the pueblo, an anguished Lecompte knew the FARC would not be coming with his wife and that waiting any longer would be in vain. Flying back to Bogotá, Lecompte looked down at the endless green and felt intense dread, wondering if he'd ever see his wife alive. In truth, Betancourt was not ill at that time, and the release was never intended. It had all been a terrible lie. Secretariat member Raúl Reyes blamed Álvaro Uribe for the fiasco. According to Reyes, the FARC never planned on unilaterally releasing Ingrid, and certainly not to the French. Reyes also denied that Betancourt was sick at that time. "It was a vulgar delusion that Uribe created to give the French the impression that the FARC do not keep their word," he said.

While Lecompte (and for a week before him Betancourt's sister, Astrid) had been waiting for Betancourt in Brazil, she and Clara Rojas were together in their jungle prison hundreds of miles away. Several months after their capture in 2002, the two women had planned to escape together. Finally one morning before daylight, they were able to sneak past the twenty or thirty guerrillas who guarded them. The jungle terrain made it nearly impossible to navigate with any speed, and they made it only a short way before they were captured. Afterward, the guerrillas took no chances. "That was when her [Betancourt's] feet were chained together," said Uni, a former guerrilla who was one of the captors. The women remained chained day and night for fifteen days. Afterward, they were chained only at night. But to intimidate them further, Rojas said, the guerrillas threw snakes, tarantulas, and, once, a dead jaguar into their tent as they slept.

For a year and a half, Rojas and Betancourt had been completely isolated from all other hostages. And what made the isolation much worse was that during that period, the former friends and colleagues grew to despise each other. The rift was later reported to have been the result of a failed escape attempt. Other hostages would say that Rojas turned cold when Betancourt learned that her father, Gabriel Betancourt, had died, and the lack of solace in the intensely painful situation became an intractable wedge between the two. On August 22, 2003, the estranged pair would be introduced to a third political hostage, Luis Eladio Pérez, a former congressman from the department of Nariño, who had been kidnapped and held alone for more than two years. Pérez was beyond relieved to have the company of the women, but he could tell immediately that the tension between them was going to make things very uncomfortable.

After six weeks of living together in captivity, Pérez, Rojas, and Betancourt were moved to another, larger camp with two separate areas—one for the military hostages and one for the civilians, who were all politicians being held as part of the FARC's demand for a prisoner exchange. Betancourt, Rojas, and Pérez joined four other politicians. Fifteen days later, on October 20, 2003, the hostages were completely shocked when a group of seven guerrillas marched the three Americans to their camp. "We approached the political prisoners' camp with real anticipation," wrote Gonsalves. "It didn't take long for that feeling to be replaced by dread. In front of us stood a large compound completely surrounded by chain-link fence topped with barbed wire. For the first time, we were in a compound that reminded us of the photos we'd seen of actual POW camps."

"We were already adapting ourselves to the situation [of being in the larger group] when the foreigners arrived . . . Tom Howes, Keith

Stansell, Marc Gonsalves," Pérez wrote in his autobiography, 7 *Años Secuestrado por las FARC* (Seven Years Held Hostage by the FARC). Pérez and other civilian hostages felt that they received far worse treatment than the military hostages, possibly because the guerrillas and the soldiers came from similar backgrounds. But it seemed that the guerrillas had treated the Americans most harshly of all. Although they arrived unchained, "they were very thin, *very* thin, and their clothes were in tatters," says Consuelo González de Perdomo, a congresswoman in her fifties whose husband had died and who had become a grandmother during her captivity. "We brought them some mattresses, and to them it seemed incredible to have mattresses in captivity. They had slept on boards covered with black plastic. They did not have bedding, and they were very surprised to be able to have a sheet." To Gonsalves, seeing this group of prisoners was shocking, and he immediately asked how long they'd been held. "Some of us four years, some five, some six," one of them told Gonsalves. "I felt my stomach curdle. The group was in a bad way," he wrote.

The additional bodies made the small quarters even more cramped, causing friction and initial resentment toward the Americans. "At the beginning they were a little bit arrogant," Pérez wrote. "They felt more important than the rest of us." Pérez also thought that the way in which their young captors reacted to the tall, light-skinned gringos was incredible: "The guerrillas have always spoken against imperialism, against the United States, and against the gringos. But when they saw [the Americans], it was an adoration and complete submission. The classic submission of a Colombian before 'the American.' This surprised me very much."

One of the political hostages in the camp was clearly not happy that the Americans had arrived. Stansell recognized the woman as Ingrid Betancourt. He'd been in Colombia at the time of her kidnapping, and the CMS crew had even been given orders to fly over the area to look for her—something that he'd thought was strange: American contractors looking for a captured Colombian. While Betancourt argued with the guards and demanded they find somewhere else for the gringos, "we lingered there like unwelcome relatives who'd dropped in for a surprise visit," wrote Gonsalves. "I was trying to be open-minded and give them the benefit of the doubt."

However rough the initial meeting had been, there was one thing the camp provided that made it the best place they'd been since their capture: radios. For Stansell, Gonsalves, and Howes, who had lived without almost any news of the outside world for the entire eight months of their captivity, it was a great relief. Betancourt's demeanor changed as she and others told the Americans about the radio station that families of kidnapped victims could use to send messages. "Your mother has been all over the airwaves," she told Gonsalves. "We hear her messages all the time. Clearly she loves you very much." The men were told that their families were okay and that Northrop Grumman was taking care of them. "Hearing those words brought tremendous relief for all of us," wrote Gonsalves, "We had talked about and worried about whether the company was taking care of our families since we'd first crashed."

Stansell, Gonsalves, and Howes were eager to tell the other hostages what they had been through. "We began to hear the stories of the gringos, how they had been isolated one from each other, how they had been prohibited to talk among themselves," says González de Perdomo. Howes was the only one who could communicate in Spanish. Stansell spoke very little, and Gonsalves none at all. In the weeks and months that followed, Stansell and Gonsalves became willing students of the congresswoman and of Orlando Beltrán, a congressman from Huila captured in 2001. "Marc had a lot of interest in learning the basics of Spanish," says González de Perdomo. "We asked a favor of the military hostages, if they would be able to loan us a Bible that they had in English, and Marc dedicated himself to try to read the Bible, to translate it." González de Perdomo wrote a page of essential Spanish conjugated verbs for Gonsalves—*ser, haber, tener, estar, comer, dormir*—which he studied judiciously. Stansell gave English classes to Beltrán and González de Perdomo. "But it was for a very short time because we were disorderly—the teacher and the students. I taught Keith and Marc to play *banca rusa* [a card game] and we played a lot, two hours, three in a row, with Marc winning time after time," she says.

The hostages slept in cabins that surrounded a small open area. The compound was enclosed by a chain-link fence and barbed wire. One hostage each day was in charge of food service to the others and of organizing the camp and cleaning the bathroom. The guerrillas took two-hour shifts guarding the hostages while another guerrilla circled the camp, keeping an eye on the other guards. The guerrillas were forbidden to speak to the hostages except on occasions when the hostages requested permission for certain necessities.

Living in a camp was extremely difficult, but still preferable to being marched through the jungle. After months in one camp, without any explanation, "they would give us a limited time to arrange our things to set off on a march of two months. They would say, 'Prepare your equipment because we're going. We recommend the least heavy equipment possible because the march is going to be long,'" says González de Perdomo. If it was during a period when the Colombian hostages were chained, each hostage was made to carry his own chains (which weighed between ten and fifteen pounds) around his waist or neck. While many of the Colombian hostages, especially Betancourt, often rebelled against the captors and made escape attempts, the Americans did not, and they remained unchained. Stansell and Gonsalves "never rebelled, or protested like Ingrid and me," wrote Pérez. Howes was the exception, and Pérez remembers that on one occasion Howes screamed furiously at the guerrillas during a brutal march that lasted forty days.

"The circumstances were always so arduous that they brought out the worst side of everyone," wrote Pérez. Betancourt received the most ire, especially from the military hostages. "She was the best in swimming, in physical exercise, the one who the media emphasized, the one who spoke various languages." Pérez would come to the conclusion that being with so many others in such bad circumstances was actually more difficult than the two years he had spent as a lone captive in the mountains. The stress in the camps became even greater when the Colombian military was near. Constant flyovers by Colombian army planes and helicopters made both the hostages and the guerrillas edgy.

For some of the hostages, the only break in the monotonous, torturous routine was the Saturday-night radio broadcast *Las Voces del*

Secuestro. "Everything revolved around this program," wrote Pérez. "Not for everyone, because many were not sent any messages. I'm referring to the military and the National Police officers. Some military, some police and the three Americans, for example, received very few messages." For the three Americans, the messages they did receive came mainly from Gonsalves's mother, Jo Rosano, and Stansell's Colombian girlfriend, Patricia Medina (Stansell heard only one message from his fiancée, Malia Phillips). "When they listened to the first messages from their families, they became extremely emotional," says González de Perdomo. "They cried in happiness because it had been a long time since they had heard anything from them." It was through a radio message from Medina that Stansell learned about the arrival of his twin sons. "So then he began to feel an immense love for Patricia, because of the messages that she sent him, because of the way she took care of his sons," wrote Pérez.

What the Americans did not hear on the radio during the long years of their captivity—even on Voice of America (the U.S. government-funded international radio broadcast) news programs— was anything about their kidnapping. "They felt very abandoned by the US government," wrote Pérez. "They did not understand this vacuum of five years—five long years where there had not been a clear attitude on the part of the government of their country to look for a solution to their problem. President Bush was in Cartagena [in November 2004] but did not make any announcement about them. When Condoleezza Rice visited Medellín [in January 2008] she didn't mention the issue, either. So they felt like pariahs in their country." Even the U.S. ambassador in Colombia, William Wood (who held the post from August 2003 to March 2007), seemed completely uninterested in the captives. "During his tenure as ambassador, Wood only seemed to talk about drugs and counterdrugs, saying nothing about us hostages," wrote Howes.

To figure out what she could do to help, Marc Gonsalves's mother, Jo Rosano, an Italian-American who had no previous knowledge of Colombian politics, became a quick study of the Colombian conflict. Rosano also refused to believe that keeping quiet about the men would do anything to help their situation, and she accused the Colombian and

U.S. governments of doing nothing to free her son and the other hostages. She met with the Portuguese government to seek help, because Gonsalves's father is Portuguese. She traveled to Washington, D.C., to meet with senators and congresspeople, several of whom promised to help but could ultimately do little. She flew to Bogotá to march with the families of other hostages. She searched the Internet for news many times each day, kept in contact with dozens of journalists, and, most important to her, she prayed. Always accompanying her was her very frail second husband, Mike Rosano. The two had severe health problems and very little income, but according to Rosano, her strength came from the Holy Father. Even her intense faith could not dampen her seething anger toward Gonsalves's wife, Shane, who, she believed, was carelessly spending her son's money and doing nothing to help free him. Shane no longer took calls from Northrop Grumman or the government agents who called to give her updates on the situation. She refused to leave radio messages for her husband, even though Northrop Grumman made sure that all the families had the ability to record messages for broadcast on Colombian radio programs. According to Luis Eladio Pérez, while Gonsalves received many radio messages from his mother, he was worried "because his wife had not sent any messages to him, and he thought she had abandoned him."

Stansell's American fiancée, Malia Phillips, later moved out of the house she had shared with Stansell and left his children in the care of his parents and the children's mother. Northrop Grumman kept Phillips's cell phone active, on the outside chance that Stansell or one of the kidnappers would call. In Bogotá, Patricia Medina continued to send messages to Stansell via *Las Voces del Secuestro*. "I would tell him what happened that day, and then I put the kids on. I would tell them, 'We're going to speak to Papa.' One day, I regretted it, because I told one of the boys, 'We're going to leave a message for Papa.' He grabbed the phone and said, 'Hello? Hello?' waiting for someone to say something. Then I said, 'No, sweetie, Papa is not going to speak to you, but he can hear you.' I saw the frustration on his face because he wanted to hear his father on the other end of the line." Medina would also read to Stansell news articles that mentioned his two children in the United States because she was worried that Lauren and Kyle weren't able to leave messages very often. Medina created a photo album as a way to keep the twins' father in their consciousness. She would routinely show them the few photos she had gathered of her and Stansell together, those that Stansell had given her of himself hunting, and photos of the twins as babies and as they grew. "This is your papa. He is very smart and handsome and strong. He loves to hunt deer and bears," she would tell them. "I could not tell the boys a lot about Keith, because in ten months, I hadn't shared many things with him."

Several miles from the apartment of Medina and her family, in the foothills of central Bogotá, Juan Carlos Lecompte continued to live in the luxury apartment he had shared with his wife, Ingrid Betancourt. The two-story penthouse, with its tremendous view of Bogotá and the sunsets over the altiplano, had belonged to Betancourt before the couple married. During the years of his wife's captivity, Lecompte changed nothing in the apartment because he wanted everything to be exactly the way Betancourt had left it when she returned. The only thing that continued to pile up through the years were shrinelike items to Betancourt—paintings of her from well-wishers and fans, and books that had been written about her in her absence. The maid still came several times a week to mop the floors and dust pictures of the couple at their wedding in Tahiti or kissing in front of the Eiffel Tower. But as the years passed, things had changed. The deep red furniture and matching drapes had faded in the high-altitude sun. The terra-cotta tiles in the living room were cracking and coming loose. There was no longer the clicking sound of Betancourt's yellow Labrador's nails across the tile floors; the much-loved dog had passed away. The small Colombian flag that had flown proudly from the balcony planter during the presidential election of 2002 was reduced to tattered threads of faded yellow, blue, and red.

Lecompte continued to do everything he could to help get Betancourt and Rojas liberated—haranguing President Uribe for his abandonment of the hostages and pleading with the media not to forget her. And when the Congress voted to disband Betancourt's political party, the Oxygen Green party, retroactively, he took a trash can full of horse manure from a friend's finca and dumped it on the steps of the Congress building. Lecompte wrote about the act in his book, *Buscando a*

Ingrid (Looking for Ingrid). " 'For corruption!' we shouted as we launched shit against the enormous stone columns. 'For cowardice!' And we dumped more shit. 'For restricting democracy!' " The stunt landed him in a freezing jail until after midnight, but Lecompte was happy that he had made his point and brought more attention to Betancourt's situation. Lecompte's antics infuriated Betancourt's mother and sister, who were of the mind that more diplomatic means should be used. When he could think of nothing else to do, Lecompte chartered a plane and dropped thousands of flyers with up-to-date photos of Betancourt's children over the jungle, hoping that one would reach her and give her comfort.

Lecompte's desperate maneuvers made Jorge Enrique Botero feel very sorry for him. Despite the many times he had interviewed the families of hostages, he was never able to escape an overwhelming sense of sadness for them. Botero never quit his push to get to Betancourt, Rojas, and the three Americans, and on another trip to the jungle in June 2005 to try to secure permission to interview one or all of the hostages, he would come across a story that, for him, embodied all that was wrong with his country and yet, at the same time, represented a rebirth of possibility.

For several years, it had been rumored that Betancourt had become pregnant in captivity. But Botero learned that it was actually Clara Rojas, Betancourt's former friend and campaign manager, who had become a mother in April 2004. Botero wrote about the startling story he'd heard from his guerrilla sources in a book titled *Últimas Noticias de la Guerra* (Latest News from the War), which was published in early 2006. Botero chose to make the book partly fictitious because the details he had were few. What Botero didn't know, and his report didn't speculate or fictionalize, was what had happened to the baby. And at the time the book was released, Clara Rojas, who was still being held along with the other political prisoners, also had no idea what had happened to her son, Emmanuel.

Rojas's pregnancy had briefly reunited her with Ingrid Betancourt, and Betancourt may have been the only hostage who viewed Rojas's pregnancy as a happy occasion. Most were angry. "We were concerned about the circumstances that would surround the arrival of this child, the difficulties that were going to exist for the child and for Clara, because we knew that the limitations were great," says González de Perdomo. Luis Eladio Pérez was deeply affected because he had lost his son to illness when the baby was just eighteen months old. "I was not happy at all because it seemed like an enormously irresponsible act, in such circumstances, in captivity, in the jungle, in these conditions, to bring a baby into the world to suffer," he wrote. The guerrillas removed Rojas from the main group prior to the April 16, 2004, birth, but they took the baby to meet the other hostages shortly after. Luis Eladio Pérez recalls, "In that moment we noticed the fracture [of Emmanuel's arm], we spoiled him, we changed him, he peed on us. We doted on him. He became a factor of happiness, but also of sadness because the baby had a fixed gaze, always toward the horizon. We made signs and movements to see if he would react, but nothing." At first, some of the hostages speculated that Emmanuel was blind, but they found out that the guerrillas were giving the baby pain medicine because of the broken arm he incurred during delivery. González de Perdomo remembers how all of the hostages, even the Americans, adored the child. "Keith carried him and put him in his hammock," she says, "and I sang to him. We were very concerned about the baby's health condition, about his arm." According to Pérez, keeping the baby in the jungle became a risk and a danger for everyone, including the guerrillas, because it was impossible to keep him quiet. The guerrillas' solution was to remove the baby from Rojas for all but forty-five minutes a day. Keith Stansell remembers seeing Rojas standing at the fence of their compound, shrieking in agony in the direction where a group of female guerrillas was taking care of Emmanuel. And at night, "We [her fellow hostages] would hear the haunting sound of Clara singing lullabies as loud as she could to her absent child," Stansell wrote. When the baby was eight months old, the guerrillas told the hostages they were taking Emmanuel from the camp in order to get him medical care. Pérez remembers that the guerrillas marched the baby off—he was carried in a pouch on the back of one of the captors—chubby, babbling, and laughing, delighted with his jungle world.

Últimas Noticias de la Guerra was a best seller in Colombia. The story shocked the nation, and Botero was delighted with his most successful book to date, and glad that the country's consciousness had finally returned to the kidnapped victims. But not everyone was happy. Manuel Marulanda and the FARC Secretariat were angry that Botero had divulged a matter that they'd wanted to keep private. In one chapter of the book, he revealed that a top FARC commander had been killed by his lover. The woman had returned from prison after five years and found that her partner, the commander, had strayed. Botero thought it was an absurd thing for them to be angry about. "They didn't want anyone to know *how* he died. It was an embarrassment to them that one of their own was killed for love instead of war, and to them it was a sign of weakness." The reaction was not something Botero was expecting, but he had learned that accurately predicting the behavior of the guerrillas was impossible. What worried him most about angering the top commanders was his continuing coverage of the hostage situation. "I knew I would have to try to make them forget how angry they were with me in order to get back into the jungle," he says.

Once again, Botero found himself in the crosshairs of the Colombian government and the mainstream media, which accused him of using the touching story of the hostage child to sway the government into talks with the "terrorists." "In media interviews of top military leaders, many generals said, 'Botero is the press secretary for Mono Jojoy.' In the editorial meetings of newspapers and radio and television stations, my name often came up. 'Watch, when Botero goes missing— surely he will arrive with new news about the FARC.' At the beginning, it made me laugh. I thought, This is pure envy of my colleagues who couldn't get the scoop." When Botero later interviewed Secretariat member Raúl Reyes for another book, Botero says, "Reyes told me, 'I hope that your new book won't be like the one about Clara Rojas. That book is complete filth.' I thought, If the FARC aren't satisfied with my work and neither is the government, it is because I am doing things well. It would be terrible if either of them applauded me."

By fall 2004, the full weight of the Colombian military seemed to be bearing down on FARC territories in southern Colombia. For Uribe, money from the United States continued to be a great windfall in the war against the FARC. President Andrés Pastrana (who remained uncredited for any of the army's success against the FARC after his term) had left Uribe with a more powerful and capable army than the country had ever seen. And with continuing American support during Uribe's first two years, thousands more Colombian troops were on the ground, and the army's airpower had significantly increased. Bombing raids killed guerrillas by the dozens and pushed the FARC front lines farther and farther into the jungle. Uribe was hailed as a hero and his approval rating in Colombia shot upward of 80 percent. In Colombia, the multibillion-dollar Plan Colombia package was part of what was known as Plan Patriota. To an American audience that was footing the bill, Uribe, rather than highlight his military success to fight the "terrorists," promoted the success of Plan Colombia in its eradication efforts. "In one year of my administration, we have destroyed 70 percent of illegal drugs," Uribe told PBS during a 2003 visit to the United States to secure continued funding from Congress and the administration. "Our determination is to overcome this problem. We no longer want drugs in Colombia, but we need American help with budget, with technology and with the attitude of the American citizens. Whenever one American citizen consumes coca, cocaine or poppy [heroin], this consumption helps the traffickers, helps the terrorists." However, the same year, John Walters, the head of the U.S. Office of National Drug Control Policy, admitted that the $3.3 billion Plan Colombia—in its fourth year—was having no significant effect in stopping the trafficking of drugs out of Colombia. Although the number of hectares of coca cultivated had significantly dropped from 420,000 in 2001 to 280,000 in 2003, Ted Galen Carpenter, vice president for Defense and Foreign Policy Studies at the Cato Institute, argued that the numbers were statistically misleading because they ignored the fact that the area of coca under cultivation in Peru and Bolivia had risen sharply. Carpenter also argued that coca growers had become more efficient and could produce the same amount of cocaine from a smaller number of plants. Walters did add that he expected to see progress in the following year or shortly thereafter.

A decidedly unfortunate consequence of the billions of American dollars supporting the war against the FARC was that it was putting the three American hostages in grave danger. "If President Uribe's objective with his *Plan Patriota* was to flush out the FARC and get them on the run in order to wipe them out, then his efforts nearly did the same to us," wrote Howes. With the intense military pressure on all sides, the guerrillas broke up the permanent hostage camp, and on September 28, 2004, the politicians, the military hostages, and the Americans were told to pack up and move out. "The brutality of the 40 days we marched after we abandoned Camp Caribe rivaled anything we'd been through before," wrote Howes. Provisions had been at an all-time low for the hostages in their last months in the camp. They were all terribly weak as they pushed through the dense foliage and mud, carrying on their backs as many of their belongings as they could. "At one point," Howes recalled, "I stumbled, fell, and lay there in the mud thinking that it would be easy to just stay where I was, but I didn't. I picked myself up and kept putting one foot in front of the other. From knee-high mud through neck-deep water and up and down hills that were high enough to tire out dogs—into shivering nights when our bodies were so depleted of calories that we could not stay warm. We stretched the limits of what we thought we could endure."

When the long march finally came to an end, the three Americans were separated from the other hostages and taken via boat and then by truck to the Macarena Mountains, a mile-high range east of the Eastern Cordillera. Over the next two years, the FARC would continue to move the men throughout the mountains and jungle of central Colombia, what Gonsalves would refer to as their "wandering phase." During that period, they never gave up hope that there were American troops looking for them—possibly overhead, possibly on the ground—and they continued to wonder what was happening on their behalf in the United States. By spring 2005, with almost no U.S. media coverage about the hostages, several other Americans working on Plan Colombia made the news when they were arrested for drug trafficking and illegal arms trading. On March 28, five American soldiers flew a U.S. military plane from the Apiay air base southeast of Bogotá to El Paso, Texas. Their payload included more than fifteen kilos of cocaine, with a street value of approximately $300,000. A month later, Colombian police arrested two members of the U.S. Army Special Forces—one a colonel, the other a sergeant. The two Green Berets had been stationed at the National Army Training Center in western Colombia and had the job of training Colombian soldiers how to shoot weapons. The Americans were accused of being part of a smuggling ring and of intending to sell 32,000 rounds of stolen U.S.-supplied ammunition to paramilitaries. Because American soldiers (and also American contractors working under Plan Colombia) cannot be tried in Colombia, under the provisions of a treaty that grants them diplomatic immunity, the two were immediately taken to the United States to face a court-martial. The move infuriated many Colombian lawmakers, who called on the United States to extradite the men to face justice in Colombia "It's completely unjust that we are sending Colombians abroad to stand trial, and we can't request anyone be sent here," said Senator Jairo Clopatofsky, a member of the Colombian Foreign Affairs and Defense Committee.

For most of their captivity, Stansell, Gonsalves, and Howes would see little of the drug business that they had been employed to eradicate. But at one point in 2006, the guerrillas took them to a location where the FARC had stored five metric tons of cocaine base. "When Keith told us about the amount of coke on the premises, we all thought about the job we'd been doing before our captivity and how we had contributed to the situation the FARC was currently in," wrote Howes. "They had the drugs at our location, but they couldn't move them anywhere because of the strong military presence and heavy activity. We were glad to know that the combined efforts of the Colombians and the Americans in *Plan Patriota* were having some effect."

While the hostages were not mistaken about the fact that the guerrillas were losing territory partly due to increased military aid from the United States, the belief that the FARC's downfall was correlative to a diminishing drug production, cultivation, or exportation was completely false. In 2007, the CIA *World Fact Book* reported that Colombia remained the world's leading coca cultivator, with a 40 percent *increase* from 2003 to 2006. The report also named Colombia as the world's largest producer of coca derivatives and stated that it was the supplier of cocaine to most of the U.S. market and the great majority of other international drug markets. The bleak analysis did not deter the State Department from continuing to tout Plan Colombia's success. "Exponential growth in Colombia's cocaine production has been stopped," wrote John Negroponte, deputy secretary of state, in a *Miami Herald* op-ed piece. "In 2006 alone, combined eradication and interdiction efforts kept approximately 550 U.S. tons of cocaine off U.S. streets." (This number was not substantiated, nor did Negroponte cite data from which it had been derived.) Negroponte also argued that Plan Colombia had helped stabilize Colombia, and that the policies "also benefit everyone in [the United States] where cocaine has ruined thousands of American lives." The State Department's 2007 budget request called Plan Colombia "highly successful by all measures" and asked for $465 million in continuing support.

The fact that the FARC's decline had no visible effect on the drug business was a result of the multitudes of others involved in the illicit trade. And as had long been the pattern in Colombia (and had been seen after the demise of the cartels), the decline of one illegal group allowed for the bolstering of another. In 2005, Uribe had placated the U.S. Congress and other detractors with a widespread and highly publicized demobilization campaign (under legislation called the Justice and Peace Law), whereby paramilitary fighters were offered amnesty, jobs, and cash to disarm. The program was given a boost by the U.S. government after Congress approved twenty million dollars in its FY 2006 Appropriations Act to fund demobilization and reintegration of ex-combatants. By 2006, Uribe claimed that thirty thousand had demobilized and that Colombia was free of paramilitaries. (Because the reported figures were far greater than the estimated number of active paramilitary soldiers, many suggested that common criminals were taking the deal as well, and that the government was turning a blind eye in order to pump up the numbers.) It was also apparent that thousands of those who had taken the "demobilization" deal were back to work under their former commanders and had resumed trafficking drugs. According to *Semana* magazine, as many as nine thousand paramilitaries never disarmed at all. In some cases, the FARC and paramilitary groups even worked together in the drug business. One of the largest groups that coalesced in 2006, the Águilas Negras (Black Eagles) had four thousand members and was responsible for murdering and threatening peasants, unionists, human rights activists, and journalists; it also controlled illegal crops and produced and trafficked cocaine and heroin. While Uribe, with Plan Patriota in his pocket, continued to bear down on the FARC, the hydra-headed illegal drug industry continued to thrive.

The majority of urban Colombians backed Uribe's war against the FARC. It was also helpful to Uribe that opinions of the FARC were changing in the countryside. Many campesinos had long supported or sympathized with the guerrillas, but the children and grandchildren of those who had settled in the Amazon Basin to escape La Violencia found themselves at ground zero of the civil war. As the FARC gave up territory, abandoning the villages they had ruled for two decades, it was startlingly evident why they had lost the hearts and minds of the campesinos. Dusty streets had never been paved. No public sewers or electricity existed in most of the villages. There were no new schools. Poverty was as extreme as it had ever been. The FARC had used the villages like ATMs, coming to collect coca base and taxing the constituents, with little thought to improving their lives.

With increasing military operations against them, the guerrillas were abandoning many towns along the Caguán River. Photojournalist Carlos Villalón, who had traveled and reported extensively in the region since the early 2000s, found the pueblo of Santa Fe nearly deserted in 2007. "There were still guerrillas in the surrounding jungle, but they didn't have the presence they had in the town five or seven years before," says Villalón. "There was coca, but the business there was decimated. Since the FARC was unable to maintain a daily presence, they didn't [operate as a government] anymore." In the river outpost of Peñas Coloradas (where Sonia had once ruled over the thriving river business), every civilian had been run out by the Colombian military. In the village of Cartagena del Chairá, the FARC left the campesinos with nothing, including the thing that they had most needed from the guerrillas—protection against the paramilitaries. In many cases, the military's success was fleeting. Because the army has no long-term strategy for settling the villages after a takeover, in some areas, things eventually reverted to "normal." "When the army enters the town, the FARC leaves for the jungle," says Jorge Enrique Botero. "There's no money to start social programs, and the businesses die. But logistically, it's impossible to keep the military occupying the village. So in many cases, after three or four months, they leave, and everything goes back to the guerrillas." However, by late 2009, CNN en Español journalist Luis Vélez traveled to the village of La Macarena, in the department of Meta, where the military had run the FARC out two years earlier. Vélez found that the campesinos (who were prevented from growing coca by the military controlling the region) were suffering more under the army than they had been under the guerrillas. "These people used to grow coca; they used to sell it," says Vélez. "The FARC used to [run] the government. They had banks. They had organizations. They had laws, everything. Now the people have sixty-five percent unemployment." The military, Vélez says, "transformed a successful illegal economy into an unsuccessful legal economy."

With Uribe's popularity at an all-time high, and with the business of ending his country's "terrorist threat" unfinished, Uribe pushed Congress to amend the constitution to allow him to run for a second term in 2006—something unprecedented in Colombian history. The voices of his detractors, who claimed that Uribe's ties to paramilitaries made him unfit to remain president, were barely audible above the cheers of his supporters. (Claims surfaced that many lawmakers in Congress who were allies of Uribe were linked to paramilitaries, as well.) Also getting very little attention or acknowledgment from Uribe were the family members of the hundreds of captive Colombians, who constantly begged Uribe to negotiate with the FARC for the release of their loved ones—and not to attempt a military rescue. In May 2006, Uribe easily won the election with 62 percent of the vote. Juan Carlos Lecompte, who had spent the previous four years believing that only with a new administration would there be hope for negotiations to free his wife, Ingrid Betancourt, and the other hostages, was devastated.

16

Trial

The Mid-Atlantic region of the United States is known for violent summer thunderstorms in which rain comes in pounding sheets, sometimes for hours on end. The force of the water can make it almost impossible to walk even a short distance without getting completely soaked. Thousands of government employees in the nation's capital wait for a break in the deluge just to leave their concrete office buildings for home. It was during the summer storms of 2005 and 2006 that Ken Kohl felt the true weight of his job. "I live in the D.C. area, and whenever we'd have the prolonged rains and it would be pouring outside, I'd be in my backyard and just be thinking of those guys in the jungle and how it can go on, year after year after year. It's absolutely insane."

Kohl was a nineteen-year veteran prosecutor with the Department of Justice when he was handed the Simón Trinidad case in 2005. He'd worked on homicide cases until 2001, when he transferred to the National Security Division—the part of the DOJ that deals with terrorism cases against Americans perpetrated outside of the United States. And although numerous accused terrorists around the world have been indicted by the DOJ, "a lot of cases never see the light of day because the criminal is never apprehended overseas, or we don't accomplish extradition," Kohl says. For FARC guerrillas, there had been many indictments, but none had ever come to trial in the United States, so there was little background knowledge in the prosecutor's office about how to handle the unique case of Simón Trinidad. "I have to admit," Kohl says, "I didn't know too much about Colombia before I was added to the case." Kohl read everything he could on the subject. He traveled to Colombia and interviewed people at the U.S. Embassy. He spoke to *reinsertados*, former FARC members who had abandoned the guerrilla organization for amnesty and the promise of being assimilated into society. Learning the facts surrounding the kidnapping of Howes, Stansell, and Gonsalves was important to Kohl, but he felt it was also crucial to understand the political complexities of the guerrillas and the Colombian government. "So much of the prosecution of Simón Trinidad most certainly had a political undercurrent to it, because Simón Trinidad wanted to use the trial as a platform for espousing

U.S. federal prosecutor Ken Kohl, who tried Simón Trinidad in 2006 and 2007. The trials resulted in a conviction for conspiracy to commit hostage taking and a sixty-year sentence. Photo: Ken Kohl.

FARC ideology. So you try to keep as much of that stuff out, but you've got to understand it first," he says.

While Trinidad remained in solitary confinement in the D.C. Jail, Kohl spent countless hours investigating the Colombian conflict. The barbarity of it amazed him. "I've talked to many FARC deserters who were directly involved with hostage takings, who participated in chaining people. I really don't know how any human being does that. You join the FARC for a lot of different reasons. But once you're into that situation, how do you, each day, attach those chains, knowing that they've got children, wives, mothers, fathers at home? It's just so inhumane."

Kohl could understand the reason that poor young Colombians joined the FARC, and he even had some compassion for their plight. But for Trinidad, Kohl felt only disgust. "I think it's even more unforgivable for a guy like Simón Trinidad, who had the education, all of the benefits in life. He left all of that and very deliberately embraced what the FARC was doing." And although Kohl knew that Trinidad had never met the hostages and had not taken part in the kidnapping, he says that "Trinidad's job was to make sure that none of the Americans were released until the FARC got what they wanted. I don't think it's really an option for the U.S. to just say, 'Oh well, let's not prosecute him because we hope that the FARC will just, out of the goodness of its heart, let the hostages go.' Under the law he's a gangster. So there was no hesitation on my part to prosecute him as a senior member of this organization."

There were five counts in the indictment: three counts of hostage taking (one for each American hostage), one count of conspiracy to commit hostage taking, and one count of providing material support to a terrorist organization. In a completely separate indictment, Trinidad was charged with narco-trafficking. The drug trial would be separate and was set to follow the trial for hostage taking. In a brief written two weeks before the trial in October 2006, Paul Wolf, a human rights lawyer in Washington, D.C., accused the government of pushing the limits of U.S. conspiracy law by accusing Trinidad—as a known member of a designated "terrorist" organization—of being responsible for crimes committed by other members of the organization. "Since

Trinidad is not alleged to have had any involvement in the actual events, it would appear difficult to convict him as a principal in the crime," Wolf wrote.

In the weeks that followed, Wolf would attend much of the trial and produce a series of articles and daily synopses. The e-mail blasts became heavily relied upon by journalists covering the complicated case. The reports also found their way onto the FARC's official Web site in Spanish translation. Wolf, who had initially invited anyone to use and post his comments on their sites, made clear that he did not know how the postings got to the FARC site and that in no way did he support the FARC organization. Learning the details of the trial and how the American system of justice worked was extremely important to the top commanders because each one of them—forty-eight of the FARC's top leaders—was under indictment by the United States Department of Justice. While the FARC was on the U.S. list of foreign terrorist organizations, its members listed on the indictment were not accused of terrorist acts but of narco-trafficking. Each of the guerrilla commanders listed in the indictment knew that, if captured, any one of them could be sitting in that same cramped American jail cell, waiting for a trial that they believed would play out just like the trial of Simón Trinidad.

As Trinidad went to trial in 2006, it was becoming obvious that America's drug war in Colombia would not be separated from the war on terror. The U.S. State Department's congressional budget justification of $600 million for FY 2007 stated, "Colombia's position as the supplier of over 90 percent of the cocaine and almost 50 percent of the heroin entering the United States makes the aggressive disruption of the illicit drug trade a top USG priority. Colombia is home to three Foreign Terrorist Organizations (FTOs). These groups finance a large part of their operations with proceeds from the drug trade and are a threat to the security of the hemisphere." After paying little attention to western hemispheric security issues in the early 2000s while fighting its war on terror in the East against radical Islam, the Bush administration began to recognize a threat closer to home in menacing Venezuelan president Hugo Chávez. Chávez seemed to be champing at the bit to start a conflict with the United States and neighboring Colombia. Chávez was also believed to be aiding and abetting massive arms shipments to the guerrillas across his porous border with Colombia. Some accused him of being involved in actually arming the FARC. The governments of Brazil, Bolivia, Ecuador, and Argentina had also turned decidedly lukewarm to the United States, and therefore it became ever more important to keep Colombia as a staunch ally. "With U.S. support, Colombia is transforming into a secure, democratic, and economically prosperous country capable of undertaking a greater role in the problematic Andean region," the FY 2007 budget report said.

In addition to the legal complexities of the case against Trinidad, Kohl had another concern: "I didn't want something we did in the prosecution of Simón Trinidad to end up either harming Marc, Keith, or Tom or prolonging their captivity," says Kohl. His justification for moving forward anyway was hard for some trial watchers to digest. "As prosecutors on the case, we felt that the best thing for Marc, Keith, and Tom would be to make their hostage taking as costly as possible for the FARC, so that the FARC would recognize that kidnapping Americans is counterproductive. Not only did they get nothing in exchange for Marc, Keith, and Tom, it brought attention to their brutal and barbaric behavior." Kohl said he was also hopeful that the strategy would help pressure the FARC to release the men, but he did not elaborate on why that would be so.

The prosecution of Trinidad would turn out to be extremely difficult. Aside from the very real concern that the trial could have a negative effect on the hostage situation, there were grave safety concerns for the Colombians who would be called upon to testify. "It's not that easy to persuade people, former FARC members, even Colombian National Police officers, to come to the U.S. to testify and then go back to their posts in Colombia where the FARC had such a presence." Kohl knew that they had a reason to be concerned. Each day of the trial would be front-page news in Colombia, and every witness and each testimony was sure to be openly dissected by the media. Although Kohl was able to secure several Colombians to testify about Trinidad's involvement in the FARC, the biggest challenge for the prosecutor was that for the actual kidnapping of Howes, Stansell, and Gonsalves there were no witnesses. Kohl would have to rely on journalist Jorge Enrique Botero's video footage of the hostages as evidence and let the Americans tell the story of their kidnapping in their own words. Evidentiary rules mandated that to use the video in the trial, Kohl would have to supply an expert witness to validate the video's authenticity. And the only person who could do that was Jorge Enrique Botero.

When first asked to testify as a witness for the prosecution of Trinidad, Botero was concerned. "A Colombian prosecutor and an FBI agent told me that the only thing they would ask at the trial is that I certify that the video of the three Americans was authentic and that I recorded it. I asked if Trinidad's lawyer would also be able to ask me questions. After assuring me that he would, I agreed to testify at the trial." With his first visa to travel to the United States in fifteen years and a round-trip ticket from Bogotá to Washington, D.C., in hand, Botero became very nervous. "I was worried that some in the Colombian government or the paramilitaries would think that I was working for the defense of Trinidad, and the death threats would come again. I was also worried that the FARC would think that my testimony could do damage to Simón and I would lose access to my contacts and sources." But there was one thing that couldn't keep him from the trial no matter the risk: his curiosity as a journalist. After quickly landing a book deal to write a biography of Trinidad, he headed to the United States, content that he had the good fortune to be traveling on the U.S. government's dime.

Because Botero was a witness, he was not allowed to attend the trial on the days prior to his testimony. So he was not in the courtroom on October 16, 2006, when, after almost two years of solitary confinement in the D.C. Jail, Simón Trinidad emerged to stand trial in U.S. federal court. The guerrilla commander had looked haggard and unkempt in his orange cotton jumpsuit in the days prior to his trial. But by the day of opening arguments, he had transformed. In a stunning wood-paneled courtroom on the fourth floor of the courthouse, the defendant resembled a composed university professor. Had his mother been able to see him, she might have been very proud of how dignified he looked as he entered the courtroom and sat at the table along with his counsel, public defender Robert Tucker. Trinidad was pale from two years without any sunlight. His skin had almost a gray tint, and he was very thin. For many years, it had been reported that he suffered from cancer, and from the look of him, some thought it could be true. Trinidad wore a well-fitted navy blue suit and tie. He was clean-shaven, but short stubble sprouted from his balding head.

With his hands folded, the defendant sat at a long table, along with Tucker and two other members of the defense team. Although Trinidad seemed comfortable with his public defender, Tucker could understand only a few words of Spanish, and Trinidad spoke almost no English. Over the past two years, Tucker had spent many Sunday mornings visiting Trinidad at the D.C. Jail. On those visits, Trinidad, shackled and handcuffed, was led to a small room to meet with his lawyer. Occasionally, the guards would remove one handcuff so that Trinidad could write. On some of those visits, Lara Quint, an assistant federal public defender, would accompany Tucker and translate for the men.

Tucker liked Trinidad and would call him "a really nice guy" and "a total gentleman." And although the two couldn't communicate well, Tucker says, "we somehow managed to get along." Tucker had been assigned to Trinidad's case because several years earlier he'd defended another extradited Colombian, Nelson Vargas. Vargas had been accused of being a top FARC leader whose nickname was "El Marrano" ("the Pig") and part of a group responsible for the 1999 kidnapping and killing of three Americans who were working with Colombian indigenous populations. Having met and defended many accused terrorists from all over the world, Tucker was not accustomed to wondering whether his clients were guilty of their crimes. "Most of the time these guys are caught coming off the airplane with a machine gun," he says. But with Vargas, "something didn't ring right," according to Tucker. To him, Vargas hardly seemed the portrait of a murderous terrorist. The simple Colombian, whose leg had been amputated after he'd been shot while in a Colombian jail, expressed no bravado or revolutionary fervor. "After talking to him for about an hour, I asked him how he got into this mess." Vargas looked at his gringo lawyer earnestly and replied with what would become one of Tucker's favorite lines in any of his cases: "It all started with a woman."

Vargas had been discovered having an affair with a married woman by the woman's husband. The scorned spouse went directly to authorities and said, "I know who El Marrano is. He is Nelson Vargas."

Because of the high-profile murder of the three Americans, El Marrano was one of the most wanted criminals in Colombia. The husband then told the police where to find Vargas. The hapless Vargas was captured and convicted of rebellion in a Colombian court with the help of two witnesses who were former FARC members allegedly on the payroll of the government. Then with a lot of fanfare, Álvaro Uribe signed the extradition order for what everyone said was the first FARC guerrilla to be sent to the United States. Vargas was shipped off to Washington to stand trial for the murders. Tucker, who knew nothing about Colombia or the FARC when he met Vargas, made four trips to research the case. His plan was to present Vargas as what Tucker knew he was, an innocent man, and to paint the FARC as an evil terrorist organization that Vargas certainly wouldn't have belonged to. But Tucker never had to make the argument. Colombian prosecutors could no longer find the witness who could put Vargas at the scene of the crime. The case was dismissed before it went to trial, and Vargas was sent back to Colombia, where he was also exonerated of the murders and of being a member of the FARC. For Simón Trinidad's trial two years later in Washington, D.C., Tucker would twist his argument about the FARC 180 degrees from the defense he'd planned for Vargas.

As the trial began, the defense team spoke quietly as Trinidad slid on his translation headset and eyed the members of the jury, who were settling into their box. John Crabb, the assistant prosecutor working with Kohl, gave the opening arguments. The young, handsome, and very polished attorney looked straight out of a Hollywood movie as he argued that Trinidad was a terrorist, responsible for kidnapping the three Americans. He was responsible for their kidnapping because he was part of the FARC, a known terrorist organization that used kidnapping to further its terrorist agenda. "The FARC is led by a small group of men," Crabb told the jury in a well-rehearsed speech. "One of their leaders, in fact one of the FARC's most important leaders is here today." Crabb pointed to the defendant. "It's that man, Simón Trinidad. Now Simón Trinidad didn't order that Marc, Keith and Tom be taken hostage. But this is what he did do. Once they were taken hostage by the FARC he tried to exploit the situation for the FARC's benefit. . . .

Ladies and gentlemen, Simón Trinidad tried to use Tom Howes, Keith Stansell and Marc Gonsalves as get-out-of-jail free cards for FARC criminals that are in Colombian jails. That's why we're here today, ladies and gentlemen. My name is John Crabb, along with my colleague, Ken Kohl. We'll present the evidence of this crime to you."

The tall, balding public defender was the stark opposite of Crabb. During his opening arguments, Robert Tucker spoke so softly that three times the interpreters said they couldn't hear him and asked him to speak up or speak more directly into his lapel microphone. In a long and confusing speech to the jury, a laid-back Tucker waxed on about Colombia's civil war, the history of the FARC, and the assassinations of Unión Patriótica members in the 1980s. The jury appeared lost. Tucker said that it was not part of his agenda to prove that Trinidad was not a member of the FARC, nor to argue that the FARC was not a brutal organization. What he would establish, Tucker said, was that the FARC was an army fighting a war against another brutal army—that of the established Colombian government. The American hostages were prisoners of that war. Trinidad was only a soldier in that army who was ordered by his commander to go to Ecuador and reestablish communication with United Nations representative James LeMoyne. All Trinidad did, Tucker told the jury, was follow orders. "I suggest to you, ladies and gentlemen, that you'll find at the end that he had nothing to do with this. Nothing. And if you think about what the government [prosecution] said, what did they really tell you this man had to do about the three Americans? They didn't tell you anything. He had nothing to do with it."

In the trial's opening days, there were testimonies from James Hollaway, the program manager of California Microwave Systems, and Derek Harvey, an administrative coordinator for the SOUTHCOM Reconnaissance System program at the U.S. Embassy in Bogotá, who described the type of work that Stansell, Gonsalves, and Howes had performed. The Colombian colonel Gustavo Enrique Avendaño and the Colombian National Police officer Juan Carlos Sánchez discussed the crash and the attempted rescue by Colombian forces, and expounded on the horrors of the FARC's grip on Colombia. On the trial's fourth day, Jorge Enrique Botero took the witness stand. It was clear that Botero felt friendly toward the guerrilla commander, whom he'd spent many hours interviewing in Colombia's DMZ and during the large hostage exchange in 2001. He winked and smiled at Trinidad as he settled into the witness chair. When Kohl asked Botero if he could identify Trinidad in the courtroom, Botero pointed at Trinidad. "He's seated next to the defense attorney. He is wearing an elegant tie and a dark suit." Over the course of his testimony, Botero became irritated when he felt that Kohl was trying to paint him as a guerrilla sympathizer, maybe even a FARC member. And Kohl seemed unnerved by Botero, who refused to condemn the FARC or Trinidad. Botero testified that the only time he had met Trinidad was during the very public and political negotiation period when the FARC had the DMZ, and that Trinidad was never in any of the hostage camps that he had visited.

After Botero's testimony, Kohl was free to present the proof-of-life video of Stansell, Gonsalves, and Howes to the jury. Although Kohl had tried to rally support for prosecuting Trinidad from the families of the hostages, none of them attended the trial except Jo Rosano. While distrustful of the government's motives, Rosano once again used the opportunity to try to bring attention to her son's kidnapping. Rosano sat in the front row of the courtroom gallery, flanked by her husband, Mike, and a young FBI agent who had been given the job of keeping tabs on the outspoken Rosano. The video had been strategically edited by the prosecutor's office, and the very first clip was of Marc Gonsalves speaking directly to the camera and sending a message to his mother and family:

> Mom, I got your message, and I thank you for doing what you had to, to get that message sent to me. I love you, too, and I want you to know that I am being strong. I'm not being hurt or tortured. I'm just waiting to come home. I really, Shane, I love you, and I've been waiting to tell you that I think about you every day. And just wait for me, baby. Joey, Cody, and Destiney, I love you guys. And I'm just waiting to come home. So just wait for me. And I'm waiting to get back to you. I love you guys so much. That's it.

The jurors could hear Rosano choke back tears as her son's face appeared on the wide-screen monitor. The U.S. attorney general's office had paid for her travel to Washington, D.C., and FBI agent Chris Voss had spent an hour going over a written script she was to recite when speaking to the media, which amounted to how glad she was that they were trying a Colombian terrorist for her son's kidnapping and how important the work was for the war on drugs. True to character, Rosano didn't follow the script. "The script I was supposed to read said, 'I am just a simple-minded woman. . . . I went onto the FARC's Web site, and it says they oppose drug trafficking, so why are they holding my son, who was helping them?' I thought they must be joking. I said, 'I'm not going to say that.' Instead, I said, 'What are they doing trying him here? Why isn't he being tried in Colombia?' " For these comments and many others condemning the Uribe and Bush administrations' handling of the crisis, Rosano had unknowingly earned the respect of Marulanda and the top FARC commanders, who, the following year, would begin to consider releasing some of the hostages.

The following week, other witnesses who would take the stand were clearly less friendly to the defendant than Botero had been. Trinidad's former university colleague Elías Ochoa and his wife, Carmen Alicia Medina, had come to Washington, D.C., to testify about Trinidad's involvement in Elías's and his brother's kidnapping in 1998. Human rights attorney Paul Wolf was critical of Kohl's tactic of using the Ochoa kidnapping to help convict Trinidad for the kidnapping of Stansell, Gonsalves, and Howes. After Medina's dramatic testimony about her husband's kidnapping, Wolf wrote in his daily e-mail analysis:

> To prove that Trinidad is a kidnapper, the prosecutor wants to introduce evidence of other kidnappings. This is a prohibited use of character evidence, but never mind that. . . . Although none of [the kidnappings] are related to the Cessna incident, the judge is allowing the jury to hear about them to prove Trinidad's "state of mind" and knowledge of FARC's activities. . . . This "trial within a trial" was really unnecessary because if Trinidad went to Ecuador to arrange for a prisoner exchange, then obviously he knew that the FARC took prison-

ers. This was the purported reason the judge allowed all of this
in, is to prove that Trinidad knew that the FARC took hostages.
Although I think Trinidad's chances are slim anyway, the intro-
duction of this evidence was hugely prejudicial, unnecessary,
and unfair.

While Kohl's goal was to keep FARC politics out of the courtroom,
the fact that Trinidad testified in his own defense made this completely
impossible. Trinidad proved to be a skilled and evasive debater. Kohl
was visibly frustrated as he examined Trinidad in a lengthy back-and-
forth, in which Trinidad said that he agreed with stopping drug traffic
but disagreed with U.S. methods, which were destroying humans, ani-
mals, rivers, and crops. When Kohl continued to press the guerrilla to
admit that Americans flying drug-reconnaissance planes were targets of
the FARC, Trinidad evaded the question and responded, "The thing is
that the war against drugs is a façade. And behind it is a war against
guerrilla organizations among which the FARC is one in the country."

During closing arguments, Botero sat in the gallery and watched
Kohl give a powerful summary of the prosecution's case. The prosecutor detailed the copious and horrific acts of terrorism by the FARC and
tied Trinidad into it all through guilt by association. Then, to Botero's
horror, Kohl stated that the proof-of-life video of Stansell, Gonsalves,
and Howes had been made by the FARC to further their hostage-taking
conspiracy. "If this were true," wrote attorney Paul Wolf, "Botero
would have been more involved in the kidnapping than the defendant
himself. . . . Botero clearly had his own reasons for making the video—
it was made into a CBS documentary—but the waters are treacherous.
The prosecutors accuse their own witness of a serious crime, on the
record." Botero was stunned by Kohl's accusation. "The first thing I
thought was that Kohl wanted revenge because I was not helpful to him
during my testimony." If Kohl's comments about the video were
reported in the Colombian media, Botero was sure he would arrive
home to death threats. Botero implored his Colombian journalist
friends covering the trial not to report the dangerous allegations
about him.

When Kohl was through, Tucker delivered a rambling and disjointed closing argument. Wolf wrote of the summation:

> If Tucker presented an alternative theory, or a defense, I do not know what it was. He mainly focused on Trinidad's [lack of] knowledge of the FARC's demands for the release of the three North Americans. This was unconvincing, because we had seen so many pictures of Trinidad with the FARC Secretariat and with European diplomats. It was hard to believe Trinidad didn't understand what he was doing, or know that the FARC takes prisoners and exchanges them. Tucker also made comparisons to Malcolm X . . . quoted from the U.S. Declaration of Independence, and finally from Shakespeare's *Hamlet*. . . . I don't think it was effective. The defense did not present any clear idea that the jury could use.

Many court observers seconded Wolf's comments and believed that the jury would hurriedly return a guilty verdict. Especially confident that Trinidad would be found guilty was the prosecution team. So Ken Kohl was in red-faced disbelief on November 21, 2006, when the jury foreman returned a third note to the judge, claiming that the jury could not reach a unanimous decision on whether Simón Trinidad was guilty of conspiring to kidnap the three Americans. The result was a mistrial. "Obviously, we were disappointed," says Kohl. "The vast majority of the jurors felt that he was guilty. It was ten to two for conviction." The trial had cost millions, and Kohl immediately announced a retrial. "We were concerned, because we knew that we'd have to bring all these witnesses back. Retrials are never fun for a prosecutor, but it's part of how the process works. You have to proceed."

Three months later, down the hallway in the same the federal courthouse, it was much easier to convict Anayibe Rojas Valderrama, aka Sonia, for narcotics trafficking. The prosecution presented the pale guerrilla as the finance officer for the FARC's Fourteenth Front in the area of El Caguán. Witnesses testified about Sonia's deep involvement in the cocaine trade. After five weeks of testimony from twenty prosecution witnesses and four days of deliberations, Sonia was found guilty of conspiring to import cocaine into the United States and of manufacturing or distributing cocaine, knowing or intending that it would be imported into the United States. Her public defender, Carmen Hernández, never called a single witness in her defense.

At her sentencing hearing, Sonia took the opportunity to speak publicly for the first time. She looked directly at the judge and said, "I am innocent," and denied being a drug trafficker or a terrorist. Then she asked to be removed from solitary confinement in the jail. "How could I be a danger to society?" she asked the court. "I'm not an addict. I'm not an alcoholic. I'm not mentally ill. What danger could I represent?" Between sobs, she implored Judge James Robertson not to send her to a maximum-security prison. "I want to study, to take advantage of the years of my sentence to learn the language and to have a career. Your Honor, today I would be insane if it wasn't for God and my willpower." Then she said that she did not want to be part of any prisoner exchange for hostages held by the FARC, and that she hoped all the hostages would soon be freed. Robertson sentenced her to sixteen and a half years in prison. Sonia's attorney vowed she would appeal.

Jorge Enrique Botero, still in Washington after Trinidad's mistrial, went to the D.C. Jail to visit Sonia. He was very curious to meet her, but he also knew that if he could speak privately with her, the FARC Secretariat would want to meet with him to learn about Sonia's experience in the United States. He would then use the meeting as an opportunity to ask for an interview with the hostages. For all his travels in conflict zones, Botero couldn't remember being more nervous than he was entering the D.C. Jail. As he filled out paperwork to visit inmate DCDC number 304314, Anayibe Rojas Valderrama, Botero couldn't believe how stringent all of the rules at the jail were. "The guards would not let me take anything in with me, so I didn't even have a pen. They also confiscated the magazines and a copy of my book that I was going to give her." Sonia appeared behind a wall of thick soundproof glass, handcuffed and wearing an orange jumpsuit. At first, the guerrilla didn't know what to make of the visitor, but she picked up the telephone handset to hear Botero. "She didn't immediately know who I was," says Botero, whose ego was slightly bruised. "When I told her that I was the one who wrote the book about Clara Rojas and the baby, then she said she had heard of me. Then she did not stop talking." It was the first time in two years of captivity that Sonia, who spoke no English, had been able to speak to anyone other than her attorney and, once, a visiting nun. "When she spoke to me, with her words and accent of a nearly illiterate *campesina*, I thought, How was it possible for the federal prosecutors to make a jury believe that this woman is a great narco-trafficker? Is condemning someone like Sonia the way the gringos aspire to win the war against drugs?"

Sonia told Botero that she had no idea of what was happening in the world or in Colombia. Then she surprised Botero with her candor. "Sonia gave me a message for the heads of the FARC. She said she was very angry with them. She felt abandoned. She dedicated her life to the revolution, and she had received neither a letter, nor a call, nor any money in the entire two years of her imprisonment." She also told Botero that during the two years she'd been in the same jail in Washington, D.C., as Simón Trinidad, she'd seen the commander only twice. Although the thirty-nine-year-old mother had been a guerrilla for nearly two decades, she'd never encountered Trinidad in person until they'd passed each other in a hallway of the American jail. Sonia was not impressed. "On television he looked so big and strong, but he's a real shrimp. The first time he saw me, he yelled across the hall, '¡Viva las FARC! ¡Viva el Libertador Simón Bolívar!' " Sonia told Botero she thought Trinidad was nuts. After the hour-long visit came to an end, an enormous guard came to take Sonia back to her cell. "She cried a little, and she told me to try to locate her son. She said, 'Tell him that I love him, and that he is always in my thoughts.' " Botero promised to look for Sonia's son as soon as he returned to Colombia.

Because of his well-known access to the hostage camps, Botero was in great demand in Washington, D.C. He was approached numerous times by FBI agents who wanted to meet with him. For the most part, he had succeeded in evading them. Gary Noesner continued to push for a meeting with Botero as well, and Botero finally agreed. For Botero's part, he wanted to get access to the American families to interview them for a book he was writing, and he felt that Noesner was the person who could make it happen. Botero also wanted to understand how the kidnapping case was being handled from the side of the U.S. government, and Noesner was not a U.S. government agent, which Botero considered an advantage, since he wanted to avoid contact with government operatives. He felt that FBI agents or others would try to convince him to take messages to the FARC, putting him in the dangerous position of being an intermediary on the part of the U.S. government. Noesner was very happy finally to have Botero's ear, and Northrop Grumman executives "were open and receptive to the idea of having Botero's help," says Noesner. "Up to that point, we had nothing. All the contacts and efforts that my company [Control Risks] and I had made through the church and the Red Cross and others—we were only getting way out on the fringes. We couldn't penetrate deep into the FARC organization, and Jorge had that access."

Botero also felt fortunate to make the connection with the former FBI boss. "When I met Gary, I was immediately struck by his intelligence. It was obvious he had a lot of experience, and a lot of ideas on how to get the FARC to release Tom, Marc, and Keith." Noesner's plan was that Botero get another interview with the hostages, then deliver the video to him before U.S. agents got hold of it. Noesner knew the U.S. government was still backing a rescue attempt, something that he was very concerned about, believing it would get the hostages killed. He hoped that if the proofs came out in the media, it would generate helpful publicity that might pressure the U.S. government to negotiate for the Americans' release. Gary was also determined to do his job well, and that meant doing everything he could on behalf of Northrop Grumman. What the company wanted was for the families to have some peace of mind, to realize that something was being done to get the hostages released, or at least to know that Stansell, Gonsalves, and Howes were still alive. He was not used to having so little success on a case, which was incredibly frustrating.

Before Botero left for Bogotá, Noesner arranged for him to meet with Northrop Grumman's director of security, Patricia Tomaselli. Tomaselli had never met the American hostages, but she felt very moved by the case and was dedicated to doing whatever she could to help free them. Tomaselli hoped that, at the very least, Botero could deliver messages to the hostages from their families. Every six months since the kidnapping, Northrop Grumman had helped the families write letters and record audio messages, in the hope that there would be some way to get them in. They had tried several routes, including the Red Cross and some FARC informants, but so far, they had not had any success. They had also had the families record messages to play on the radio programs for hostages. However, the company had no way of knowing if the messages were ever received or if the men had access to a radio.

Tomaselli gave Botero letters from each of the hostages' families, and three letters from Northrop Grumman, one to each man, stating that the company was doing everything it could and promising to take care of the men's families. She also gave Botero a CD with the audio messages. When Botero was alone, he put the CD into his computer. The first message he heard was from Kyle Stansell to his father. "I'm a freshman in high school now. I'm, like, six two now—about one hundred and sixty pounds. We miss you a lot. You're in our prayers. . . . I think about you all the time. I miss you." How can it be that a child has to tell his father what grade he's in? Botero thought. The messages brought tears to his eyes. As many times as he'd heard someone leave a message to a father, a mother, or a child who was being held hostage, he never got used to it. He took the families' letters and the CD and hid them in his backpack. The letters written by Northrop Grumman and the envelope with the company's logo he tore into tiny pieces and flushed down the toilet in the apartment where he was staying, which belonged to a Colombian journalist friend. He could not risk going into FARC territory looking like an envoy for a North American defense contractor.

In January 2007, when Botero next met with Raúl Reyes, he gave the guerrilla commander the letters from the families and a copy of John McCain's memoir *Faith of My Fathers* that he'd picked up in Washington, D.C. He felt that the words of a U.S. presidential candidate, someone who had also gone through a long period of captivity, might bring the men some solace and hope. Botero knew that the hostages were probably hundreds of miles from Reyes's camp, but he was confident that the letters and the book would reach the Americans. He had seen that the guerrillas had a robust network of couriers who delivered goods, letters, cards, and gifts throughout the jungle, and Reyes had taken the package readily and noted the contents in his notebook. Noesner had also asked Botero to let the guerrillas know that the families wanted to find a "solution" to the kidnapping. What Noesner had inferred to Botero was that the company wanted to explore all possible options. In essence: If the guerrillas were starting to realize that the exchange was not going to happen, would they accept a ransom for the hostages' freedom? Noesner knew that the U.S. government might not allow a ransom to be paid, but he also knew that getting the FARC to ask for something tangible in exchange for the release of the hostages—something that could open up a dialogue—could be helpful. Botero told Noesner that he would pass along the message, but he wasn't hopeful that the FARC would be interested.

Four years into the crisis and no closer to a hostage release, the government remained static in its policy. A letter from National Security Advisor Stephen J. Hadley to Northrop Grumman's vice president, James Pitts, indicated the government's continuing trajectory in dealing with the crisis: "I want to reiterate our commitment to rescuing our American citizens and update you on our efforts to bring your employees home safely. . . . The Department of State and Defense and our Embassy in Colombia, together with National Security Council staff, continue to review our strategy to ensure we are fully leveraging all intelligence and available national resources and capabilities to locate and rescue our Americans." Ever since the kidnapping, Gary Noesner had been pushing Northrop Grumman executives to take a stand against the government's refusal to look for any solution other than a rescue, and finally, his ideas were gaining credibility within the company. Along with Northrop Grumman's security team, Noesner helped craft a reply from Pitts to Hadley, stating the company's concern over the risks of a rescue attempt and asking that "the government should thoroughly explore alternatives, such as the use of intermediaries or other diplomatic avenues. I recognize the difficulties involved in such alternatives; however, with four years having passed since the kidnapping and given the inherent dangers in a military rescue, it is critical that other options be pursued." The letter included a request for a meeting with National Security Advisor Hadley, but according to Noesner, the meeting never took place.

In August 2007, with the case at a standstill, Noesner and Botero met again in Washington, D.C. This time, Botero had an idea, and he would need Noesner's help. Botero had been trying to get the FARC to agree to let him make a documentary film about Jo Rosano's search for her son, Marc Gonsalves. Botero had used the same narrative structure before, filming the travels of Marleny Orjuela, who was able to secure the release of her cousin and hundreds more in 2001. Afterward, Orjuela became a constant crusader for the release of the rest of the victims, holding rallies and lobbying the government to do something on behalf on the hostages. Recording Orjuela's travels, Botero says, was "my way of narrating the drama of these people and getting the public interested and moved by the topic."

Jo Rosano's story seemed a perfect way to bring the attention of the American public to the plight of the hostages. "I was hoping to take Jo to the deepest parts of the jungle to find Marc. I wanted to film that reunion. If we weren't able to reach Marc, I could film Jo traveling many regions of the country in search of her son. I was hoping that I could film something very emotional, something that would shake the opinion of people in the U.S. so that people there would call for a negotiation to free them." When Noesner heard Botero's proposal, he implored Botero not to go forward. "My concern went back to my FBI days. To me, sending an American citizen into harm's way was always something that frightened me. I was worried that the FARC would— for some twisted reason—decide to grab Jo." Noesner had been involved with a Lebanese hostage crisis in the 1980s. During the ten-year-long case, Terry Waite, an American envoy helping with negotiations, was captured by Hezbollah in 1987. "You always worry that you're sending someone into danger or encouraging risky behavior that risks their life." Noesner was especially concerned because of Rosano's precarious health and her emotional state. He also felt that Jo was especially susceptible to being manipulated in different situations and probably couldn't handle such an arduous trip. "She has to be given enormous credit for being a mother really devoted to doing whatever's necessary to get her son out. I could certainly understand why Botero wanted to make the documentary. I just felt it was my role to inform him that there were some downsides to it."

"At first, I was furious when Gary opposed my idea so strongly," Botero recalls. "I had already practically convinced the FARC to grant me access, so I felt like we were on the verge of making progress again." Botero admonished Noesner for treating him like a subordinate. He could easily have called Rosano, whom he'd met several times, and asked her to go to Colombia, but it would have been logistically very difficult without Noesner's blessing. "Later, I understood he had good arguments. I thought, Maybe I wouldn't have been able to handle this woman who could be so emotionally volatile. Maybe I would have been putting her in danger and would also have endangered myself." The mountain, once again, seemed immovable.

17

Emmanuel

Two months before the June 4, 2007, retrial of Simón Trinidad, Thomas Hogan, the judge who presided over the first trial, would step down from the case. The surprising turn of events came about after a pretrial hearing, when Ken Kohl let slip that he had spoken to the jury foreman to find out why the first jury could not return a guilty verdict. This was news to Trinidad's defense attorney, Robert Tucker, who had no idea that Hogan had secretly authorized Kohl to contact the jury foreman. The ex parte contact between Hogan, who was the chief judge of the U.S. district court, and Kohl was prohibited because the law states that if one party to a case communicates with the judge, the other side has a right to present its argument at the same meeting. Tucker pressured Hogan to disqualify himself, since his "impartiality could reasonably be questioned." Hogan announced that he had done nothing wrong, but for the sake of proving to the Colombian people that Simón Trinidad was getting a fair trial, he would resign. For his part, Kohl was unrepentant about the underhanded move: "When we prosecute the case the second time, we want to make sure that the jury finds the defendant guilty. The government naturally wants to do its homework," he said.

The retrial of Simón Trinidad was to be essentially the same as the

Venezuelan president Hugo Chávez (center, holding González de Perdomo's grand-daughter) and Colombian senator Piedad Córdoba (far right) welcome recently released Colombian hostages Clara Rojas (second from right) and Consuelo González de Perdomo (far left) at the presidential palace in Caracas, Venezuela, January 10, 2008. Photo: Pedro Rey/AFP/Getty Images.

first trial, with one startling new development: John Frank Pinchao, a hostage who had escaped from the same camp where Thomas Howes, Keith Stansell, and Marc Gonsalves were being held, would testify. To free himself from his captors, Pinchao, a member of the National Police who had been captured in a raid in 1998, had worked for weeks to break a link in the chain around his neck by prying it with a small stick and continually twisting it until the link finally broke. Then he spent a harrowing seventeen days trekking through the jungle, mostly without food or water, until he ran into an antinarcotics patrol. Pinchao's account of the hostage camp and his life in captivity gave some relief to the families of the Americans; all three were in relatively good health, he said, although Marc Gonsalves was suffering from hepatitis. About Ingrid Betancourt, who was also in the same camp, Pinchao said that she was faring far worse than the gringos; she was thin and ill, and she was chained by the neck to her bed every night—a punishment for numerous escape attempts. And not only did she suffer abuse at the hands of the guerrillas; she was harassed by some of the military hostages as well. However relieved Pinchao was to be free, those that he'd left behind were clearly weighing on him. "I hope they make it back soon, one way or another," Pinchao said in his first press conference after his escape. "I know that someday they will see the light of liberty. I would like to send all of them a hug from here. I ask God to protect them. I know they must be paying the price because of me."

The hostages were indeed paying the price. According to Luis Eladio Pérez, the guerrillas had never calculated that any of the military hostages would attempt to escape, believing the soldiers and National Policemen would know it would be impossible to make it out of the jungle alive. To make sure that none of the other hostages would try to follow Pinchao's lead, the guerrillas brought heavier chains, weighing between seventeen and twenty pounds, nearly double the size that Pinchao had been able to break. "With those they would tie us to a tree or to another hostage, and we had to carry them individually on the marches," wrote Pérez. After having avoided chains for the entirety of their captivity, the Americans were now regularly chained as well, and Pérez would spend the final six months of his captivity chained by the neck to Thomas Howes.

As Trinidad's second trial opened with a new jury, which both Tucker and Kohl hoped would be swayed by their arguments, the fact that Pinchao had been covertly brought to Washington, D.C., by the prosecutors was a poorly kept secret. It was rumored among the Colombian press corps covering the trial that Kohl had brought Pinchao to testify that Trinidad had visited the American hostages regularly. So it was quite a surprise that when it came time for Pinchao's testimony, and Kohl asked whether he had seen Trinidad in the hostage camps, Pinchao shot his answer back to the prosecutor with an emphatic "*Nunca*" ("Never"). In addition, Pinchao's testimony portrayed the FARC as a highly organized military force, a description that attorney Paul Wolf thought was helpful to Tucker's argument that the Americans were prisoners of war. As in the first trial, Trinidad himself took the witness stand to tell the tale of his entry into the revolutionary army, while testifying for his own defense. He appeared composed and spoke with an intense precision.

Trinidad, knowing his words would be reported in the news and reach the FARC Secretariat, also made it clear to those in the court-room, that he did not want to be an "obstacle" to any prisoner exchange. He said that he was thinking of those in captivity on both sides, not just the FARC guerrillas in jail, and that a prisoner exchange would be a step toward peace. As in the first trial, Trinidad remained a difficult witness for Kohl and repeatedly turned Kohl's loaded questions into long back-and-forths filled with political overtones. "Basically," wrote attorney Paul Wolf, "it looked like Kohl kept trying to get him to admit he was a hostage-taking terrorist, and Trinidad was making the point that if Kohl would stop interrupting him like that, he could explain everything." At one point, a frustrated Kohl posed a question that seemed ridiculous considering the circumstances: "You don't want to go to jail now, do you?" the prosecutor demanded. Trinidad replied calmly, "Whatever the reality is, I will take it and be strong. In this case, concretely, my word is under oath. I respect this court. I respect Judge Lamberth. I respect the jury. I respect the lawyers. I respect the govern-ment representatives here, and the public. And most of all, I have self-respect. Here I am telling the truth."

After the closing arguments, one juror asked to be excused from the case because she felt that her religious beliefs made it impossible for her to judge Trinidad. Sara, a twenty-nine-year-old alternate juror, replaced her. Sara had attended the entire trial and had been keenly interested in the case. She was absolutely sure that Trinidad was not guilty of kidnapping the Americans. So she was greatly surprised when deliberations began and she realized that all of the other jury members were convinced of Trinidad's absolute guilt. In a small, claustrophobic-feeling room, heated deliberations began. Sara says she felt under attack as her fellow jurors tried to convince her that Trinidad was guilty. After four days of deliberations, Sara was incredibly conflicted. She decided that since Trinidad had gone to Quito to try to negotiate for a humanitarian agreement, perhaps he *had* played a very small role in the hostage situation. But she told the rest of the jury she wasn't ready to convict him for conspiracy. Anxious to reach a verdict, the foreman sent a note to the judge, asking for clarification: "How large a role must one have in a crime to be convicted of conspiracy?" "Judge Lamberth answered back that no matter how small a role Trinidad played, participation is participation. The judge also emphasized that the role could be intentional or unintentional. And to me, there was no evidence that showed his intent," Sara says. She and the other jurors debated the degree of Trinidad's role and his intention, but, Sara adds, "I felt like, since I had admitted to the other jurors that he had a very small role, I had to follow the rules and return a guilty verdict for conspiracy." Kohl had fought to convict on four other counts, but those counts were based on the charge that Trinidad had taken part in the actual kidnapping and provided material support to terrorists, something that Sara was adamant there was no evidence for. The jury returned a guilty verdict on the one count of conspiracy to commit hostage taking, and a mistrial was called on the four other counts. The announcement of the verdict was a great success for the prosecution. But in the jungle, at the headquarters of the FARC leaders, it was actually a victory as well—two trials, five counts each, and only one conviction. Marulanda and the Secretariat leaders were quite ignorant of the American justice and political system, and even though Trinidad had been convicted, they still believed that somehow, under the table, they could negotiate an exchange of Trinidad and Sonia for the three Americans.

On July 9, 2007, when the verdict was announced, attorney Paul Wolf was among the observers who were stunned by Kohl's comments afterward to the press. "After the final verdicts came the surprising announcement by prosecutor Ken Kohl," wrote Wolf, "that if the FARC were to release the three Americans within the next two months, he would seek a reduced sentence for Simón Trinidad." Many trial observers and members of the press felt that Kohl had made an offer to the terrorist group, but in a 2008 interview, Kohl would defend his comments: "In the end, I didn't care much about Trinidad. We all wanted Marc, Tom and Keith to be released. What I said after the sentencing and what the [U.S.] Ambassador elaborated on in Colombia, was that when the defendant commits a crime of hostage taking, one of the factors that a sentencing judge must consider is the length of time the victims have been held, and a longer term will be imposed based on how long you've held the hostage. So if the FARC had unilaterally released Marc, Keith and Tom, and they appeared at the sentencing, it would have been a factor that the judge was required to take into consideration. That's not any concession to the FARC, that's the law. There was no bargaining with the FARC. It was just explaining publicly how our sentencing works."

Kohl never again publicly mentioned that a unilateral release of the Americans by the FARC could have reduced Trinidad's sentence. Under the radar of the media and perhaps many in the U.S. government, a different offer was made. Jorge Enrique Botero, who had made his way back to Bogotá after the trial, received a call from Trinidad's public defender, Robert Tucker. "Perhaps because the prosecution realized there was no way the FARC was going to release the Americans, Tucker told me that if I could get a meeting with one of the FARC commanders, I should let them know that Simón's sentence could be lighter if the FARC would give proof-of-life images of the gringos. I was stunned because after all, this 'bargain' must have come from Ken Kohl, and the bottom line was that I felt it amounted to negotiation with terrorists. I began to wonder if this was the whole strategy of the U.S. in the beginning—to convict Trinidad and then negotiate with the FARC to release the gringos by offering a lesser sentence?" The idea seemed preposterous and contradictory to the stated policy, but contacting Raúl Reyes with a message from Trinidad's public defender would be a great opportunity to try to get permission for an interview with the hostages, Botero realized.

As Trinidad waited in solitary confinement for his November 2007 sentencing hearing, and Botero made contact with the FARC, a strange series of events cast Venezuelan president Hugo Chávez in a starring role in the Colombian hostage drama. The controversial populist leader had become a nightmare for Washington, with his unending oil reserves and vocal hatred for President Bush—which he often expounded upon during his weekly television program, *Aló Presidente*. And it was on one of these Sunday broadcasts, in August 2007, that a flashy left-wing Colombian senator named Piedad Córdoba appeared on the program and asked for the Venezuelan leader's help in her country's hostage crisis. It may have been at that moment that a lightbulb snapped on for Chávez: What could be better than a theatrical media blitz showing American hostages released into the arms of Hugo Chávez?

Chávez wasted no time in holding a press conference, where he announced his intentions to negotiate a hostage release. In September, he invited the families of the Americans (including Patricia Medina and her twin sons) to come and meet with him in Venezuela. Behind the scenes, Chávez demanded that the guerrillas produce proofs of life of the hostages and deliver them directly to him, something Chávez expected would give him even more clout in the negotiation process, make a big media splash, and especially incense George W. Bush's government. Rumors abounded that Chávez might actually be buying the hostages out of captivity for as much as fifty million dollars. However the relationship was blossoming, FARC high commander Manuel Marulanda and the FARC Secretariat were delighted to have the recognition and involvement of their rich leftist neighbor. It was a direct affront to the Colombian government. An infuriated Uribe could do little to stop Chávez without appearing to impede the release of the hostages, and so he grudgingly sanctioned Chávez's participation. To keep a Colombian presence in the process, Uribe gave Piedad Córdoba a green light to make contact with FARC commanders and begin negotiations for a humanitarian exchange.

Córdoba had high political aspirations and knew it would be great for her career to be the one to finally put an end to the hostage situation. But she had a very personal reason to want the hostages released, as well. In 1999, she had been taken hostage by the AUC paramilitary group. Córdoba says that after she exposed several military commanders for being involved in many human rights violations, "military and paramilitary forces agreed to act against me. The order was to kidnap and kill me." The public outcry to release the well-loved senator was tremendous. Horacio Serpa, a former minister of the interior, who had been involved in many peace negotiations, asked the AUC leader, Carlos Castaño, to take him captive in her place. Two other Colombian congresspeople met with Castaño to push for Córdoba's release, "but the paramilitaries told them to forget about me because their purpose was to kill me," Córdoba says. "That same day Báez [one of the paramilitary commanders] came to talk to me, almost to say good-bye, to tell me that he had asked Castaño for permission to see me because he wanted to meet me before they shot me. We talked for a couple of hours. He tried to convince me to change my ideas, not to attack them anymore, and maybe they would change their decision to kill me. I told him that I was not going to change my views about them or about what was happening in the country." Finally, due to fierce political pressure, including a demand for her release from U.N. Secretary-General Kofi Annan, she was released. "Castaño himself told me, 'I'm going to have to let you go because I can't stand the pressure from my friends in the Colombian government,' " she says.

In her new position as hostage negotiator, the first thing Córdoba did was contact Jorge Enrique Botero. She knew that Botero was an expert at navigating FARC pathways, and she needed all the advice the seasoned reporter could give her. From 2004 to 2006, Botero had tried to distance himself from the hostage stories. He had become acquainted with Córdoba when he was covering the trial of President Ernesto Samper. "So when I heard her on the radio, saying she wanted to work on the topic of the hostage exchange, to work with both sides, I called her and told her I was doing a book about guerrillas in jail," Botero says. "I took her to the Buen Pastor jail twice, and we began to work together." One of the first trips they took together was to visit Raúl Reyes, the FARC Secretariat member and spokesperson who was based near the border between Colombia and Ecuador. Botero had been to see Reyes numerous times, but this trip was like no other he had ever taken. Usually, Botero traveled under the radar, trying his best to blend in and not arouse suspicion. But Córdoba was an extremely flamboyant woman. She often wore bright African head wraps and boldly patterned tunics or body-hugging blouses over her robust bosom. She was rarely seen without enormous false eyelashes and sparkling eye shadow. In the jungle, she toned down her look with a green turban and matching green velvet running suits, but she was still impossible to miss—especially in remote villages where Córdoba was well known and well loved. "It was like traveling through the jungle with a Hollywood celebrity," Botero says. But since Córdoba had received Uribe's blessing to negotiate for the hostages, Botero knew he would get coveted inside information by acting as the senator's personal press corps. Córdoba and Botero traveled from the jungle, where they met with Raúl Reyes, to Caracas to meet with Hugo Chávez. They even made trips to Washington, D.C., where several U.S. congresspeople were trying to rally support for a humanitarian exchange.

Botero had passed along Tucker's message to Raúl Reyes that proofs of life could help lower Trinidad's sentence, but the proofs were already in the works; Hugo Chávez had requested them to present to French president Nicolas Sarkozy on an upcoming visit, sending FARC commanders into a frenzy to comply. However, the logistics of producing and delivering proofs of life were complicated. As quickly as possible, a plan was devised, and in late October 2007, more than four years after they had last sent messages to the outside world, Ingrid Betancourt, Marc Gonsalves, Keith Stansell, Thomas Howes, and twelve other prisoners found themselves in front of a video camera. Several of them were allowed to write letters as well. Luis Eladio Pérez was not happy when they came to remove his chains and told him to speak in front of the video camera. "I wanted to be with the chains on," Pérez wrote. "And I told them, 'Be men. Film me as you have me, like an animal. Don't be ashamed to show the world your behavior.' " Stansell, Howes, and Gonsalves also demanded that they be filmed in the chains they were forced to wear, but the guerrillas didn't allow it. Pérez convinced many of the hostages not to speak on camera, which he believed would impede what the guerrillas were trying to do. "It was to pressure the guerrillas, because what were they going to negotiate; what were they going to show the world if all of us refused to give them a proof of life?" wrote Pérez.

The videos, photos, and letters were put in an envelope and given to a young guerrilla sympathizer, who was instructed to take them to Bogotá. To ensure that the girl would guard the package with her life, the guerrillas told her that it was full of cash. She was told that once she got to Bogotá, she was to make contact with another FARC member, who would travel from Venezuela to meet her and take the package. But the transfer never happened. Colombian agents had picked up the trail of one or possibly both of the women. The women arrived in Bogotá completely unaware that they were being followed. When the two met on a busy street in Bogotá to exchange the package, they were slammed facedown on the pavement and the envelope was confiscated. The Colombian government immediately released the videos to media around the world. What the government did not do—for a change—was verbally condemn the FARC for acts of terrorism. If they wanted proof of the FARC's atrocities, the videos spoke volumes. The image of Ingrid Betancourt was most shocking. She appeared emaciated, her skin gray and stretched over bone, and her hair hung to her waist. Even more heartbreaking was a long letter to her mother, Yolanda Pulecio. It seemed that after almost six years in captivity, the former senator, who had survived a hunger strike and numerous death threats, was totally and completely shattered.

Betancourt told her mother that she was in poor physical heath and mentally numb. Her hair was falling out, and she could not eat. She said her life in captivity was not a life at all, but, rather, a dismal waste of time. "Here nothing is one's own," she wrote. "Nothing lasts, uncertainty and precariousness are the only constant." Her sole luxury was a Bible, and her only lifeline to the outside world came in the form of radio messages, sent mostly from her mother and her children. Hearing about her children, she said, was the only thing that made her happy. She asked her mother to give a message to her husband, Juan Carlos Lecompte, who, although he continued working for her liberation, rarely left her messages on the radio. "Tell him to be at peace with himself and with me. That if life gives us the opportunity, we will come out fortified from this test," she wrote.

Betancourt's letter had been leaked by someone in the government and published by the Colombian press. Her mother was outraged. *El Tiempo* reported that Pulecio was considering legal action against the prosecutor's office. But the letter created a firestorm, and a new light was shone on the horrors of captivity. Many left-leaning intellectuals who had once been sympathetic to the FARC were aghast at the hostages' treatment. In France, the push to do something for Betancourt intensified as it was rumored she was near death. In front of the Hôtel du Ville (Paris's town hall), a campaign portrait of Betancourt had been hanging since February 2005, but in December 2007, a six-foot image of Betancourt in captivity replaced the smiling photo, and an electronic device ticked away the days of her captivity.

In three separate videos, the American hostages seemed to be doing much better than Betancourt, and the images provided some solace for their families. Keith Stansell stood completely still, his arms still muscular, his haircut neat as a marine's. The camera microphone picked up jungle sounds in the background as Stansell glared icily toward the camera, arms crossed defiantly over his chest, chiseled jaw clenched. In a separate video, Marc Gonsalves looked down at the ground, his hands behind his back, revealing a receding hairline and swatting at a fly on his neck. Of the three Americans, only Thomas Howes spoke to the camera. Pérez says that it was because Howes, who was plagued by health problems, had little hope of making it out of captivity alive. "Hi, Mariana, I'm sending you this video on the twenty-second of October, 2007. I was very proud to hear your voice on the radio a short time ago. I love you very much," Howes said. "You and the boys. Please send my best to the family. I've got a letter for you. And a will, and a last testament that I'm going to give. Hopefully it'll get passed to you. Again I love you very much, Mariana. To my company, thank you very much for taking care of our families, and I ask that you please continue to do so. Thank you."

Although the proofs of life had resulted in a major debacle for the guerrillas, Manuel Marulanda and the FARC Secretariat assumed that the American prosecutors would take the proofs into account in Trinidad's sentencing. But neither Kohl nor anyone else in the U.S. government was impressed by the FARC's olive branch. Gary Noesner tried to convince the DOJ otherwise, in the hope that it would encourage some kind of deal to send Trinidad back to Colombia, or at least reduce Trinidad's sentence, something that could be helpful for the hostage situation. But Kohl and others didn't count the proofs as having fulfilled the FARC's end of the bargain, because they'd been confiscated, not released. With the sentencing scheduled to take place two days later, it was rumored that Kohl would seek the maximum sixty-year sentence for the fifty-seven-year-old guerrilla.

In the meantime, Álvaro Uribe, sick of Chávez's posturing and cozying up to FARC leaders in dozens of media ops and furious that Chávez had spoken behind his back to Gen. Mario Montoya, the head of the Colombian army, demanded that the Venezuelan president stay out of the hostage negotiation business for good. An enraged Chávez took the opportunity to cut all ties to Uribe and announced that relations with Colombia were in the "deep freezer." But Chávez was now more determined than ever to be the one to deliver the hostages to freedom. Just before Christmas in 2007, Chávez announced that the FARC would release three hostages to him. The names of those to be released shocked Colombians and observers around the world. While the French government had spent millions of dollars and endless hours lobbying for the release of Ingrid Betancourt, instead it would be her former friend and colleague Clara Rojas who would go free. Along with Rojas, the FARC promised to release Rojas's three-year-old son, Emmanuel, and former Colombian congresswoman Consuelo González de Perdomo, who'd been held for over six years.

There was much speculation about why the Secretariat chose the two women and the child. The story of Rojas giving birth in captivity had shocked the nation, creating intense public pressure for the FARC to release Emmanuel. Consuelo González de Perdomo was one of the few women held by the FARC, and her daughters had worked hard to win her freedom, which impressed the guerrillas. The Secretariat believed that after the unilateral releases the public would recognize the guerrillas' generosity and surely support the idea of a humanitarian exchange for the rest of the captives. Moreover, for the FARC it was a good way to get closer to Chávez, whom they had always admired and considered an ally.

A delighted Chávez dubbed the mission "Operation Emmanuel," after the child, and invited more than one hundred journalists and observers from eight countries to meet in the Colombian city of Villavicencio on December 28, 2007, where they would wait for instructions from the FARC. The first day passed uneventfully while rescue crews in Venezuelan helicopters bearing Red Cross emblems stood by to receive coordinates where they would collect the hostages.

President Chávez had promised Rojas's and González de Perdomo's families that the women would be home to ring in the new year. But days passed and all Chávez was left with were excuses from the FARC. On January 2, 2008, the FARC finally released a message, claiming that they couldn't orchestrate the releases because President Uribe had called for intense military activity in the area where the hostages were being held. Hollywood director Oliver Stone, who was a fan of Hugo Chávez and had gone to Venezuela to film the documentary *South of the Border*, told *The Observer*, "It's Colombia's fault. Colombia did not want it to happen, and I think there were other outside forces, like Bush. . . . Every Colombian that I spoke to was scared of the military in some way or another; they're the most dangerous people, not the FARC." That same day, Uribe appeared in Villavicencio and made an astonishing announcement at a press conference: The reason the FARC was not releasing the hostages was because they did not have Emmanuel in their possession. "The FARC terrorist group doesn't have any excuse. They've fooled Colombia and now they want to fool the international community," Uribe told the massive congregation of journalists, who were skeptical of his intentions. The child had been found living in foster care in Bogotá, Uribe said, and was now safely in the custody of the state. Many believed it was a ridiculous ploy by Uribe to remove Chávez from the negotiations and to make the FARC look bad in their time of obvious humanitarianism. But it *was* true. And to prove it, Rojas's brother had given a DNA sample to compare with the boy's. The FARC looked ridiculous and so did Hugo Chávez, who was furious with the bumbling guerrillas. Chávez quickly called his people out of Villavicencio, and behind the scenes, he demanded that the FARC hand over Rojas and González de Perdomo to him immediately.

Eight days later, on January 10, 2008, Rojas and González de Perdomo were released to a Red Cross and Venezuelan commission. In video footage, Rojas and González de Perdomo appeared healthy and enormously relieved as they spoke by satellite phone to Hugo Chávez. "Mr. President, oh Mr. President, a million thanks for all of your humanitarian efforts," said González de Perdomo. "Please, Mr. President, don't let your guard down, Mr. President. Those who are still there told us to give you that message. We have to continue working. A thousand thanks, Mr. President. Yes, sir. Thank you. And you are helping us, Mr. President, to return to life." An equally jubilant Rojas took the satellite phone: "Mr. President, I am thankful from the bottom of my heart for these people that you have sent us. A million thanks. Yes, we are being reborn."

It was several days before Rojas would be reunited with her son and learn the details of his difficult journey. The story quickly emerged that Emmanuel had been taken from Rojas when he was eight months old, under the guise that he would receive treatment for a tropical disease and his broken arm. Instead, Emmanuel had been taken to a nearby village and handed over to a poor campesino family who could barely afford to feed him. Sometime later, a sickly baby with no known history arrived in the foster care system, a ward of the Colombian state. He was undernourished and his broken arm remained untreated.

How Rojas had managed to become pregnant in captivity was a matter of great speculation, and some wondered whether she had been raped by one of her captors. According to Rojas, that was not the case. Nor would she confirm Botero's speculation that she'd had a consensual relationship with one of the guerrillas. Luis Eladio Pérez wrote in his book that Rojas had secured permission to have sexual relations and was supplied with condoms to prevent pregnancy. Some speculated that she had planned to get pregnant, in the hope that the guerrillas would free her. Rojas told members of the media, who were understandably fascinated with her story, that she had no idea if the father of her son was still alive. Some of the hostages believed he was not. Martín Sombra, the commander in charge of Rojas during her pregnancy, was captured by Colombian forces in February 2008. From jail, Sombra told Ingrid Betancourt's husband that the guerrilla soldier suspected of being the father of Emmanuel had been executed for his part in the conception. Other guerrillas would tell Jorge Enrique Botero that Emmanuel's father hadn't been killed, but was sentenced to hard labor and stripped of his weapon for more than a year.

18

Tucker on the Mountain

On the northern part of the border between Colombia and Venezuela, the land juts out into an enormous peninsula of temperate desert called La Guajira. Giant dunes reach down to the Caribbean Sea on the Colombian side and into the Gulf of Venezuela on the neighboring coast. Heading south along this same political boundary, a huge mountain range rises. The northernmost extension of the Andes, it is called the Serranía de Perijá, and it was in this region that Simón Trinidad began his career as a guerrilla. On one side of the wild virgin mountains is the Venezuelan state of Zulia. On the other side is the region that the family of Simón Trinidad was from—the department of César.

"It's impossible, really impossible, unless you're an expert or you have a GPS, to know whether you are in Venezuelan territory or Colombian territory," says Botero, for whom the mountains had become a more and more common destination. His target each time was the camp of FARC Secretariat member and Caribbean Bloc commander Iván Márquez. Traveling to see Márquez was difficult, but less so than the trip to see Raúl Reyes near the Ecuadorian border or the weeks-long trek to the hostage camps in the jungle. After several days of travel, Botero would meet a guerrilla who would guide him up the rustic footpaths, or *trochas*, through the mountains along the border.

The trip to the camp was an arduous two-day journey by foot and on mules. The reason that Márquez's camp had become so important to the journalist was that it had become a sort of "international relations" headquarters for the FARC. And while Raúl Reyes was still the main Secretariat member dealing with hostage negotiations, Márquez and several other high-level commanders had also become players.

Each trip into FARC territory fascinated Botero. He never ceased to be amazed by the way the guerrillas acted and defined themselves— what he saw as a throwback to a Marxist guerrilla movement in a world where Marxism no longer existed. But no trip into FARC territory had ever been as unusual as the one Botero made on January 20, 2008. As he hiked up the muddy mountainside, he could hardly comprehend how he found himself with such strange traveling companions. In front of him on the *trocha* was the enormous American public defender Robert

Robert Tucker, Simón Trinidad's public defender in four federal trials held between 2006 and 2008, and Lara Quint, assistant federal public defender, who helped translate exchanges between Trinidad and Tucker during the trials. Photo: Jorge Enrique Botero.

Tucker, and behind Tucker was an American woman Tucker had brought along to act as his translator.

"When Mr. Tucker first called me and asked if I could get him an audience with a FARC commander, I was very impressed by his interest, his capacity to take a risk and to do something that was obviously going to be dangerous. I was also sort of stunned because what he was asking seemed to be very much against the U.S. policy not to negotiate with the FARC." Tucker asked Botero to make sure that he could meet with a commander who could make the decision to release Stansell, Gonsalves, and Howes in exchange for an offer that Tucker would bring with him. "I told him that this was very difficult because it would have to be a collective decision of the Secretariat, and all of the Secretariat members would never be in the same place at one time." It was early January 2008, and Trinidad's sentencing date of January 28 (which had been postponed from November 2007) was swiftly approaching. Botero wasn't optimistic about making the meeting happen, since the FARC usually took months to agree to anything so out of the ordinary. So he was shocked when only ten days later, he received an e-mail response to his inquiry from Raúl Reyes, who said that the FARC would be very interested in talking with Trinidad's lawyer. Reyes and all of the Secretariat members had been closely following Tucker's work through Colombian news reports and the trial chronicles of attorney Paul Wolf. "They all felt that Tucker did a great job for Trinidad, even though the guerrilla commander was convicted in the end," says Botero. "Several commanders told me that they respected Tucker very much. They said, 'Here is a man that is not earning money from this defense; he's a public defender. We have to applaud him because he did not leave his client hanging. He did a very professional job.' " Botero was informed that he and Tucker would be received by Iván Márquez. Tucker agreed and coordinated with Botero about making the trip. Although Botero was dying to know what offer Tucker was going to make, as a journalist, he did not want to be in the business of negotiations, and so he didn't ask.

The journey into the mountains began in the early morning, and Botero was immediately impressed by his gringo companions. "Tucker was really calm. He was never nervous. He was always looking around with a lot of curiosity. He was joking like a person who is not thinking that he is in danger." Tucker's translator was calm as well, but the Americans did have one concern. "They kept asking about weapons—if the guerrillas were going to be armed. I told him that yes, the guerrillas would be armed, very armed." At dusk, Botero, Tucker, and the translator arrived at a small house belonging to a campesino family in the Serranía de Perijá and were told to wait for the arrival of the guerrilla commanders. Hours later, fifty-two-year-old Secretariat member Iván Márquez, a thickly built man with dark curly hair and a neatly trimmed beard, arrived with his entourage. All of the guerrillas were dressed in combat fatigues and were carrying semiautomatic rifles. The group consisted of Márquez; his companion, Lucia; and a senior guerrilla named Rodrigo Granda, along with half a dozen young soldiers, both men and women.

Botero had met Granda thirty years before, when the two were both university students participating in political marches. Tucker also knew who Granda was because of the guerrilla's interesting history. Granda had been captured in Caracas in January 2004 by Colombian police commandos (reportedly without the authorization of the Venezuelan government) and secretly transported to Colombia in the trunk of a car. His capture was a coup for Uribe because Granda was the FARC's acting "foreign minister." Granda was held for over three years in a Colombian prison, and his liberation came in a most unusual way. In May 2007, with enormous pressure mounting on newly elected French president Nicolas Sarkozy to do something to help free Ingrid Betancourt, Sarkozy persuaded Álvaro Uribe to release Granda from prison. Sarkozy's argument was that the FARC would be thrilled to get their high-level commander out of jail and therefore would be so thankful to the Colombian government that they would respond with a similar gesture and release Betancourt. Uribe initially resisted Sarkozy's appeal, because with so many Colombians in captivity, he did not want to give the impression that Betancourt's freedom was more important to the government than the freedom of any of the other hostages. However, Uribe finally gave in to Sarkozy, and upon Granda's release, the guerrilla commander was made to swear he would not return to the FARC. Sarkozy then publicly asked the guerrillas to make a "similar gesture," and thousands of French people waited for the FARC to respond with the release of their beloved Betancourt. Nothing happened. The FARC completely ignored the request to reciprocate. Colombians were not surprised. Within weeks of his release, Granda was once again in the mountains with Iván Márquez, his AK-47, and his revolutionary rhetoric. "I will never demobilize or call for an end to armed struggle until our objectives are met," he said in an interview with a French newspaper in May 2007. For Sarkozy, it was a painful embarrassment. For Uribe, it was a successfully calculated move: those in France and the international community who said he was not doing enough through diplomacy to free the hostages were temporarily silenced.

However frightening the assemblage of armed guerrillas looked, the reception they gave Tucker at the campesino house was quite warm. Márquez, Granda, and a group of guerrillas who were part of Márquez's personal guard sat down at a table near the kitchen to greet one another. "It was bizarre because I introduced them as if I were introducing business associates: 'Mr. Tucker, this is Iván Márquez; Mr. Márquez, this is Trinidad's lawyer,' " says Botero. At the same time, the presence of the attractive *gringa* translator had dampened any climate of hostility. "All the guerrillas stared at her because she was so pretty, so nice, and always smiling. She awoke many sighs among the guerrillas," says Botero. Márquez began the meeting by thanking Tucker for the effort and the professionalism with which he had handled the case. Then to Tucker's astonishment, Granda and Márquez cited various things that had impressed them about Tucker's defense of Trinidad during the trial. "While we were talking, the guerrillas began preparing dinner on a woodstove, and just before we were served, Tucker told the FARC commanders that he wanted to discuss an offer. He said, 'If you release the three Americans, the prosecutor could request a shorter sentence for Simón.' " Granda and Márquez looked at each other in disbelief. Botero was speechless. He had expected something more substantial in Tucker's offer. It was the same offer that Ken Kohl had made publicly, a proposal that the guerrillas had categorically rejected. Botero knew that Márquez was expecting Tucker to offer Trinidad's and Sonia's freedom for the liberation of the three Americans. "Márquez told Tucker that his proposal would be 'taken to the Secretariat,' but he was also firmly discouraging," says Botero. "They took the offer a little bit like it was a joke. They said, 'How long of a sentence are you talking about? Forty years? So Simón only has to live to be one hundred years old, not *one hundred and twenty years old*, to get out of prison? Well, that's fine. Thanks a lot, Mr. Tucker, but this is not sufficient.' Tucker was a little taken aback, like he hoped for something more, like he hoped for more flexibility, more pragmatism. But he didn't think it had been a waste of time. He said, 'Well, I've done as much as possible to try to help my client.' " After the frustrating exchange, the mood lightened and the meeting went the way of revolutionary music and conversation. There were Cuban cigars and rum. Before noon the following day, Tucker, the translator, and Botero headed down the mountain.

In an August 2008 interview, Ken Kohl said that he had never made a specific offer for Tucker to deliver to the FARC, but he added, "Certainly, we wouldn't be against whatever [Trinidad's] attorney wanted to do to try to get those guys out. And if they were successful, we certainly would recognize that in sentencing Trinidad." But days before the hearing, Tucker was empty-handed; he had nothing to offer the prosecutor when Trinidad's sentencing day arrived.

On January 28, 2008, in the same courtroom where Simón Trinidad had been convicted for conspiracy to commit hostage taking, Ken Kohl asked Judge Royce Lamberth to condemn Trinidad to the maximum sentence allowed in the extradition agreement—sixty years in prison. In Kohl's argument, he compared Trinidad to Osama bin Laden and said that the guerrilla should be punished as a terrorist. Kohl pointed dramatically at Trinidad in front of a courtroom packed with reporters, saying, "Because that's what he is—a terrorist." In Tucker's subsequent statement, he rejected the comparison to bin Laden and told the court that, contrary to what the prosecution argued, a harsh sentence would not encourage the FARC to release the three Americans. Then Tucker—freshly back from his secret meeting in the mountains—argued that the U.S. government *should* allow negotiations for the release of hostages and that it should amend its policy regarding negotiations. Judge Lamberth, unmoved by the public defender's proposal for changing U.S. policy, announced to Tucker and the packed courtroom that he, as a judge, had nothing to do with the U.S. policy on negotiation.

Then Trinidad spoke. Reading from a long speech for over an hour, he denounced terrorism in all its forms and said it was his sincerest wish that the three Americans be returned safely to their loved ones. He said that when he joined the FARC, he knew he could lose his life and liberty fighting for justice and peace in his country. He concluded what would likely be his last public speech with the declaration of a dedicated revolutionary: "Long live Manuel Marulanda. Long live the FARC. Long live Simón Bolívar, whose sword of freedom continues to run through America." After Trinidad's speech came the judge's sentencing decision. Attorney Paul Wolf summarized Lamberth's final comments:

> Judge Lamberth looked Trinidad in the eyes, said he respected Trinidad's intelligence, sincerity, and eloquence, and then proceeded to sentence him to 60 years—the longest sentence ever imposed on a Colombian. Trinidad had gone over the line, explained the judge, when he joined this conspiracy. His crime was terrorism, a heinous and barbaric crime that violated the law of nations. No civilized nation will tolerate terrorism, he concluded, and this was a court of law. The maximum sentence allowed for hostage taking was life imprisonment, said the judge. But he would abide by the wishes of the Colombian government and only impose a term of 60 years. "Good luck to you, Mr. Palmera Piñeda."

Colombian senator Piedad Córdoba sat in the courtroom gallery, fuming and holding back tears. Córdoba had not stopped working to help free the remaining political hostages, including Stansell, Howes, and Gonsalves, and she knew that Trinidad's incredibly harsh sentence could severely damage prospects for getting any more hostages out. Gary Noesner and those at Northrop Grumman were disheartened because they felt like the sentence would be a major detriment to getting the Americans released, and it seemed like they had run completely out of options. The hostages' families feared it was a terrible maneuver by the U.S. government. But none were more distressed than the hostages themselves, who immediately learned of Trinidad's sentence through radio broadcasts. Luis Eladio Pérez wrote that Stansell, Gonsalves, and Howes were "tormented by the topic of Simón Trinidad and Sonia with their respective sentences [Simón Trinidad with sixty years and Sonia with sixteen and a half years]. But particularly that of Simón Trinidad, because they had heard some guerrillas declare openly that they would be sentenced to the same number of years as Simón Trinidad, but in the jungle." Several weeks later, the FARC would make its position clear through an interview with Iván Márquez posted on the Web site of the Bolivarian Press Agency (ABP): "The Colombian government and the White House should think about not putting more obstacles in the way of a humanitarian exchange with sentences like this, which in the end amount to 60 years of prison in the jungle for the three Americans held by FARC."

While the prospect of the Americans' freedom being gained through negotiations seemed to be completely erased by the DOJ's sentencing of Trinidad, a month later, several other political prisoners were on the verge of being released unilaterally by the guerrillas. In February 2008, with the FARC Secretariat itching to unload the burden of the hostages and also to repair relations with Hugo Chávez, Luis Eladio Pérez was unchained from Thomas Howes and told that he would be released. Before he left the camp, Pérez's fellow hostages wrote letters for him to carry out. None of the letters passed the guerrillas' censorship, and they were taken away. But Pérez had read and memorized their contents, and he promised that he would visit all of the families and deliver the messages to each intended recipient. On February 27, after seven years in captivity, Pérez was marched out of the jungle, along with three other political hostages, and delivered with great fanfare to Hugo Chávez.

For the most part, each visit Pérez would make to the families of the hostages he'd left behind would be a difficult, heart-wrenching experience. But there was one instance when Pérez was delighted to be the messenger. Hearing that Pérez had something to tell her, Keith Stansell's girlfriend, Patricia Medina, went to the airport to meet Pérez on his arrival in Bogotá. Pérez wrote of the moment he saw Medina:

"Right then, someone came up to me with a bouquet of flowers, and I grabbed a rose. 'This is the most beautiful message that I could give to a woman: Take this rose in the name of Keith. He wants to know if you would like to marry him.'" Medina froze. The young mother had spent five years bracing herself for the possibility that Stansell would not want to be with her when he returned. "When Luis Eladio told me that Keith wanted to marry me, it caught me by surprise, because Keith never sent a message to me in the video by Jorge Enrique Botero. Keith never sent *any* message to me. But when Luis Eladio told me that Keith said that he wanted to marry me, I swear, that was the day I had most yearned for in my life." Medina stood completely still, clutching the rose that Pérez had given her, tears streaming down her face. "Luis Eladio said, 'Well, yes or no?' And I said, 'Yes, yes.'" Then Pérez smiled and made Medina promise that he could be the best man at the wedding. (Stansell would later say in the book *Out of Captivity* that he didn't exactly offer a marriage proposal, but that Pérez had interpreted it as such.)

Pérez also visited Ingrid Betancourt's husband, Juan Carlos Lecompte. During their years of captivity together, Betancourt had earned Pérez's great admiration and respect. He told Lecompte that Betancourt had been exceptionally brave in the face of terrible abuse by the guerrillas. She had saved Pérez's life and forfeited her own freedom when the two tried to escape together and Pérez had become too ill to continue. She was defiant and strong and incredibly spiritual. Lecompte was so impressed by what Pérez told him about his wife, he was overwhelmed with emotion. "It just made me love her that much more," he said in a June 2008 interview.

On behalf of Stansell, Gonsalves, and Howes, Pérez made his way to the United States to meet with their families. He felt the visits were very important for their emotional well-being because he could give them details about their loved ones that they'd been unable to know for over five years: Stansell was a leader among the prisoners, strong but fair; Howes was a joker, good-natured and friendly with almost all the others; Gonsalves was kindhearted and devoted to his Bible. But there were other meetings that Pérez hoped to have in Washington, D.C., ones where he might accomplish something he felt was even more important: support for a humanitarian exchange to free the hostages. And he hoped the catalyst would be the very strong messages from the American hostages to their own government. "In their letters, Marc and Keith both expressed their loyalty to the United States and said that they were disappointed in the behavior of the government, because during the five years, it had not made any statements with respect to them. Without a doubt, this abandonment affected them a lot," Pérez wrote. "The letters weren't only directed at President Bush, but also to the Congress, to Nancy Pelosi, and to a coalition led by Massachusetts congressmen Jim McGovern and Bill Delahunt, who the Americans knew had been working to find a political solution to the situation." The three Americans also wrote letters to *The New York Times* and *The Washington Post* asking for more coverage of their plight. Three more letters were directed to the possible future presidents of the United States: Hillary Clinton, Barack Obama, and John McCain. Pérez was able to convey the contents of the letters only to McCain, who, Pérez wrote, "was very touched by their situation."

After Pérez's release, Hugo Chávez and Piedad Córdoba continued to push the FARC to release more hostages, and the families of the Americans were hopeful that Stansell, Gonsalves, and Howes could be the beneficiaries of those negotiations. However, the U.S. government flatly refused any type of collaboration with the Venezuelans on the case. Even Córdoba, because of her association with Chávez and proximity to FARC commanders, became persona non grata in Washington, D.C., on her visits to try to secure support for a hostage exchange. Noesner believed that the snubbing of Córdoba was another in a long list of mistakes by the U.S. government. "The problem in the government is that they always look at anybody who has access as being duped by the FARC or secretly pursuing the FARC's agenda," he said. "To me it reflects a naïveté about who you have to deal with in a hostage crisis. You have to deal with people who have access and influence, and those aren't going to be people who 100 percent share your political ideology."

In mid-February 2008, just after the fifth anniversary of the kidnapping of the Americans and a week before Pérez's release, Northrop Grumman had organized a meeting for the family members to give them an update on the status of the case. As they had for the meetings held each year since the kidnapping, the company once again invited spokespeople from the FBI and the State Department, Gary Noesner from Control Risks, a military spokesperson, and the U.S. ambassador to Colombia, who in 2008 was a veteran diplomat named William Brownfield. They also invited the recently released Colombian hostage Clara Rojas. From Rojas, the families learned more about how their loved ones were faring in captivity, which gave them some solace, although Rojas had not been with the men for more than two years. And because she had been released through the work of Piedad Córdoba and Hugo Chávez, they began to see a possibility that Stansell, Gonsalves, and Howes could benefit from the work of Chávez, as well. Unfortunately, none of the speakers from the government or the corporation could report any new progress on the case. There was, however, one new guest who had recently been face-to-face with the FARC commanders responsible for the men's fate. Noesner had convinced Northrop Grumman executives to invite Jorge Enrique Botero to the meeting to give the families an inside analysis of the FARC and to detail what he believed were the guerrillas' plans for the hostages. When it was time for the families to ask questions, Keith Stansell's nineteen-year-old daughter, Lauren, asked Botero if he thought that the FARC would authorize him to tape another interview. He said, "Lauren, my dear, it is not time to talk about interviews. It is time to talk about releases." The family members let out a collective gasp. Botero knew that Córdoba had been pushing for the release of at least one of the Americans as a way to get the U.S. government involved. This was encouraging because Botero knew that the FARC were eager to please Chávez and would probably be very eager to do his bidding. Botero could not tell the families any more specifics. Instead, Botero spoke about Córdoba's and Chávez's continuing interest in working toward some sort of an agreement for the release of all the hostages. For the first time in five years, everyone left the company meeting in high spirits. Noesner and Botero ate lunch together in a Fort Lauderdale café, thrilled with the possibility of progress after so many disappointing years.

Eleven days later, just after midnight on March 1, 2008, Colombian military bombs rained down on the camp of Raúl Reyes, instantly killing the commander and sixteen of his men. Immediately after, Colombian troops stormed the wreckage, collecting the body of Reyes and all of the evidence they could find on the FARC organization. The attack was a complete surprise, and many of the dead guerrillas were found wearing underwear or nightclothes. (Defense Minister Juan Manuel Santos later admitted paying $2.7 million to an informant for information that led to the successful strike.) The attack had come after Colombian bombers entered more than a mile into Ecuador and struck Reyes's camp while flying north. The enraged Ecuadorian president, Rafael Correa, announced that the action was a violation of Ecuador's airspace and that he considered Colombian troops on the ground a military invasion. Hugo Chávez moved Venezuelan troops near the border with Colombia and recalled all personnel from the Venezuelan embassy in Colombia. A similar strike inside Venezuela, Chávez warned, would be considered a "cause for war." Chávez was still ardently supporting the guerrillas and arguing that they should be considered a "belligerent army" rather than an "international terrorist organization"—a political distinction that the Venezuelans said had no legal effect but which showed Chavez's support for the guerrillas. Relations were smoothed over a week later when Uribe met with Chávez and Correa in the Dominican Republic. After first offering insults, the three ended the meeting with an apology from Uribe, followed by handshakes and hugs among the frosty neighbors.

Just two days after Reyes's death, on March 3, Iván Ríos, the youngest member of the Secretariat and commander of the FARC's Northwestern Bloc, was also dead. But this time, it was impossible for the guerrillas to place the blame directly on the Colombian army. Ríos had been killed by his own security chief, Pedro Pablo Montoya, aka Rojas, who put a bullet through Ríos's forehead and murdered the commander's girlfriend as well. Three days later, Montoya delivered his boss's severed right hand, a laptop computer, and Ríos's ID card to the Colombian military and asked for amnesty and a big payoff. Fingerprint results proved that the hand was indeed that of Ríos. It was unclear what motivated Montoya to kill his boss, but it was speculated that there had been so much pressure on the guerrillas to capture Ríos that Montoya decided to put a definitive end to being at the wrong end of the chase. It was also reported that Ríos had become increasingly paranoid about infiltrators and had executed more than two hundred of his own men. "I did it to save my life and that of my girlfriend and another companion," Montoya said as he was paraded in front of reporters by Colombian authorities. Shortly after, Defense Minister Santos said that a payment of 800 million pesos ($320,000) had been made to Montoya. The payoff was highly criticized by many within the government, who argued that it amounted to rewarding someone for murder. Santos argued that the policy to pay someone to deliver a FARC commander was helping fight the guerrillas and should be upheld regardless of how the delivery transpired.

Analysts said that Ríos's murder was telling because it showed the rebels were beginning to turn on one another. Adam Isacson of the Center for International Policy felt that Rojas's act of treason was indicative of a much greater problem that ran through the entire organization—an inability to communicate. "Not only on a national level—every communiqué looks like it was written by Marxists in the 1960s—but also at the local level where they're feared instead of loved [by the campesinos]. And now it's looking like they're even feared and not loved by a lot of their own recruits, their own rank and file. We're hearing so many rumors now about [FARC commanders] having *consejos de guerra*, war tribunals, and trying to root out would-be traitors—just killing people by the dozen within their own ranks. So the Colombian government's strategy of making clear that those who desert will not be mistreated, and may even get a reward, probably is having a huge impact." (In February 2009, Montoya remained in jail, where he'd been since his celebrated murder of Iván Ríos and his departure from the guerrillas a year earlier. Prosecutors had frozen the reward money, and Montoya was under investigation for terrorism, theft, and murder. "With this kind of treatment for a deserter," an annoyed Montoya told the Associated Press from jail, "what guerrilla is going to turn himself in?")

Nonetheless, over two thousand guerrillas entered the Colombian government's reinsertion program in 2008. The highly publicized deal offered incentives such as health coverage, stipends, and job training. Deputy Defense Minister Sergio Jaramillo said that not only was the number of desertions staggering but that commanders were also leaving the ranks in numbers never before seen. "More than quantity, what is interesting is the quality of the people who are demobilizing. You see more and more people with command positions." Jaramillo said that the FARC, although it was one of the world's oldest guerrilla movements, was becoming inexperienced due to the loss of its more senior members.

In April 2008, a deserter from the Caribbean Bloc told the *San Francisco Chronicle* that intense ground attacks and aerial bombardments forced his comrades out of their area of influence, and by late 2007, 80 percent of his regiment had deserted. "Our money, our food and our economic support all began running low," he said. Another deserter told the *Chronicle* that he and his girlfriend deserted after being told that their baby daughter would have to be given away or killed because the child was a security risk. A ten-year veteran who quit the guerrillas in 2008 told Reuters, "To say the FARC are finished is a mistake. The FARC have been around for 40 years and could be for 50. But the FARC are stuck, and what future is there in growing old there?" he said. "I believed in the FARC once, but now, they are infiltrated and some bosses are corrupted by drugs."

While the mass desertions were commonly written off by the Secretariat as just a downward phase of a long war, the deaths of Secretariat members Ríos and Reyes were undeniably the worst hit in the army's entire forty-five-year history. It was an especially debilitating defeat for the commander in chief, Manuel Marulanda, who was believed to be close to eighty years old. On March 26, less than a month after the deaths of two of the seven Secretariat members, Marulanda told his companion, Sandra, a much younger woman who'd been with him for the past decade, that he had a very bad stomachache. Sandra was sure it was gastritis, not only because of the symptoms but because Marulanda had been plagued with the ailment various times and hadn't been feeling well for several days. One of his attendants gave him a generic medicine to take away the pain, and by 5:30 p.m., Marulanda said that he felt much better and asked for dinner. They gave him food, and he said, "Ah, now I feel well." At 6:30 p.m., Marulanda was resting, when he had a sudden and massive heart attack. Sandra grabbed him and held him, but there was nothing she could do.

"Immediately, the people who were with Marulanda communicated the news to the members of the Secretariat," says Jorge Enrique Botero. The death of Marulanda was reported by Defense Minister Santos two months later. The Colombian military had intercepted several communications about Marulanda's death, and on May 25, Santos presented the evidence in a press conference. He apparently doubted the FARC's account that their commander had died of a heart attack. "Whether Marulanda died in an air raid or of natural causes," Santos said, "this would be the hardest blow that this terrorist group has taken, because Tirofijo was the one who kept the criminal organization united." The day following Marulanda's death, the FARC Secretariat had a virtual meeting via radio to elect the commander in chief's successor. "There was no division over the death of Marulanda," says Botero. "They were unified. It was like, 'Our father died, so we should unite to overcome this moment.' The whole group agreed that Marulanda's successor should be Secretariat member and FARC ideologue Alfonso Cano." The new leader of the FARC would be Botero's former friend from his days with the Juventud Comunista.

That same month in Washington, D.C., U.S. federal prosecutor Ron McNeil began what was likely hoped to be a big publicity boon for the war on drugs in Colombia: Simón Trinidad's drug-trafficking trial. Many court observers felt that the trial was an unnecessary waste of time and money, since Trinidad had already been convicted and sentenced to sixty years in prison. Even Judge Lamberth, who had sentenced Trinidad, was indignant. At the status conference that preceded the March drug trial, Lamberth asked the prosecutor, "Will the government explain why we are doing this? In light of what happened in the previous case?" Trinidad had also already been tried for drug trafficking once before, in fall 2007. The jury deadlocked seven to five, favoring an acquittal, and the judge declared a mistrial.

For the drug-trafficking retrial, Robert Tucker once again defended Trinidad. The government's case was based purely on informant testimony by former guerrillas who had taken the Colombian government's reinsertion deal. Several experts gave background evidence on drug-trafficking routes, the structure of the FARC (in which Trinidad was erroneously described as an alternate member of the seven-member Secretariat), and how cocaine is made. Of material evidence, there was none; no drugs had been seized, no telephone calls recorded. The jury deadlocked once again, and Judge Lamberth declared a mistrial. The strategy to tie a high-level FARC commander to the narco-trafficking business to justify the U.S. policy in Colombia had fallen on its face. Jury members interviewed after the trial said that they believed that the FARC were in the illegal drug business but that there was no evidence that Trinidad had anything to do with it. After spending millions of dollars on four trials and receiving only one conspiracy conviction, the U.S. Department of Justice quietly closed the case of Simón Trinidad.

In Bogotá, Patricia Medina had accepted Stansell's marriage proposal via a radio message. The extraordinary and romantic story was widely reported in the Colombian news and immediately reached the camp where the American hostages were being held. Stansell realized immediately that his message to Patricia must have been embellished by Luis Eladio Pérez. "When I first heard about the captive American who had proposed to his Colombian girlfriend, I was stunned," Stansell wrote. And although Patricia's increasingly loving messages were a great comfort, Stansell "wasn't sure that a wedding was in our immediate future, but I was eager to see her again, and she wasn't going to be simply a monthly notation in my checkbook—she was going to be someone I would spend significant time with." While Medina dreamed about their future wedding, she was also deeply troubled by the chaos within the FARC ranks. "After Raúl Reyes was killed, Piedad Córdoba, the senator, came out and said that things were very difficult. She had always been very positive that the hostages would be released. But at that time, Piedad said we would have to wait to see how things would be solved, and that they were very bad." Patricia felt conflicted between the happiness of knowing she would marry the man she loved and sadness, "because the moment that Keith would return to freedom was getting further away."

Three months later, in June 2008, thousands of files discovered on

Raúl Reyes's computer became another cause of FARC-inspired grief for Hugo Chávez. The Colombian National Police chief, Óscar Naranjo, reported that one document mentioned financial support to the tune of $300 million from Chávez to the FARC for the purpose of purchasing arms, and another file mentioned approximately $150,000 in the other direction, when the FARC gave money to Chávez as he vied for power in 1998. There were reportedly dozens more e-mails detailing an extensive relationship between the FARC and the Venezuelan leader. Chávez and the FARC Secretariat claimed the documents were fakes. But to make matters worse for Chávez, on Saturday, June 7, a Venezuelan National Guard officer was caught inside Colombia with forty thousand rifle cartridges that he was trying to deliver to the rebels. For Chávez (who had little popular support in his own country for his continuing dalliances in the Colombian hostage crisis), it was time to publicly and viscerally rid himself of his problematic guerrilla neighbors. On June 8, the FARC's most valuable ally made a crushing about-face in his weekly television program, *Aló Presidente:* "The guerrilla war is *history.* At this moment in Latin America, an armed guerrilla movement is out of place," said a livid Chávez. "The time has come to free all the prisoners you have, in exchange—for *nothing.*"

19

Operación Jaque

By June 2008, the responsibility for fifteen of the FARC's most valuable hostages, including Ingrid Betancourt, Marc Gonsalves,
Thomas Howes, and Keith Stansell, belonged to the commander of the
First Front, a guerrilla by the name of César. Because of César's great
success in military operations and his dedication to the insurgent army,
the forty-nine-year-old guerrilla had risen to the prominent position of
controlling a vast area of jungle within the department of Guaviare, in
the northern part of the Colombian Amazon region. Not only was the
massive land area a perfect hiding place for hostages because of its pure
inaccessibility but, under César, it had become a pot of gold for the
FARC. Adam Isacson called the area "Colombia's coca-growing heart-
land." In addition to overseeing financial matters dealing with coca
production and trafficking, César, like other front commanders, was
responsible for all FARC activities in his geographical area. And
because of all of his responsibilities, he had little direct contact with the
hostages under his command. Instead, he put them under the control of
subordinate commanders. One of the most cruel of those commanders
was a guerrilla named Enrique, who was in charge of Betancourt and
the Americans toward the end of their captivity. Those held under
Enrique were threatened with death and chained to trees and to one

Stansell (front to back), Gonsalves, Howes, and Gen. Mario Montoya, head of the Colombian army, immediately after the men were rescued in Operación Jaque on July 2, 2008. Photo: U.S. Embassy.

another. And, in a sick and degrading practice, women hostages were filmed going to the bathroom and then the videos were shown to the rank-and-file guerrillas.

In his book *Operación Jaque: La Verdadera Historia,* Juan Carlos Torres describes communication between César and other guerrilla commanders. To communicate with Enrique and other subordinate commanders, César would send orders via his radio operator, a female guerrilla called India. César's superior commander, Mono Jojoy, who was in charge of more than twenty fronts in the Eastern Bloc, would communicate with César and his other front commanders via radio operators as well. Each day, the radio operators would go on predetermined channels to hear news or orders given in FARC radio code, a complicated set of numbers and letters that, according to César, consisted of over five thousand words. Text messages on satellite phones and e-mail were also used to send messages. But FARC commanders found that communicating among themselves had become very difficult. Since the death of Raúl Reyes, which the guerrillas believed to have been the result of intelligence breaches, radio contact had been kept to a bare minimum. Things had been especially difficult for César and the First Front. After hostage John Pinchao escaped from captivity in May 2007, César said that the Colombian army's manpower on the ground, in the air, and on the rivers had greatly increased. He suspected that he was surrounded by tens of thousands of Colombian troops, leaving him virtually paralyzed. He was not imagining things. By April, Álvaro Uribe had ordered the military to conduct what he termed a "*cerco humanitario*"—a "humanitarian cordon." The idea was to move thousands of troops in, encircling the general area of the hostage camps, to pressure the guerrillas to turn over the hostages. On May 31, 2008, César received a decoded message from Secretariat member and military chief commander Mono Jojoy asking about the hostages: "How is *la carga*? [The hostages were literally referred to as "cargo."] How are they distributed? How are the conditions to receive an international commission?" It would be an entire day before César could have his radio operator, India, reply at the designated time, "Comrade Jorge [referring to Mono Jojoy, who was also known as Jorge Briceño], *saludos. La carga* is good." Then, as per her orders from César, India described the geographic locations of the three groups of hostages under César's command. One group was near the Inírida River, by Puerto Nápoles; another was in Carurú, near the Vaupés River; and another was situated between the Jirisa and the Itilla rivers. The three groups were dispersed throughout a nearly one-hundred-mile radius because of the recent intense military pressure. If one group was attacked and the hostages were rescued or killed, César would still have the other valuable *carga*. A little more than a week later, on June 11, 2008, César received another message from Mono Jojoy: "Reunite all of *la carga*. Create all the conditions to receive an international commission in a safe place. When you are ready, send a message. *Saludos,* Jorge."

"César said that the situation didn't seem right. It wasn't clear at all," says attorney Rodolfo Ríos, who briefly represented César after his capture. "They sent César a message that said, 'Gather them in one place.'" Ríos said César didn't like the idea. "He said, 'But they repeated the order, and I had to carry out the order. It was an order of the Secretariat, and you just follow orders.'" César felt a little uneasy, but "he said that the radio code they used was perfect, that there was no way that it could be an imposter," says Ríos. "Besides, the news radio had been full of reports that some sort of hostage exchange was going to take place." In mid-June, radio broadcasts carried rumors that Betancourt and some of the other hostages might be released. In an interview with *El Espectador*, Luis Eladio Pérez, who had been freed in February 2008, sounded very convincing when he, too, said that a release was imminent: "Without a doubt, I think that several of the hostages are already walking toward their freedom. The country will hear news very soon." César also understood from radio broadcasts that a meeting was in the works with delegates from France and Switzerland and the newly appointed commander in chief, Alfonso Cano. "Those media reports got César's attention," says Ríos. "He was very conscientious. He figured that moving the hostages was connected to this 'international commission' from France and Switzerland and that perhaps there would be some kind of negotiations."

On June 11, César received another message from Mono Jojoy: "Keep the plan secret. Do not include people who are not under your command. How is everything going? Your mission is to guarantee the life of the prisoners. We cannot commit mistakes like those of the Valle. [On June 28, 2007, eleven hostages held since 2002 had been gunned down by their captors when the guerrillas mistakenly thought they were under attack by the Colombian army.] Prepare a special meal for them the day of the visit. Have them all dressed in white T-shirts with messages about the exchange. Motivate them. Prepare a press release for this visit. *Saludos,* Jorge." The following day, César sent a response through his radio operator: "Comrade Jorge, everything's going well.

We are moving slowly to guarantee the secret. In five days we will all be together and we will communicate. *Saludos*, César." On June 23, 2008, César sent a message assuring Mono Jojoy that although he could feel the Colombian military's presence in the area, all was still on track.

While César pushed his subordinate commanders to unite the hostage groups, the captives themselves were becoming very uneasy about the impromptu march, wrote Torres. At times, the hostages were forced into boats and moved down the rivers, their bodies hidden under tarps in the stifling heat. At other times, the guerrillas would set up a temporary prison camp and wait for several days. As usual, the hostages were not given any information about why they were being moved or where they were going, but this trip seemed somehow different from the others. They had also heard the news reports that a French and a Swiss delegation might be coming to speak with Cano about a possible humanitarian exchange. Although years of lies, false hopes, and disappointments had worn away any confidence in rumors of impending releases, the hostages still felt that something big was about to happen, according to Torres. At one of the temporary camps erected in mid-June, Enrique presented the hostages with new clothes, increased their rations, and gave them special food they had not eaten in years. The hostages were suspicious of the kindness coming from this captor, who had never shown any mercy before. For days they discussed the possibilities: Would someone be released? Would a journalist come? Were they going to be transferred to another front? Would more proofs of life be filmed? Some of the hostages thought that Betancourt would be released, because the FARC had been so reviled after the release of her last proof of life that the secretariat would seek some kind of international forgiveness. The situation became all the more curious when, some days later, they arrived at a rustic house utilized by the guerrillas. According to Torres, the hostages took advantage of finally being out of the jungle to enjoy the sun. Betancourt shared stories from her new encyclopedia, which the guerrillas had recently given her after years of her begging for one. The hostages were fed a meal of meat, milk, fruit, and sweets and then were presented with new jeans and long-sleeved dress shirts. To the three Americans, the clothing was absurd. "Our new clothes consisted of cheap blue jeans, the kind we'd seen poorer

Colombians wearing when they came into the city in their good clothes," wrote Howes. "With the pants, we were handed campesino-style western dress shirts. All we needed was a straw hat and we would have looked like we'd stepped off the set of one of the Mexican B movies we'd watched on the DVD players." Thinking that they would be dressed up to film a proof-of-life video, they all revolted. After an intense argument, during which Stansell, Gonsalves, and Howes threw their clothes into a pile, Enrique angrily relented. "If you don't want to use them, fine," he said. "Don't say we never gave you anything."

On June 24, César transmitted a message: "We already have a command at the site, and we are twenty kilometers away. All is well. Coordinates 0218113, 07203193." On June 28, a reply arrived for César. He was informed that the Secretariat had decided to move the hostages by helicopter to meet with Alfonso Cano in the mountains of western Colombia. They also told César that he would be traveling in the helicopter with the hostages because he had been personally invited to meet with the commander in chief. "All is clandestine," the message said. "Do not use the [satellite telephones]. *Saludos*, Jorge." Torres speculated that César jumped at the chance to be recognized by Cano: "The arrogant César, like a mouse in a trap with cheese, had bitten the most tantalizing piece of all. Finally, the high commander of the FARC would recognize his work." César's reply to the invitation came quickly: "Agreed. *Saludos*, César."

Unfortunately for César, the message that he was to hold court with Cano—and all of the other messages that he'd received since May 31—were not from his superior commander, Mono Jojoy, or from anyone else in the FARC. Unbeknownst to César, he had been taking orders directly from the Colombian military. What neither César nor Mono Jojoy knew was that a small team of Colombian intelligence officers had intercepted their communications and broken their code. The guerrillas believed that they were communicating with each other, while all the time they had been communicating directly with impersonators from the Colombian military who had learned to mimic Mono Jojoy's and César's radio operators' tones and voices. In the nearby mountains, on a day when there wasn't communication between the two camps, the team had seized the opportunity to contact

César's camp and using an impostor radio operator tell him that they would be changing the radio channel and the designated time to transmit. César obeyed the order. From then on, César's radio operator, India, was communicating with a fake radio operator pretending to transmit messages from Mono Jojoy. Another intelligence officer impersonating India continued the usual communications with Mono Jojoy's camp.

The groundwork for what would become an ingenious military deception had been conceived far in advance, with an exemplary shift in the way the Colombian military began to approach their war against the FARC. In July 2006, Juan Manuel Santos, Colombia's newly appointed defense minister, began to transform Colombia's military through a combination of information sharing among the forces, a focus on military intelligence, and incentives meant to increase FARC desertions. In 2008, a *Semana* magazine editorial gave kudos to Santos for the successful shift: "If Plan Colombia has helped in the technological and logistical modernization of the defense sector, Santos has contributed in a significant way to modernize the thinking of the military and its war doctrine. . . . One of his best moves was to seek Israeli advisors who would help identify the missing link in intelligence, that is, to connect the information with tactical operations and to modernize the methods and procedures in decision making. Santos put the advice in practice with an elite group of special operations forces with the capacity to infiltrate in the jungle for weeks." Santos also sought out advice from the British Secret Intelligence Service.

"What has worked against the FARC the best has been encouraging the demobilization of rank and file guerrillas and actually using people in intelligence to find and pressure the leaders," said Adam Isacson. "Instead of these massive, scorched earth, 18,000 troops-in-the-jungle offensives, are these smaller, cheaper efforts. In the last year or two, as far as counterinsurgency goes, the Colombians have done way better than anything the United States has tried in Iraq or Afghanistan. Defense Minister Juan Manuel Santos has been pushing for this. And this is the stuff that's yielding the most results." In fact, on February 16, 2008, a superclandestine Colombian commando team specially trained to remain unsupported for a month in the jungle would actually see

Stansell, Gonsalves, and Howes and several other hostages bathing in a river in the department of Guaviare. Juan Carlos Torres wrote in *Operación Jaque* that after four days, the guerrillas moved the hostages out of the area and the troops lost their trail. (It was rumored that U.S. Special Forces troops were also involved in the mission. However, a source inside SOUTHCOM says that there were never any American troops on the ground.)

When it came to figuring out creative ways to beat the enemy, Santos gave those under his command a wide berth. He was very fond of a line that he recited to his intelligence troops over and over: "Think the unthinkable." The midlevel intelligence officers took Santos at his word, and their out-of-the-box thinking resulted in an idea that would morph into Operación Jaque (Operation Check, as in chess). The idea was to corner the FARC hostage captors through a series of subversive moves. It was fervently hoped that the guerrillas would release the hostages, believing this was a legitimate handover sanctioned by the Secretariat. And to do so, the mission would be made to look nearly identical to the operation that freed Clara Rojas and Consuelo González de Perdomo. By June 29, 2008, the highly secretive military operation, under the guise of an international humanitarian organization, neared its D-day. In an office building in Bogotá, Misión Humanitaria Internacional prepared for the ultimate ruse. A group of intelligence officers pored over images from the previous two Venezuelan-led humanitarian missions. The Colombian team consisted of majors, lieutenants, a military medic, a nurse who had no former military intelligence experience, and a former guerrilla who had deserted from the FARC many years earlier. They prepared for their roles as sloppily dressed and whiskered humanitarian workers, members of a pushy Venezuelan television crew, an Italian delegation leader, an Arab Red Cross worker, an Australian with bleached-blond hair who spoke no Spanish, a doctor, three nurses, and two guerrillas. In the weeks leading up to the operation, each of the participants developed his or her character by creating false life histories. They changed physical characteristics such as hair color and facial hair, found the best costumes and props, developed foreign accents, and erased all traces of military training from their speech and physical demeanor. The team members also took a crash course in acting and improvisation at a Bogotá drama school. On the Tolemaida military base, four helicopter pilots and four crew members were instructed that they were to prepare to play the roles of civilians in a special humanitarian mission, but they were told nothing more. Within three days, the exteriors of two Russian Mi-17 military helicopters morphed into replicas of those used in the earlier Hugo Chávez–sponsored missions: a shiny white exterior with bright orange trim and the logo of the imaginary humanitarian organization.

On June 29, the fake Mono Jojoy radio operator sent César another message: "Wednesday at eight o'clock in the morning, await communication as the situation develops in the same coordinates that you had established on the twenty-fourth. A cameraman will come. . . . Coordinate with the helicopters on VHF in the frequency 174300. Extreme security measures and only what is necessary. *Saludos*, Jorge."

Since the kidnapping of Howes, Stansell, and Gonsalves, President Uribe had promised the U.S. government that he would seek its approval prior to any military rescue. At first, some of the mission organizers considered it unnecessary to inform the United States of the top secret mission, since it deviated from a typical combat rescue operation and the team did not plan to use weapons of any kind. But in mid-June, members of the U.S. military in Colombia (who, under Plan Colombia, worked to collect intelligence on the FARC) intercepted messages between César and his subordinates. On June 17, the Americans asked Colombian army officials if they knew anything about César's movements of the hostages. They received no response. "But the questions didn't stop," wrote Torres. "The gringos knew that something was cooking in the jungle and they wouldn't drop the subject." Defense Minister Santos became concerned that the Americans might unintentionally sabotage the operation during their own intelligence gathering. On June 18, when Santos finally told President Uribe of the pending mission, Uribe insisted the details should be shared with the Americans.

Upon hearing the plan, William Brownfield, the U.S. ambassador, who had been posted in Colombia since September 2007, was concerned. He had been much more interested in finding a less risky solution than a rescue. At the February 2008 meeting with Northrop Grumman, Brownfield had assured the hostages' families that he would do anything he could to ensure the men's safe return—including going beyond the bounds of what the U.S. government would publicly sanction. But after learning the details of Operación Jaque and securing permission from Washington to go ahead, Brownfield agreed to the mission. "We took a deep breath," he told *The Washington Post*, "and said, 'Proceed.'"

The Americans offered technical support for the operation, and a team of embassy personnel (who'd been working on plans for recovery and reintegration of the hostages since March 2004) prepared for the possibility of a rescue. A video recorded by the Colombian military documenting the mission shows three men who appear to be American civilian contractors installing communications equipment in the helicopter crews' helmets. Another microphone placed in the video camera of the "Venezuelan cameraman" would permit the pilots to listen to everything that was happening on the ground. If something went awry, plan B would come into play. The helicopter crew would call to nearby army, navy, air force, and National Police troops, who would surround the area and pressure César to negotiate. It was hardly an ideal plan, and one with very little possibility of success. No one wanted plan B to be implemented.

The Operación Jaque helicopter was scheduled to depart from the Tolemaida military base on July 2, but a forecast of stormy weather caused the team to move the helicopters from Bogotá over the Eastern Cordillera a day earlier to a remote, carefully chosen campesino ranch in the department of Meta, in central Colombia. A final send-off from Gen. Mario Montoya, the Colombian army commander who'd overseen the entire operation, encouraged the team. Torres wrote that although all of the team members were committed wholeheartedly to the mission, they couldn't help but worry that they, too, might end up as hostages of the FARC, or be killed if the operation was compromised. The helicopters carrying the eleven-member "commission" and eight-person flight crew lifted off and flew into the thin air above the mountain range. After landing in a clearing near the farmhouse, the team quickly covered the helicopters with camouflage green tarps. They ate a dinner of roast chicken and beef, chatted with the campesino family that lived in the house, reviewed their roles over and over in their heads, and fought off an army of mosquitoes the likes of which they'd never seen. Less than one hundred miles away, Betancourt, Howes, Gonsalves, Stansell, and the other hostages spent the night together in a large room of what one of the guerrillas had told Stansell was an old whorehouse. Lying on mattresses for the first time in a long while and listening to the radio, the hostages pondered what was to come. "Until well past dark," Stansell wrote, "we chattered excitedly like kids at a sleepover."

A little before midnight, the Operación Jaque team members were falling asleep when a Black Hawk helicopter noisily arrived. Its crew had special instructions for the group. Less than twenty-four hours before the mission was to commence, César had sent a message requesting that a total of six guerrillas accompany the hostages to what he thought would be Alfonso Cano's camp. The Operación Jaque mission commanders were worried that without weapons in the helicopters, the situation could turn ugly and the six guerrillas might overtake them. The team decided that to prevent César from being able to take the others on board, only one of the helicopters would land. With a maximum capacity of thirty, there would be room only for César, one of his subordinate commanders, the nine team members, the four crew members, and the fifteen hostages.

The unexpected change turned out to be fortuitous. The second helicopter would hover above the site, and in the case of clouds or bad weather, it would provide a clear communication link from the helicopter on the ground to a U.S. platform airplane monitoring from forty miles away. A Colombian military source who was part of the mission says that the helicopter pilots were to speak in code because the FARC would almost certainly be listening to their communications. "The second helicopter was also important to ensure the deception," says the source. "Because in the other liberations, there were always two helicopters, and the terrorists were expecting two helicopters."

Skies were clear on the morning of July 2, but the Operación Jaque team knew that at any moment, a procession of black clouds could obscure the landscape. They ate breakfast and received orders to prepare. The mission would begin in a few hours, and although they had rehearsed every step again and again, a frantic atmosphere pervaded their preparations. All dressed in the clothing of their respective role: Pilots donned matching beige jumpsuits; "delegates" wore vests with the Misión Humanitaria Internacional logo on the back; the "journalist" and "cameraman" wore red T-shirts and black vests adorned with the logo of Hugo Chávez's television network, Telesur; the "guerrillas" dressed in black T-shirts emblazoned with the popular revolutionary image of Che Guevara; and the "Arab delegate" wore a Red Cross bib over his shirt. (After the mission, the use of the Red Cross symbol in a military operation elicited criticism from some humanitarian organizations.)

The morning began stressfully for the Colombian intelligence agents, who were stationed on a mountain post, impersonating the guerrilla radio operators. Because of interference caused by bad weather, a final message to César was significantly delayed. Finally, the message reached him. "The head of the commission is a Señor José Luis Russi. . . . *La carga* should go tied up. We are waiting here for you to tell us when they arrive. *Saludos*, Jorge." At 12:30 p.m., the team received word; they peeled tarps off the helicopters, loaded in, and the operation took off.

Nearly forty-five minutes later, among acres of waist-high coca bushes, the hostages waited with great speculation. Earlier that day, Betancourt had heard that the hostages were going to be taken to another front. One of the hostages mentioned to Betancourt that they should hijack the helicopter to avoid being taken to another hostage camp, after which Betancourt secretly handed him her scissors and nail clippers. Once again, the guerrillas gave the hostages new clothes— T-shirts that said, ¡SÍ AL ACUERDO HUMANITARIO!—YES TO THE HUMANITARIAN EXCHANGE! Again, they refused to wear them.

As the helicopters approached, the hostages became even more unnerved because the guerrillas forced them to hurry *toward* the helicopters, while for so many years they'd been made to run and hide when they'd heard any aircraft overhead. "Keith and I stood frozen, weighing our options. Nearly everything in me said to run, but something held me back," wrote Gonsalves. "Maybe it was just the idea that as far as we knew, the FARC had no helicopters. Whoever was coming in would likely be better than the guerrillas."

As the Operación Jaque team hovered above the scene, there was a moment of panic with the mission crew, as well. All of the hostages were supposed to be in white T-shirts so that they could be easily identified, which is why they had ordered César to have the shirts made and to have the hostages wear them. Now, from above, the mission commanders couldn't even tell if there *were* hostages on the ground. Torres wrote that the helicopters made three circles and called by radio to the guerrillas, who were supposed to give them an okay to land, but they couldn't raise the guerrillas on the radio. With great trepidation, the Misión Humanitaria Internacional team decided to land.

The helicopter carrying the crew touched down at 1:15 p.m., while the second helicopter hovered a few thousand feet above. Dozens of armed guerrilla troops stood threateningly in two rows and watched with interest as the people dressed as humanitarian workers and Telesur journalists began to disembark. César and Enrique, who were dressed in civilian clothes, carefully approached the strange-looking foreigners, but they relaxed when they saw two "guerrillas" in Che Guevara T-shirts who addressed them with a common guerrilla greeting: "What's up, comrade?" César also felt confident, he said later, "because the helicopters looked just like those used when the Venezuelan commissions came to pick up the other hostages." As soon as they were off the aircraft, the "Telesur" team approached César for an interview. He relaxed, thinking he recognized one of the journalists as the person who had covered hostage releases in the past. "I thought he was the journalist that wrote a book about the guerrillas, Jorge Enrique Botero. And when I saw him, he looked just like the journalist, so I felt confident." In his best impersonation of a pushy television reporter, one of the creators of Operación Jaque went immediately to César and said, "Can we ask you just one question?" César protested. In the scene being shot by the imposter cameraman (the entire mission was actually being recorded and the video was later released by the authorities), César says coyly, "It's not my place to make statements. No, we will talk in the helicopter." The video shows César with a wide grin that exposes a row of perfect white teeth under a thick black mustache. The guerrilla commander didn't seem at all nervous: he just appeared tickled to be the star of the show. The fake reporter kept insisting, "Just one question. Just one question." César again said that he didn't want to give an interview.

Then he told the person he thought was the delegation leader to bring the humanitarian team inside one of the houses to have a drink. The leader was thinking of how to handle César's invitation, knowing that it could put them in a dangerous position, when India, César's radio operator, came running with an urgent message, which she said was from Mono Jojoy: They had to get the helicopters and hostages out immediately. The men pretending to be the reporter and the cameraman distracted the guerrilla troops with their filming while the remaining participants talked with the hostages and tried to get them ready to board the helicopter. But convincing the hostages to go with this strange crowd was not as easy as the team had anticipated. The hostages, having been hardened by all of the FARC's games, did not want to go, especially when the supposed humanitarian workers said that they were going to have to handcuff them before they got on the helicopter, something that concerned the guerrillas as well. "That got César's attention," says attorney Rodolfo Ríos. "He said, 'Why do the members of the Cruz Roja Internacional [International Red Cross] have to tie them?' He asked one of the foreigners, 'What's going on here? Why do they tie their hands?' Then the foreigner told him, 'This is the routine procedure of the humanitarian action.' So César said, 'Oh, okay, then.' "

The man pretending to be the Australian delegate tried to move the Americans away from the others so he could speak to Howes in English. "Are you U.S. Army?" Howes asked the blond man with the strange accent. The man knew that what he was about to say could jeopardize the entire mission, but he knew if he didn't act quickly, the Americans would refuse to get on the plane, so he answered in a whisper, "We're Colombian army." Immediately and loudly, Howes said, "Okay, we're going," and agreed to be handcuffed with the plastic ties. Stansell wrote: "I could hear Tom's voice above the engine noise: 'Everyone just be calm and cooperate. This is just a precaution. Get in the helo quickly so that it doesn't burn too much fuel.' " The video shows the team's "nurse" and some guerrillas securing the hostages' wrists with plastic zip ties—a necessary precaution they'd decided on to prevent the hostages from making an attempt to take down the helicopter before the rescuers could reveal who they were.

Inter Press Service reported that at first César protested leaving his guerrilla unit and wanted another guerrilla to go in his place. But the two "guerrillas" with the mission reassured him that Alfonso Cano needed him: "Okay, Commander, the idea is that you come with us; you are in charge. You are the person that the superiors need. The Secretariat needs to talk to you." It was apparent that César had chosen his second in command, Enrique, to accompany him on the trip. As the two boarded the helicopter, the crew members knew that the guerrillas were always armed and that it would be imperative to take their guns away. "You can't bring any weapons in the helicopter. This is a humanitarian action," one of the crew said, pointing at a sign that had just been made days before showing a machine gun in a red circle with a line through it. "You have to leave your guns. . . . Give them to us. The pilot will keep them." Enrique reluctantly handed over his 9mm pistol. César removed a weapon from his backpack and relinquished it to the crew. Just before departing, a member of the crew stepped out of the plane and set two cases of beer on the ground as a gift for César's troops, who stood watching. Moments later, the helicopter lifted off. The entire mission on the ground had lasted only twenty-two minutes.

One of the guerrillas was videotaping as the helicopter flew overhead, carrying their commanders, César and Enrique, to what they believed would be a meeting with FARC high commander Alfonso Cano. On the video, one guerrilla, seemingly unconcerned that anything is awry, remarks, "The comrades have left, man." The video (which was later obtained and broadcast by an independent Colombian television station) shows the conversation quickly turning to the cases of beer left by the fake aid workers. A female voice off camera happily says, "You know what he said to me, the guy from the Red Cross? He said, 'Take this as a little gift. Good-bye, comrades!' "

Almost immediately after the helicopter lifted off, one of the team members grabbed César in a choke hold and repeatedly slammed his head into the fuselage. César, fighting him off, tried to get up. "César was hoping to rush the cockpit, tackle the pilot, and make the plane crash," says Rodolfo Ríos. "And at that moment they started hitting him. He was knocked out by a slew of fists from the crew." Gonsalves was sitting directly across from César with his hands and feet bound. "I did notice that Keith had broken his binds off," Gonsalves told CNN, "and all I saw was a scuffle right next to Keith. . . . I got up, tried to get up to get to Keith because the scuffle was right next to him, and I wanted to try to keep him out of it . . . in the chaos and excitement, I couldn't move, I was tied." Several of the hostages, including Stansell, joined the melee and attacked César, while Enrique was subdued in the front of the aircraft. The man playing the part of the doctor grabbed a hypodermic needle and jabbed it into César, who was unconscious seconds later. "One of the aid workers grabbed me, kind of put his arms around me and put me down, and he said, 'We are army. We are army.' And that's when I found out I was free," said Gonsalves.

All of the hostages reacted with euphoria and disbelief. "It was like somebody just released from a tar pit," said Thomas Howes. "You're just suddenly free. I was dazed by it. The second thing I thought was, Man, I'm in a Russian helicopter. I hope this damned thing doesn't crash, because I want to make it through to enjoy this freedom." For a moment, Gonsalves thought he was dreaming because he'd dreamed of freedom so many times. "And to think that, to actually think that it was going to happen, it was difficult to take it in." There were exclamations of joy, euphoric shouts, hugs, laughter, and sobs. Betancourt was afraid the helicopter would crash from all the jubilant jumping up and down, and she tried in vain to calm the others, "Be still! Calm down! Sit down!" she yelled at them, praying to God that they wouldn't fall from the sky.

An hour later, the helicopter landed at the military base in San José del Guaviare. The mission team members jumped off the helicopter as a jubilant General Montoya, the commander of the army, hugged each of them as they ran from the helicopter to an awaiting plane. "Mama, I'm alive! I'm free! Mama, the army rescued me," said Betancourt, speaking to her mother by phone for the first time in nearly six and half years. Marc Gonsalves, Keith Stansell, and Thomas Howes were immediately flown to Bogotá and welcomed by Ambassador Brownfield and a group of U.S. military personnel, contractors, and intelligence people before being transferred to a U.S. Air Force C-17. Several hours later, they headed to Lackland Air Force Base, in Texas, and then were transferred in a Black Hawk helicopter to the Brooke Army Medical

Center, in San Antonio, where they were to be "reintegrated" with their families. The newly freed Colombians headed to Bogotá and stepped off the plane to be enveloped by their family members amid the collective euphoria of millions of Colombians who followed every detail of their homecoming by radio and television. "Thank you, Colombia! Welcome to freedom!" shouted one of the newly freed hostages to an ecstatic crowd of well-wishers and members of the media.

One of the few Colombian journalists who missed the celebration was Jorge Enrique Botero. The previous day, on July 1, Botero was in the United States, where he'd had the second of what he believed would be several meetings with New Mexico's governor, Bill Richardson. Richardson had already met with Hugo Chávez in Venezuela and expressed interest in helping find ways to achieve a diplomatic solution to the hostage crisis. Botero was thrilled because Richardson was by far the highest-profile politician to show a real interest in the case, and obviously a heavy hitter in international diplomacy. In fact, Richardson's Web site for his presidential campaign offered a publicity page touting his prowess in the field of hostage crises: "Bill has gone toe-to-toe with some of the world's toughest characters—Saddam Hussein, North Korean generals, Burmese military leaders, Sudanese President al-Bashir and Fidel Castro—to name a few. Presidents, Secretaries of State, and Prime Ministers soon came to know Bill as the go-to guy for tough hostage negotiations." Botero figured if Richardson had dealt with Saddam Hussein, he would have no problem with the FARC Secretariat. "I asked if he would be open to having a meeting with the guerrillas, and he said he would," says Botero. "He said that Tom, Marc, and Keith were his countrymen, that he had done this in other countries, and that he was ready to go to Colombia."

On his way back to Washington, D.C., the following day, Botero got a glimpse of a news report on one of the airport television monitors. "I thought, What is this? What is this? Ingrid Betancourt with [Minister of Defense] Juan Manuel Santos? How strange." Botero thought he was watching archival footage, since there was no sound on the television monitor, so he boarded his flight without knowing what had happened. When he landed, he was greeted by a colleague who informed him of the rescue. To Botero, the feeling was surreal. "Imagine it; I had been following this topic for so many years. I felt happiness, of course—that was my first sensation—that more people recovered their freedom, but I was also beside myself for not being in Colombia." That night, Botero kept a planned dinner meeting with Gary Noesner. The two men had initially planned to meet and discuss new strategies for the case. Instead, they celebrated. "I remember that we were all very happy. We cheered, celebrated," says Botero. The two men spent the evening speculating about how the rescue had been pulled off. Noesner was absolutely positive that someone—a guerrilla on the inside—must have been paid off. Botero was not so sure. For Noesner, the longest hostage case he had ever worked on had finally come to a flawless ending. "Gary was euphoric," says Botero, "as if a nightmare he had lived with for so many years had finally vanished."

Earlier that same afternoon, the two guerrilla commanders who had inadvertently lost their freedom by stepping onto a Colombian army helicopter sat on the grass, back-to-back in their underwear, coming out of a drug-induced haze. César told attorney Rodolfo Ríos that when he awoke, "he tried to understand what was happening, but he was very groggy, and he was a beaten mess." The military commander at the campesino ranch from which the team had departed that morning ordered the zip ties to be removed from César's and Enrique's feet. "I asked them how they felt, and they said that they were tricked," says the commander. "César told me that he really swallowed the story. He and Enrique looked like two people who were totally deceived."

The stunningly flawless rescue operation caused much speculation in the days, weeks, and months that followed. No one could quite understand how it had been pulled off—including the two guerrillas who sat in a Colombian jail, having already been indicted by the United States. In the jungle, the FARC Secretariat, enraged by their stunning loss at the hands of the military, immediately released an official statement condemning César and Enrique for treason: "The escape of the 15 prisoners of war last Wednesday, July 2, was the direct result of the despicable conduct of (Gerardo Aguilar) 'César' and (Alexander Farfán) 'Enrique,' who betrayed their revolutionary principles and the confidence placed in them."

When defense attorney Rodolfo Ríos came to meet César with the idea of possibly handling his case, he brought a copy of the FARC communiqué. "I noticed that he was so sad. He felt a lot of pain when the FARC made those comments," Ríos says. "He stood up and told me, 'I want you to tell the comrades of the FARC, I want you to tell the Colombian Communists and the world, through the media, that I'm a complete revolutionary. I am a convinced Communist. I am a man who's not easily fooled. And I have not betrayed the FARC.' He was trembling and tears almost appeared in his eyes. He said, 'Look, I am a guerrilla fighter, I am an ideologue, I am a politician of the FARC. Not yesterday, nor today, nor ever will I give up the FARC, nor will I give up the political fight.' "

20

Reintegration

On July 7, 2008, after five days as part of a reintegration program run by the U.S. military, Marc Gonsalves, Keith Stansell, and Thomas Howes emerged in front of a packed crowd of journalists and soldiers at the Brooke Army Medical Center in San Antonio, Texas. Bright yellow bows decorated each isle and the podium at the center of the auditorium stage. At the press conference, which had been dubbed a "yellow ribbon ceremony" by the military brass, Gonsalves stood flanked by Stansell and Howes and proudly held up a small American flag. In the first three rows, several dozen soldiers dressed in desert fatigues cheered and applauded. The tall, graying Stansell, although much thinner than before his capture, was still a remarkable presence. Turning around and pointing to an enormous flag behind him and choking back emotion, Stansell addressed the audience of soldiers, journalists, and the men's family members and began by thanking the United States of America, "who never forgot me, *never.*" Reporters in the audience scribbled notes and took photos. A dozen television cameras lined the back of the room. Several journalists who had learned about the story only five days earlier whispered questions to colleagues about the case but got mostly shrugged shoulders. The three former hostages took turns speaking to the crowd. While Howes and Stansell made brief statements, Gonsalves—in a lengthy and politically charged speech, which he read in both Spanish and English—described the horrific five and a half years that the three men had spent under the control of the guerrillas. "I want to send a message to the FARC: *FARC, you guys are terrorists. You deny that you are. You say with words that you're not terrorists, but your words don't have any value. Don't tell us that you're not terrorists. Show us that you're not terrorists.*" Gonsalves continued in a soft but resolute voice: "They say that they want equality, they say that they just want to make Colombia a better place, but that's all a lie."

For Maj. Gen. Keith Huber, who was the acting head of the U.S. Army South (the army component of SOUTHCOM), the positive press surrounding the release of the Americans was a windfall rarely seen by the U.S. military, and Huber squeezed out every ounce of publicity he could, while completely confining the men from actual media contact. The day before the yellow ribbon ceremony, Huber held his own press conference, beaming as he told reporters, "I will tell you that

Keith Stansell reunited with his family at Brooke Army Medical Center, San Antonio, Texas, days after his rescue from five and a half years of captivity. Photo: U.S. military.

they greeted me with a strong handshake and clear eyes and an incredible smile. . . . On the tail end of their first private reunion in five years and five months, I can tell you that it made us all very proud—that there were children there who were thrilled to see their parents, and there were parents there who were overwhelmed with seeing their son back safe," Huber said. "At the human dimension level, that's what we're all here for."

The yellow ribbon ceremony was held without allowing any questions from reporters, and the men's families were shielded from the press by FBI and army escorts. Satellite trucks from every major station sat in the parking lot while producers from CNN's *Larry King Live*, CBS News, and ABC vied to get the first interview with the men, but they were repeatedly turned away. The U.S. Army South public information officer (PIO) released a handful of photos of family members hugging and dining together during their limited meetings, which were structured parts of the reintegration program. On July 10, the PIO sent out a press release stating that an exclusive interview with the former hostages would be given to a CNN Headline News morning anchor named Robin Meade, a former Miss America finalist, whose show was normally broadcast from CNN headquarters in Atlanta. "At their request, Marc Gonsalves, Thomas Howes and Keith Stansell will conduct a taped interview with Robin Meade of Headline News at 10:30 a.m. today in the U.S. Army South Headquarters at Fort Sam Houston, Texas." Rumors abounded among the network producers that Meade was a personal friend of Major General Huber, hence the amazing scoop for the lightweight news show, *Morning Express with Robin Meade*. The day before, Meade recorded herself in a "Behind the Scenes" video blog as she got ready for the interview, clearly nervous and gushing to a bouncing camera she held. "I'm putting pressure on myself because I want to make them feel so comfortable so they can give us the details and tell us about what they've been through and do justice to their story." In the highly promoted one-hour interview with the three Americans, Meade asked the men about their life in captivity and what type of things had surprised them on their return to a world they'd been absent from for nearly six years.

Journalists clamored for information on what the role, if any, of the

United States had been in Operación Jaque. The U.S. Southern Command released a list of numbers they claimed represented efforts and monies expended by the U.S. military over the five and a half years of the men's captivity.

U.S. SOUTHERN COMMAND LEVEL OF EFFORT ON US HOSTAGES
(kidnapped 13 February 2003—rescued 2 July 2008)

- US Hostages: Marc Gonsalves, Keith Stansell, Thomas Howes
- 1,967 Days held Hostage by FARC
- 3,600 Intelligence, Surveillance and Reconnaissance (ISR) sorties
- 17,000 Flight Hours during 54 operational deployments in Colombia
- 175 intelligence leads
- 6 major Crisis Action Planning events involving 300 DOD and IA* personnel
- 35 full-time personnel with full-time primary SRS** duties
- $50 M spent annually in direct & indirect hostage recovery operations
- $250 M executed since February 2003

* Interagency
** SOUTHCOM Reconnaissance System

"This hundreds of millions of dollars—that is pure bullshit," says Gary Noesner, who had suggested to Northrop Grumman that the men would receive much better care in a private program rather than one sponsored by the military, which he felt was completely exploiting the men and the situation. "They left Tom, Marc, and Keith with an impression that hundreds and hundreds of people were working on their behalf every day. In my mind, the question is, How much of this money was directly related to the recovery of the hostages versus other operational objectives relating to our support of Colombian military operations? If they spent two hundred and fifty million dollars on hostage recovery, then a bunch of people should be indicted for fraud or fired for incompetence." Noesner says that when he first saw the report, "I said, 'Hey, if they'd just spent one million dollars on negotiations, we'd probably have had them out three years earlier.' People in the government would be absolutely shocked to hear me talk like this, because they legitimately believe their own propaganda." SOUTHCOM spokesperson Jose Ruiz defended the figures, saying they could seem misleading because of the many costs associated with hostage-recovery missions.

Contractors working in conjunction with the U.S. Embassy in Bogotá had a similar take on the level of U.S. military effort to secure a release of the hostages during their five and a half years of captivity. "We are not trustworthy as a government," says a colleague who worked closely with Stansell, Gonsalves, and Howes. "Contractors are an easy way for the government to hire someone who can be thrown away without any responsibility to anybody. That's the definition of *contractor* these days." But in contrast to the anger and abandonment that they expressed to fellow hostages while in captivity, in Texas the three men and their families heaped praise on Huber and the U.S. military. In a prepared statement given to journalists and posted on the U.S. Army Southern Command's Web site, the three men expressed their joy at being free, thanked the Colombian government and Colombian military, and offered generous praise to the U.S. government and to those involved in their reintegration program.

"I think the way the military and this General Huber guy controlled the men and their families in San Antonio is scandalous," says Noesner. "But the guys aren't going to protest. Their families think everybody down there [Brooke Army Medical Center] walks on water, so everybody's happy. But the way they set up an interview for these guys I think was very unprofessional, at a minimum. And it was so blatantly self-serving on the part of the military to manipulate Tom, Marc, and Keith so that they would come away feeling a certain way and saying a certain thing about the U.S. government. But it was successful. The government pulled it off. They won. The families and the guys have bought it hook, line, and sinker."

The Pentagon backed off from taking credit for Operación Jaque, with a DOD spokesperson saying only that "the two countries' militaries have a strong relationship that includes 'a certain amount of cooperation and information sharing.' " However, the U.S. ambassador to Colombia, William Brownfield, painted a somewhat different picture in an exclusive interview he gave to *The Washington Post*. "This mission was a Colombian concept, a Colombian plan, a Colombian training operation, then a Colombian operation. We, however, had been working with them more than five years on every single element that came to pass that pulled off this operation, as well as the small bits that we did on this operation," Brownfield said. The *Post* article also reported that "a special 100-person unit made up of Special Forces planners, hostage negotiators and intelligence analysts worked to keep track of the hostages. They also awaited the moment when they would spring into action to help Colombian forces carry out a rescue."

Journalists who called the U.S. Embassy in Bogotá to follow up on the role played by the United States were told that Brownfield would not be doing any more interviews. Noesner believes Brownfield's assessment is highly inaccurate. "If you take away the purely military components that were focused on a rescue, it was probably never more than a handful of people who ever worked this case at any time." And according to Noesner, there was never an FBI negotiator deployed to Colombia to work on the case except for very brief periods.

After the men had undergone a comprehensive medical check, which found them to be in generally good health, and after they had been in the reintegration program for a full week, Huber reportedly ignored the base psychologist, who said the men were ready to return home, and kept them on the base an additional three days. On the day they were to leave, the men were put before the press at another event at the military base. Standing in front of their waiting plane on the tarmac, the three made brief statements about how much they were looking forward to going home but took no questions.

On July 12, 2008, ten days after their rescue, Stansell, Gonsalves, and Howes left the sheltered confines of the military base to begin the process of living as free men. Five and a half years of absence had taken a toll on the personal lives of Gonsalves and Howes. Gonsalves returned to a wife he loved, who had dug him into a world of debt and had no desire to have him home. While he dealt with the real challenges of rebuilding his financial life, Gonsalves worked to reestablish a relationship with his stepsons and his teenage daughter, whom he'd not seen since she was ten. Howes and his wife, Mariana, separated shortly after his release. Only Keith Stansell came back to a complete family, although not the same one that he'd left behind when he was kidnapped. Stansell and Patricia Medina found a house in Florida to share with their twin boys and Stansell's two older children. And on Medina's birthday at the end of July, Stansell's twenty-year-old daughter, Lauren, baked Medina a birthday cake. Medina says, "They gave me a framed photo of our family: Keith, Kyle, Lauren, Nicholas, Keith Jr. [the twins], and me. It was the most meaningful gift for me, and it tells me that we will be together forever." On November 22, 2009, Medina and Stansell were married in Bradenton Beach, Florida.

Several weeks after their release, Northrop Grumman invited Howes, Stansell, and Gonsalves to a dinner in their honor in Maryland. The meeting was a chance for Northrop Grumman executives, as well as others who had worked on the men's case from the private sector, to meet the former hostages. Gary Noesner attended the meeting and was surprised by the men's reaction when the topic turned to Botero. "Jorge's name came up," says Noesner, "and Marc made some very disparaging comments about him. He said, 'Yeah, he was working for the FARC the whole time.' That's when I pulled Marc aside and said, 'No. There's more than meets the eye here, Marc. There's a lot more than you may realize. Botero was actually very helpful to us." Noesner gave Gonsalves his contact information and offered to fill him in on what had happened with regard to their case during the five and a half years of their captivity. Gonsalves never contacted Noesner. On February 28, 2009, Howes, Stansell, and Gonsalves released the memoir of their ordeal, *Out of Captivity*. In the book, they harshly indicted Botero for his interview of them, calling it a "propaganda scheme." "The fact that they came out of captivity with hatred toward me is very logical and normal after everything they lived through with the guerrillas," says Botero, who admits to feeling hurt and upset by the charges, even though he understands their animosity. "The only contact that they had with the outside world was with me. So they want to associate me with the FARC."

Two weeks after the book's release and during their press tour, each of the former hostages received the DOD's Defense of Freedom Medal (the civilian equivalent of the Purple Heart) at the headquarters of the U.S. Southern Command in Florida. At the ceremony, the military once again reiterated all they had done for the men. Again, the men tearfully acknowledged the support of the U.S. government. "You were sending us reminders that you were looking for us," said Gonsalves, describing how he would hear the "buzz" of aircraft engines. "We would look up and try to see it, but we could never see it because it was up so high, and there were just so many trees. But we knew what it was, and that gave us strength to carry on. Thank you for never giving up on us. Thank you for doing everything that you did to bring us home." Howes seconded Gonsalves's sentiments: "You folks are basically my family," he said. "You spent an incredible amount of time trying to get us out and you never forgot us."

For Juan Carlos Lecompte, Ingrid Betancourt's return to freedom was nearly as difficult to comprehend as her captivity had been. After six and a half years, during which the majority of Lecompte's time, energy, and money had been put into searching for a way to win his wife's freedom, Betancourt left him less than twenty-four hours after she was rescued from captivity. Lecompte says that after the two spent her first night of freedom getting reacquainted and discussing all of the things he had done to help free her, "she told me that she wanted to be with her kids because she felt a certain guilt that she didn't see them grow up," Lecompte said. The following day, Betancourt left with the rest of her family for France, where thousands of French supporters and members of the media awaited her. After several days had passed with no word, and it was apparent that Betancourt was not planning on coming back to him, Lecompte, in what he said would be his final interview, told *Semana* magazine, "It's a complicated situation that I'm in. I don't want to have to believe that everything with Ingrid is finished. . . . Her love for me could have ended in the jungle. And what can I do? While she organizes herself, is brought up to date, you have to give things time. I've already waited six and a half years. . . . She knows where I am the day she wants to return. With Ingrid or without Ingrid

I am going to continue in the most natural way I can. And you know what I'd like? For this to be my last interview. I want to remove myself from the grip of the media." In early 2009, it was clear there would be no reconciliation: Betancourt filed for divorce, based on six and a half years of de facto separation.

In October 2008, Simón Trinidad was transferred from the D.C. Jail to a maximum-security prison in Florence, Colorado, to serve his sixty-year sentence. Although exasperated at the idea of a fifth trial, defense attorney Robert Tucker moved to appeal Trinidad's conviction. (In October 2009, the D.C. court of appeals committee agreed that there had been prejudicial evidence used in the trial by the prosecution. However, the committee deemed that it had been harmless to the defendant, and the appeal was denied.) While Trinidad remained in solitary confinement, with almost no contact with the outside world, and Sonia (who said she had no desire to ever return to Colombia or to the FARC) began her sixteen-and-a-half-year sentence in a women's prison in Texas, the movement that they had dedicated their lives to had become a shadow of its former self. After the deaths of Reyes, Ríos, and especially of Marulanda, the FARC ranks felt beaten. Operación Jaque was another major blow to morale.

Official figures released by President Álvaro Uribe's administration seemed to demonstrate that the balance of power had shifted decidedly in favor of the government. In early 2009, Uribe said that the army had caused more than fifty thousand casualties to the insurgent forces since he took office in 2002. The numbers were disputed by military analysts, who argued that if they were accurate, there would be no conflict in Colombia at all. The Colombian think tank Corporación Nuevo Arco Iris reported that between 2006 and 2008, the FARC lost a significant amount of territory and suffered constant desertions. But despite Uribe's eulogy, it also became apparent in early February 2009 that the FARC remained dedicated to continuing their waning revolution. The guerrillas remained powerful in the departments of Tolima and Huila, in central Colombia, and in the northern part of the country. The Eastern and Southern Blocs withstood continuing military strikes. Ex-governor Alan Jara, a hostage held for more than seven years, who was released in February 2009, said, "It's a mistake to think that the FARC is defeated. I witnessed during my seven years that every day more young people joined the ranks."

According to Corporación Nuevo Arco Iris, while desertions were rampant, the majority of those who abandoned the FARC between 2002 and 2008 were found to be recent recruits who had been part of the organization for only three to six months. However, in fall 2008, twenty-eight-year-old midlevel guerrilla Wilson Bueno Largo, known as "Isaza," would become a poster boy for the Colombian government's push to encourage desertions. (If a guerrilla escaped and brought a hostage with him, there would even be a substantial reward.) Isaza had been one of the jailers assigned to guard professor and former Colombian congressman Óscar Tulio Lizcano, who, after nearly seven years in captivity, was one of the FARC's longest-held political hostages. Hearing the government radio campaign offering reward money for deserting with a hostage, the twelve-year veteran guerrilla decided to take the minister of defense up on his offer. In a harrowing escape, Isaza and the sixty-two-year-old Lizcano, who was so weak that he could barely walk, traveled for three days and nights in the jungle before being intercepted by Colombian troops. Defense Minister Juan Manuel Santos made good on his promise, and Isaza received a reported $400,000. French president Nicolas Sarkozy then offered Isaza political asylum in France. The former guerrilla's traveling companion on his flight to Paris was none other than the world's most famous former hostage, Ingrid Betancourt. After touring eight Latin American countries to gain regional support to denounce the FARC, Betancourt was once again returning to France. While she was thrilled with Isaza's desertion and found great symbolism and meaning in the two of them traveling together to Paris, the story got almost no attention in the French media. Over the several months since her heroic homecoming to France immediately after her release, Betancourt's popularity had waned. For the French, there was far less adoration for a free Betancourt than there had been for the hostage. Part of the reason had to do with the fact that Betancourt appeared physically fine upon her release—not close to death, as everyone had thought. She also perturbed the proletariat by allowing herself to be photographed by the upscale magazine *Paris Match* and jetting around the world to meet the pope and several heads of state.

After the July 2008 success of Operación Jaque and the public revelations by former hostages about the brutality of the FARC, the international community rallied around Uribe's fight against Colombia's terrorist insurgency. But several months later, in November 2008, a horrifying truth, long rumored but never so blatantly exposed, would significantly tarnish the image of those seeking to put an end to the guerrillas. A gruesome story emerged that members of the Colombian military had murdered eleven young men and disguised the corpses as those of guerrillas for the purpose of gaining monetary rewards. Civilian recruiters had lured the victims from Soacha, a poor Bogotá slum. Promised quick work and easy money, the men were taken three hundred miles north of Bogotá to the department of Santander. One of the recruiters (who later turned himself in to authorities) says that he was responsible for three of the "deliveries" from Soacha. In late January 2008, the recruiter picked up the young men when they arrived at a bus terminal in the town of Ocaña. He gave them drugs and alcohol in a local bar. Then he took them to a military checkpoint so that the soldiers there could shoot them. The three deliveries earned the recruiter nearly a million pesos (five hundred dollars). The story was exposed when an undertaker handling the bodies (which were reported to him as combat fatalities) became suspicious. None of the men had any identification on them. But most disturbing of all, underneath the guerrilla uniforms that the cadavers wore were the bloody civilian clothes that the men had been murdered in. The family members of the missing men began to investigate their sons' disappearances, and when they discovered what had happened, they made a tremendous public outcry, which was widely covered by the Colombian media and impossible for Álvaro Uribe to ignore. The result was that Gen. Mario Montoya, the head of the Colombian army, who'd long been at the center of several human rights investigations and reportedly had connections with paramilitaries, was forced to resign, along with twenty-seven other army commanders. The resignation came just four months after Montoya had received international praise for his part in the hostage-rescue mis-

sion. The horrific murders exposed a pattern of similar crimes brought
about by a policy within the Colombian military that rewarded soldiers
with money, time off, or promotions for delivering dead guerrillas.
More than fifty civilians were allegedly killed by the Colombian military in extrajudicial executions between January 2007 and June 2008,
according to a 2008 report by the Colombia-Europe-United States
Coordination Group—a number almost twice that recorded during the
previous five years. The U.N. high commissioner for human rights
termed the killings "systematic and widespread" and called for investigations. "Multiple sources report that unlawful killings by the Colombian army are continuing despite efforts by the Minister of Defense to
stop it," Vermont senator Patrick Leahy said in an e-mailed statement
published in August 2008 in the *Los Angeles Times*. "After providing billions of dollars in training and equipment to the Colombian army, we
should expect better, including vigorous investigations and prosecutions of these crimes."

And just as the gruesome revelations were coming to light, Álvaro
Uribe was in Washington, D.C., hoping to land a bilateral free trade
agreement with the United States. Although President Bush gave the
bill a hard sell—"I urge the Congress to carefully consider not only the
economic interest at stake, but the national security interest at stake of
not approving this piece of legislation," he said, calling Uribe a "good
friend"—Congress did not bite. Presidential candidates Hillary Clinton and Barack Obama both said that Colombia needed a better record
on human rights in order to have a free trade deal, and the Senate
majority leader, Harry Reid, added, "Many Democrats continue to
have serious concerns about an agreement that creates the highest level
of economic integration with a country where workers and their families are routinely murdered and subjected to violence and intimidation
for seeking to exercise their most basic economic rights." The bill never
passed.

In the federal prosecutor's office in Washington, D.C., Ken Kohl
readied for a slew of extraditions of Colombian guerrillas to land in federal court. For those connected to the hostage case of the three Americans, landing a conviction would be much easier this time around, since
Gonsalves, Howes, and Stansell could actually go to court and testify as

witnesses for the prosecution. But in a surprising decision in February 2009, the Colombian Supreme Court (which has a final say in extraditions of Colombian citizens) refused to extradite Enrique, the guerrilla who had been the direct jailer of the hostages and who was captured during Operación Jacque. The Supreme Court stated that its decision— "Enrique cannot be extradited on kidnapping and terrorism charges because the crimes for which he is wanted were committed in national territory"—was based on careful consideration of Colombian law and multilateral treaties and could not be appealed. In a seemingly contradictory move in July 2009, the Supreme Court allowed the extradition of César, who had been captured in Operación Jaque and now would face charges of narco-trafficking in U.S. federal court. While the Department of Justice called to expand the charges to include the hostage taking of Stansell, Gonsalves, and Howes, the Colombian Supreme Court refused. Marc Gonsalves was incensed that neither of the captured guerrillas would be tried in the United States for their part in his kidnapping. "How is it that a terrorist who was caught red handed committing crimes against Americans is not going to be extradited to the U.S. to face American justice?" Gonsalves wrote in The Huffington Post. "As a Christian, I forgive [Enrique]; but as a citizen of the world, I want justice."

Also furious was Álvaro Uribe, who accused the Colombian Supreme Court of acting politically in the case of Enrique and of being compliant when it came to the terrorists. Uribe was also at war with constitutional court justices for impeding his bid to amend the Constitution so that he could run for a third term. Even many of those who had supported Uribe in the past felt that his bid to remain in power for another four years was putting democracy at stake. His popularity began to slide, and his approval rating, although remaining high, reached a low point in 2009. In addition, over a third of the members of the Colombian Congress—most of whom were Uribe supporters— were under investigation, on trial, or behind bars for alleged ties to paramilitaries. And by fall 2009, those who had not yet been tried faced charges of "crimes against humanity" after a September Supreme Court decision. The head of the court, Augusto Ibáñez, told reporters. "The Court will study the cases of all persons who had something to do with illegal armed groups, and if any form of support, back up or relation is found, it will be tried as crimes against humanity, according to international standards." Uribe was ultimately denied the right to run for a third term by a February 2010 constitutional court decision.

Because the guerrillas were more paranoid and distrustful than ever after Operación Jaque, Senator Piedad Córdoba's job became even more difficult, but her goal was still to see the remaining hostages freed. In mainstream Colombia, Córdoba faced an increasingly hostile audience. She was publicly heckled and harassed. Once while she boarded an international flight out of Colombia, several passengers aboard began to yell insults and to call out, "Go live in Venezuela with Hugo Chávez!" For those who hated the guerrillas and supported Uribe's hard-line tactics, Córdoba had become a high-profile target. By January 2009, Jorge Enrique Botero, who was still following Córdoba as she bounced from the Colombian jungle to Bogotá to Caracas to Washington, D.C., was suffering from exhaustion and the effects of ceaseless stress brought on by two years of near-constant travel and by being consumed with the difficult topic of kidnapping. But still, there was something that kept him tethered to Córdoba: Botero believed she was the only person who could convince the guerrillas to hand over the rest of the hostages. He had taken so many trips into the jungle to film hostages in captivity, he wanted desperately to film those hostages finding their freedom.

Finally, it looked as though Córdoba had been able to pry open the negotiations, and the guerrillas had agreed to turn over four hostages to her and delegates from the International Committee of the Red Cross. On February 1, 2009, Botero joined the group and boarded a Brazilian military helicopter adorned with giant Red Cross emblems. They landed in an initial meeting place in Caquetá, where they would rendezvous with the guerrillas to organize the handover. The area had been guaranteed by the Colombian government to be free from military activity. Córdoba and a Swiss Red Cross worker were speaking to the guerrillas when the terrifying sound of military jets rattled the cloudy skies. "It was one plane first, then two planes, three planes above us," Botero recalls. "Circling—each time getting closer. Everybody was terrified. The first thing I thought was, Uribe doesn't want this hostage release to happen. Then I thought, They're going to bomb us, but at least I'm going to be able to film this before I die." Botero quickly called in a report to Venezuelan television station Telesur, because he knew that the two major Colombian news stations wouldn't air a report showing the government impeding the handover. Soon after, the guerrillas picked up Colombian military radio transmissions. Botero filmed the guerrillas as they listened to the intercepted message. "Photograph them at the coordinates," the military commander said. "Then do a ground search in that area." The FARC soldiers told Córdoba that they were going to cancel the hostage release. The Red Cross delegate tried to reach the Colombian peace commissioner, Luis Carlos Restrepo, by satellite phone to get him to call off the military, but Restrepo's phone went to voice mail. At the time, Restrepo was holding a press conference at the Villavicencio airport, where journalists had gathered to wait for the hostages' return. The reporters had gotten wind of Botero's live report about the aggressive flyovers, and they demanded answers from Restrepo, who denied any military action was going on in the area. Finally, Córdoba and the Red Cross delegate were able to communicate with Minister of Defense Santos, who called off the military. The planes left the area. Santos later referred to the incident as a simple misunderstanding. In the end, one soldier and three members of the National Police were released to Córdoba.

In a press conference the following day, Uribe was irate that Botero had exposed the flyovers on Venezuelan television. "What's his name? The journalist Jorge Enrique Botero? He was not acting as an observer, but instead he was a *publicist of terrorism*, and that cannot be accepted. One thing is the freedom of the press, and another thing is to use the press pass to become a publicist for terrorism." Botero apologized for not following protocol. He'd been invited to be part of the release as an observer for a nongovernmental organization called Colombians for Peace. "But everyone knew I was traveling as a journalist, as well. I'd arrived in Florencia with all my camera gear, and I'd secured permission to film." Botero was smugly confident that had he not reported on the flyovers, the military would have continued their operations and the hostages would not have been released. Still, he felt Uribe's condemnation like a noose around his neck. For several days, Botero locked himself in his apartment and waited for the storm to calm down. "I believe that Uribe was very irresponsible with his accusations, and I told my children, 'If something happens to me, it will be Uribe's fault.' Some lawyer friends suggested I bring a lawsuit against Uribe in court for slander, but I preferred to keep things quiet and lie low."

While the fate of the remaining Colombian hostages had become internationally uninteresting after the release of Betancourt and the three Americans, Piedad Córdoba continued to negotiate with the FARC for the release of the remaining prisoners. For his part, Botero couldn't help but continue to follow her. There was one hostage in particular whom Botero was determined to see freed—the first hostage he'd ever interviewed in captivity in 2000, a National Police colonel named Luis Mendieta, who had been kidnapped when the FARC attacked his battalion in 1998. "What impressed me so much about him was his serenity and his capacity to keep his men united," Botero says. "It was before the 2001 prisoner exchange, and Mendieta had fifty or sixty of his men who had been kidnapped along with him. He was like a father to them." Botero was also taken with the colonel because he was cultured and sophisticated, but in a very gentle way—something Botero found very unusual for a police colonel. But the thing that made Botero feel most connected to Mendieta was the colonel's family, whom Botero had become very close to while filming the documentary *¿Cómo Voy a Olvidarte? (*How Can I Forget You?*)* about their situation. "They had so much love—the two children, Jenny and José Luis, and the colonel's wife, María Teresa." Botero says that after making his documentary and watching the heartbreaking footage over and over while editing the film, "I had many sleepless nights. For months, I awoke in the middle of the night remembering the images of that family submerged in suffering. I heard the cries of María Teresa when she read the love letters she wrote to the colonel; I saw his children cry [while] remembering their father." Twice more, Botero would receive permission to interview Mendieta in the jungle. The last time would be in 2003, just prior to his interview with Gonsalves, Stansell, and Howes.

"The colonel was destroyed. He'd lost his will to live, his ability to fight. He clung to God with a desperation that he'd never had before," says Botero. At that last meeting, Mendieta gave Botero a letter to give to his family and a religious medallion that he'd been wearing on a silver chain. Botero gave his headphones to Mendieta so he could use them to listen to his radio. Four and a half years would go by before Botero received news of Mendieta. Among a stack of letters brought out by Clara Rojas and Consuelo González de Perdomo in January 2008 was a tragic letter from Mendieta to his wife. The colonel, who had been promoted to brigadier general in absentia, wrote that he was often chained by the neck to other hostages, had chronic chest pains, and was so ill at one point that "I had to drag myself through the mud to relieve myself with only my arms because I couldn't stand up." Mendieta's daughter read excerpts of her father's letter on Caracol Radio in January 2008. The letter from Mendieta and the continuing brutality of the FARC caused a public outcry so great that less than a month later, more than two million people—the largest demonstration ever witnessed in Colombia—came together in Bogotá and other Colombian cities. The call to march against the FARC went viral on the social networking site Facebook, and thousands more joined in cities around the world on February 4, 2008, with a simple and straightforward cry: *"No more FARC!"*

As Botero returned to the jungle in early 2009 to continue reporting on the war and the hostages, he found that Marulanda's ultimate goal for his revolution was still moving forward under the leadership of Alfonso Cano. "From what I have heard personally and from the documents they've produced, the FARC have not renounced the plan to take over the country; they have postponed it—pushed it back," Botero says. "The reality is that Uribe came in and started a huge plan to annihilate them. So they've had to dedicate all of their efforts to defending themselves. But from what I've seen, they are resisting. They are continuing to recruit people." By mid-2009, Botero witnessed an obvious growth in the ranks. "I also saw a push to obtain heavy weaponry, including missiles, weapons to take down planes, high-power armaments and long-range weapons."

On February 3, 2009, Alan Jara, the former governor of Meta (who had been chained to Colonel Mendieta during his captivity), was released to Piedad Córdoba after seven and a half years in captivity. The Colombian government forbade Botero to accompany Córdoba on the mission this time, and instead he waited for Jara to arrive in Villavicencio. "I had tears in my eyes as I watched him come from the helicopter into the arms of his wife and son," says Botero, who had interviewed Jara in captivity and met Jara's family several times. In a press conference two days later, Jara would express his anger toward both sides of the conflict that had kept him captive for 2,760 days. "I think that the President's attitude hasn't helped the exchange and the liberation happen at all. It would seem that President Uribe benefits from the situation of war that the country is living through, and it seems like the FARC likes to have him in power. In one direction or the other, [Uribe and the FARC] aim the same way." Three days after Jara's release, the FARC freed the last politician they held, former assemblyman Sigifredo López, who had been a captive for six years and ten months. López had been held with eleven other lawmakers from the Valle de Cauca assembly. All of his colleagues had been murdered a year and a half earlier when their captors mistakenly thought the Colombian army was attempting a rescue. At the time, López had been chained to a tree as punishment and was missed in the massacre.

With twenty-two military and National Police hostages still on the list of exchangeables, Córdoba and Botero made another trip to Washington, D.C., to try to gain support for hostage negotiations between the FARC and the Colombian government. There was little interest on the part of U.S. lawmakers or the international media. "When the rich people were still hostage, it was an important item, but now that the politicians are free, it is not important anymore," Marleny Orjuela, director of Asfamipaz (an association of relatives of military hostages), told *Colombia Reports*. "The interest of countries like France, Switzerland and Sweden has dropped 80 percent since Ingrid Betancourt was released. We haven't heard from the Betancourt Committees ever since—nor from her." Orjuela said that she had asked for a meeting with the U.S. ambassador to Colombia, William Brownfield, and had been waiting for months but had received no response. Although there was little market for stories about the hostages, there was one specific reason Botero continued his trips to the mountains and the jungle to meet with FARC commanders. "It's because of the colonel," he says. "When Mendieta is free—and I'm afraid he may be the *last* one to be freed—when this happens, I will turn the page. Only then will I be able to close this chapter of my life."

Epilogue

During the 1,967 days that Thomas Howes, Marc Gonsalves, and Keith Stansell remained in captivity, nearly three billion dollars were invested by the U.S. government to fight the war on drugs in Colombia. Four months after their rescue, in November 2008, a glossy State Department brochure titled *Colombia: An Opportunity for Lasting Success* (published to pump up the idea of a trade agreement with Colombia) stated, "While estimates differ, coca cultivation has declined since 2002." The statement could only be interpreted as a twisted analysis of the State Department's own data, since the International Narcotics Control Strategy Report for 2007 (compiled by the State Department) actually reports an *increase* in cultivation every year since 2003. The United Nations found similar trends. In a 2008 survey, coca cultivation in South America was found to be at its highest level since 2001 due to a 27 percent rise in Colombia's crop. The executive director of the United Nations Office on Drugs and Crime, Antonio Maria Costa, called the increase "a surprise because it comes at a time when the Colombian Government is trying so hard to eradicate coca; a shock because of the magnitude of cultivation." The National Drug Intelligence Center, a division of the DOJ, reported that the price for cocaine in the first quarter of 2008 was up by about 22 percent from 2005 and purity was down. Both factors pointed to a decline in the availability of cocaine on U.S. streets. The promising trend was attributed to several exceptionally large cocaine seizures, counterdrug efforts by the Mexican government, increasing intercartel violence in Mexico, and expanding cocaine markets in Europe and South America. No credit could be attributed to any U.S.-Colombia efforts.

Although the empirical data show an absolute failure of Plan Colombia to curb coca cultivation and production, the State Department's 2007 International Narcotics Control Strategy Report, released in March 2008, indicated that the unsuccessful policy would remain essentially the same for 2009 and 2010: capturing and extraditing Colombian nationals, dismantling terrorist organizations and illegal armed groups that run the drug trade in Colombia, and continuing the chemical eradication efforts. The price tag for the 2009–2010 program would be $1 billion.

In February 2009, South American leaders from seventeen countries met in Rio de Janeiro to evaluate western hemisphere drug policies. The Latin American Commission on Drugs and Democracy presented its conclusions in an op-ed piece in *The Wall Street Journal*. "Prohibitionist policies based on the eradication of production and on the disruption of drug flows as well as on the criminalization of consumption have not yielded the expected results," the article said. "We are farther than ever from the announced goal of eradicating drugs." The commission was cochaired by former heads of state Fernando Cardoso of Brazil, César Gaviria of Colombia (who helped bring down Pablo Escobar), and Ernesto Zedillo of Mexico, all of whom were once leaders in the crusade to crack down on the drug trade by using military, law enforcement, and fumigation techniques. The commission also blamed the war on drugs for a litany of dire and costly consequences: "The expansion of organized crime, a surge of violence related to drug trafficking and pandemic corruption among law enforcement personnel from the street level on up."

"Every measure of the coca and cocaine reduction effort indicates failure," says Adam Isacson. "Whether it's the amount of coca being detected, whether it is the tonnage of cocaine being shipped, the percentage that we think we've interdicted, the price of the stuff on the streets here in the U.S., or the size of the addict population. Everything indicates no impact." Alfredo Rangel, a top Colombian security expert and a supporter of Álvaro Uribe, told *Newsweek* in January 2009, "We're capturing more cocaine and heroin than ever before. The bad news is that all that has done nothing." A former U.S. Army veteran and self-described ultra-right-winger who worked closely with Stansell, Gonsalves, and Howes was one of the first to capitalize on the massive influx of U.S. dollars that came with Plan Colombia. "If the drug war goes away, I might be unemployed," he said in a June 2008 interview. "But I think that legalization is the way. It's a lie that the drug war has changed anything. The laws in the U.S. have not changed. The DEA [Drug Enforcement Agency] spends a lot of money. The solution is to legalize and tax drugs in the States and in Mexico. Pablo Escobar is like a Boy Scout compared to the Mexicans."

By 2008, it had become apparent that the illegal drug trade, manifested in a form more brutal and deadly than ever before, had landed on the very doorstep of the United States. Long-problematic drug violence in Mexico dramatically escalated in 2006 when Mexican president Felipe Calderón declared war on seven major cartels by deploying 45,000 soldiers and 5,000 police officers across the nation. In the Wild West city of Uruapan in central Mexico, traffickers tossed five human heads onto a dance floor. In Tijuana, on the border with California, decapitated bodies of soldiers and police turned up in minimarts, and gunmen blanketed neighborhoods with gunfire. Mutilated bodies appeared with written signs taunting rival cartels. In 2009, the ghoulishness reached Hollywood horror film proportions when Santiago Meza López, known as "El Pozolero" ("the Stewmaker"), admitted he'd dissolved three hundred bodies in barrels of lye for Tijuana's Arellano Félix cartel. After his arrest, hundreds lined up with photos of missing loved ones, begging police to ask López if he recognized the faces. Between January 2008 and July 2009, over seven thousand were killed as traffickers fought over territory and smuggling routes and battled often-corrupt military and police forces. Nearly one-third of the killings took place in Ciudad Juárez, on the border with El Paso, Texas. In almost all cases, there were no arrests, no prosecutions.

The violence has not been contained behind the U.S.-Mexico border. In August 2008, in an apartment near Birmingham, Alabama, five men were tortured by electric shock before having their throats slit over a $400,000 debt to a Mexican cartel. Phoenix, Arizona, has become the kidnapping capital of the United States, with nearly four hundred known abductions in 2008 by those tied to the Mexican drug business. And in February 2009, U.S. authorities arrested forty-eight people in California, Minnesota, and Maryland as part of a twenty-one-month investigation targeting Baja California's Sinaloa cartel. In Starr County, Texas, in March 2009, the town sheriff was arrested for taking payoffs from the Gulf cartel as it moved drugs across the border. The U.S. National Drug Intelligence Center believes that Mexican cartels maintain distribution networks or supply drugs in at least 230 U.S. cities. In 2009, Secretary of Homeland Security Janet Napolitano said the Obama administration was considering swarming the border with agents and hadn't counted out the possibility of engaging the military. And while drugs and their problematic counterparts have flowed north, American weapons have poured south. Responding to a report that 90 percent of all arms in Mexico come from the United States, Eliot Engel, chairman of the House Foreign Affairs Subcommittee on the Western Hemisphere, said, "It's simply unacceptable that the United States not only consumes the majority of the drugs flowing from Mexico but also arms the very cartels that contribute to the daily violence that is devastating Mexico."

To tackle the menacing problems emerging from its southern neighbor, in June 2008, the United States began a new chapter of the war on drugs with a costly antinarcotics program called the Mérida Initiative. As with Plan Colombia, much of the $1.6 billion plan for Mexico and Central America will never leave the United States. Instead, the money will go to private U.S. contractor corporations for surveillance software, computers, ion scanners, gamma-ray scanners, satellite communication networks, and other goods and services. A large portion of the first-year budget is for aircraft and includes $104 million to Texatron, Inc., for eight Bell helicopters to transport troops and support counternarcotics missions, $106 million to the Connecticut-based Sikorsky Aircraft Corporation for three Black Hawks, and $10 million for the purchase of three single-engine Cessna Caravans, training, maintenance, and parts "for surveillance of drug trafficking areas and for a wide range of surveillance missions."

In the end, it is the many U.S. defense contractors who are the only clear winners of the unrelenting war on drugs. A 2009 State Department report showed that Virginia-based DynCorp International earned $164 million for fumigation missions in Colombia in 2007—a quarter of all aid intended for Colombia's military and police. The amount was double what DynCorp got five years earlier, in 2002, when it cited in its annual report that a "primary responsibility" of its mission would be to train Colombians to do the work themselves. Maryland-based Lockheed Martin, which subcontracted the SRS missions that Stansell, Howes, and Gonsalves performed, tripled its share over the same four years to eighty million dollars, even as Plan Colombia failed to return its promised results.

In summer 2009, changes were under way in the U.S. government's military relationship with Colombia. In August, Ecuadorian president Rafael Correa expelled U.S. antinarcotics personnel from the Manta military base on Ecuador's Pacific coast, making good on a campaign promise to end ten years of "subordination." The fifteen American troops at Manta were transferred to Colombia, where deals were in the works between the Obama and Uribe administrations to give the U.S. military long-term access to seven Colombian bases. The move created an immediate backlash from several South American leaders. "You are not going to be able to control the Americans," Ecuadorian president Rafael Correa warned Álvaro Uribe during a special summit in Argentina on August 28, calling the act a "grave danger for peace in Latin America." Bolivian president Evo Morales and Argentinean president Cristina Kirchner were also harshly critical. Even the Brazilian and Chilean governments—normally on friendly terms with the United States—called upon Barack Obama to better explain his administration's objectives. The response was predictably hostile from Hugo Chávez, who called the action a "step toward war." The following month, the Venezuelan president returned from a shopping trip to Moscow, where he purchased (with a $2.2 billion loan from the Russian government) the advanced S-300 missile defense system, Smerch missiles, and ninety-two T72-S tanks. A gleeful Chávez pored over diagrams and charts on his television show, *Aló Presidente*, showing off his purchases and addressing the United States and Colombia with a provocative call: "We're ready for you." The U.S. government said that the new arrangement was only to support Colombia's fight against drug traffickers and guerrillas involved in the illegal trade. President Obama (whose administration officially ended the use of the term *war on drugs* in May 2009) accused the detractors of "trying to play up [the use of the bases] as part of a traditional anti-Yankee rhetoric" and assured them that his government had "no intent in establishing a U.S. military base in Colombia." Uribe was under immense pressure at home, including from many of his political allies in Congress, who argued that such a deal needed congressional approval. Uribe staunchly defended the plan: "Securing agreements with countries like the United States, in order for them to help us in the battle against terrorism and drug trafficking, is the best thing for this country."

Throughout the first decade of the twenty-first century, the war on drugs has continued to ignite fervor among its supporters. Billions of dollars have been spent, thousands of people have been killed, and the protagonists, buoyed by the ideal of right versus wrong and ignoring the evidence of failure, continue to push on in search of the absurd: a utopia where drugs no longer exist. The business of illegal drugs continues its course—as it has for decades—stimulated by the law of supply and demand. Like the war on terror, the war on drugs is abstract, difficult to define, and constantly morphing into another form or taking a new path. The battlefield is now global and the possibilities are limitless. And for those who profit from the war on drugs, it has become the perfect war—a war against an enemy that has no ability to surrender.

ACKNOWLEDGMENTS

The creation of this book was an eight-year journey that began in 2002 and would not have come to fruition without the help of many people. We owe a huge debt of gratitude to our agent, Peter McGuigan, at Foundry Literary + Media, who, along with his assistant, Hannah Brown Gordon, read through many drafts of our proposal, offered essential guidance, encouraged us to keep the project alive year after year, and patiently waited for us to come back to him when it was finally ready. We couldn't have done it without you, Peter. Hannah, thank you for dealing with the many details of a book with three authors, for tirelessly answering our questions, and for giving us feedback on many fronts. We also appreciate Foundry's wonderful foreign rights director, Stéphanie Abou. Thank you, Stéphanie, for your invaluable expertise in the international market. To our editor, Edward Kastenmeier, at Knopf: We greatly appreciate that you found the value in this complicated story, even when we all had no idea what the ending would be. Your insight, thoroughness, and probing questions challenged us to dig deeper, to create a work of narrative nonfiction that we are very proud of. You are an incredible editor, and we are honored and fortunate to have worked with you.

Thanks to Tim O'Connell, associate editor, for helping us navigate the complex details of putting this book together over many months. And thank you to Maria Massey, production editor, and Carol Edwards, our copy editor, for your work in assembling our book, for making sure we've dotted all of our i's and crossed all of our t's, and much, much more.

When we initially began to cover the world of hostages in Colombia, César Pinzón, our cameraman on the documentary film *The Kidnapping of Ingrid Betancourt*, introduced us to Jorge Enrique Botero. For that, we owe César a debt of gratitude. This book would have been impossible without Botero's years of travel to the jungle and his coverage of Colombia's civil war. Thank you to our colleagues in Colombia: Mayra Rodríguez, Mauricio Mesa, Humberto Pinzón, Freddy Cusgüen, Efraín Bahamón, and Angela Botero. An additional thanks to Efraín and Angela for your kindness in hosting us on many occasions, and for the hours spent on transcriptions and translations for this book. Many people in the United States shared our desire to raise public awareness about the tragic hostage situation from the outset. Thank you, Richard Plepper, Sheila Nevins, Geof Bartz, Lisa Heller, and Sara Bernstein at HBO; Diana Holtzberg, Jan Rofekamp, and John Nadai at Films Transit International, Inc.; CBS *60 Minutes II*; the History Channel; the History Channel en Español; the Sundance Channel; and Justin Loeber at Mouth Public Relations. We are grateful to you all for working with us to bring the situation further to light.

To all of the people we interviewed for this book, including those whose names we cannot reveal: We are ever grateful for your time, and for the stories, insights, and knowledge you shared with us. An especially generous thanks to Gary Noesner, who not only agreed to be interviewed numerous times for the book but who organized our initial meeting with the FBI, Northrop Grumman executives, and the State Department when we presented them with the proof-of-life video footage of the three American hostages. Your guidance throughout was indispensable.

To Jo Rosano, the first family member to go public about the situation of the American hostages, who continued to reach out to the media throughout the five-and-a-half-year ordeal: Your trust in us to record that first special interview began a journey for us all. We greatly admire your courage, strong will, and unwavering strength.

To Adam Isacson and Sanho Tree, who have worked on Colombian issues for years: Thank you for sharing your expertise with us. Both of you have been invaluable resources. And thank you, Sanho, for working with us at the outset so we could speak to U.S. Congress members about the hostage situation.

Barbara Bruce, thank you for your willingness to read and edit our drafts again and again. Your attention to detail helped us when our eyes were too tired to see the mistakes. Barbara Gray and Lisa Tradup, we thank you not only for being supportive friends but also for your willingness to help us find buried pieces of research, and for your immediate attention to our frantic last-minute requests. Juliana, Alejandro, and Primavera, what would we have done without your help? Thank you for the hours spent on transcriptions, photo research, and general assistance (including reminding your dad to return our calls).

Carlos Villalón and Karl Penhaul, we thank you for your insights, journalistic guidance, and comforting presence in Bogotá. And to Carlos, as well as to Scott Dalton, Claudia Rubio, Felipe Caicedo, and Salud Hernández-Mora: We are honored to be able to include some of your outstanding photographs in our book. Heather Powell Crowder, thank you for your time and generosity in creating our terrific author photos. Hugo de Coloumme, we can't thank you enough for your incredible agility at cutting through red tape, for your language expertise, and for the numerous connections you helped us make. In you we have found a true friend. Tereaz, we greatly appreciate your love and support, which helped us with some of the most difficult challenges in this project.

Thank you, Paul and Alex, for being so understanding of our last-minute travels, trips that extended from days into weeks, and of our unannounced guests, who lived with us for indeterminate periods of time. Your love, support, trusted advice, and encouragement keep us going. To our families, whose love and willingness to lend a hand means more than we can express: Joe and Barb, Paula and Roger, Tim (thank you for all of the flights), Uncle Jim, Evelyn, and Catalina. And to our friends, thank you for standing by us through the many twists and turns

ACKNOWLEDGMENTS

of this long journey, for always inquiring about the current state of the hostages, and for asking if there was anything you could do to help. We love you all.

Words cannot fully express how grateful we are that the long years of captivity are finally over for those who have been rescued or who have escaped. To all of those who are still being held hostage in Colombia, we anxiously await news of your freedom.

SOURCES AND REFERENCES

"Alan Jara: 'In the Jungle, the Time Counts Double.' " Cipcol.org, February 4, 2009. Translation of *Semana* magazine's excerpts from the lengthy press conference given by Alan Jara, former governor, Meta department, Colombia.

Aló Presidente. Venezolana de Televisión, Caracas, Venezuela, June 8, 2008. Youtube.com, June 9 2008.

Alsema, Adriaan. "Paramilitary Links to Be Judged as Crime Against Humanity." Colombiareports.com, September 22, 2009.

"American hostages Rescued with Betancourt." LiveLeak.com, July 2, 2008. Originally broadcast on Caracol TV/CNN.

Americas Research Group. "Chronology of Peace Process in Colombia 1998–2001." Reliefweb.int, February 28, 2001.

Amnesty International. "Colombia / Amnesty International Report 2009"; available at thereport.amnesty.org.

Amnesty International. "Colombia: Paramilitary Infiltration of State Institutions Undermines Rule of Law." Amnesty International USA, November 29, 2006.

Amnesty International USA. "Colombia: Extradition of Paramilitary Leaders Must Not Lead to Closure of Investigations into Human Rights Violations" (press release). Amnestyusa.org, May 13, 2008.

Apuzzo, Matt. "Judge Declares Mistrial in Drug Case Against Colombian Rebel." Associated Press, April 22, 2008.

———. "Jury Deadlocks in Colombian Rebel Trial." poorbuthappy.com, October 4, 2007. Associated Press article originally appeared at news.yahoo.com.

Arango, Carlos Z. *FARC, veinte años : De Marquetalia a la Uribe.* Bogotá: Ediciones Aurora, 1984.

"Así manejan sus finanzas las FARC." Caracol Radio, January 31, 2005; available at www.caracol.com.

"Attacks on the Press 2001: Colombia." Cpj.org, March 26, 2002.

Barrionuevo, Alexei. "Chávez's Promised Hostage Release Fizzles, His Second." NYTimes.com, January 2, 2008.

Beaulac, Paul. Telegram no. 193 to U. S. secretary of state, April 9, 1948; available at www.icdc.com/~paulwolf.

———. Telegram no. 197 to U.S. secretary of state, April 9, 1948; available at www.icdc.com/~paulwolf.

———. Telegram (unnumbered) to U.S. secretary of state, April 9, 1948; available at www.icdc.com/~paulwolf.

———. Telegram no. 190 to U.S. secretary of state, April 9, 1948; available at www.icdc.com/~paulwolf.

Bedoya Lima, Jineth. *En las trincheras del Plan Patriota*. Bogotá: Intermedio Editores, 2008.

Beers, Rand. "Plan Colombia Is Well Worth US Support." *Boston Globe*, July 9, 2001.

Bertram, Eva et al. *Drug War Politics: The Price of Denial*. Berkeley: University of California Press, 1996.

Betancourt, Ingrid. *Until Death Do Us Part: My Struggle to Reclaim Colombia*. Translated by Steven Rendall. New York: HarperCollins, 2002.

Betancourt, Ingrid; Lorenzo Delloye-Betancourt; and Mélanie Delloye-Betancourt. *Letters to My Mother: A Message of Love, a Plea for Freedom*. Danbury: Harry N. Abrams, 2008.

"Betancourt's Running Mate and Fellow Hostage Breaks with Candidate." Laht.com, January 29, 2009.

Boadle, Anthony. "Obama Denies US Creating Military Bases in Colombia." Reuters.com, August 7, 2009.

Botero, Jorge Enrique. *Simón Trinidad, el hombre de hierro*. Bogotá: Random House Mondadori, 2008.

———. *Últimas noticias de la guerra*. Bogotá: Random House Mondadori, 2006.

Bowman, Tom. "U.S. Role Seen in Colombia Hostage Rescue." NPR.org, July 3, 2008.

Brice, Arthur, and Mariano Castillo. "17 Patients Killed in Shooting at Mexican Drug Rehab Center." CNN.com, September 3, 2009.

Bridges, Tyler. "Despite Setbacks, FARC Far from Out." *Miami Herald*, March 9, 2008.

"Bush Sends 150 Soldiers to Search for U.S. Hostages." USAToday.com, February 22, 2003.

"Can Colombia Win the War?" CNN.com, September 30, 2009. *Backstory* sat down with CNN en Español correspondent and Colombian citizen Luis Velez after an embed with the Colombian military.

Cancel, Daniel. "Chávez Agrees to $2.2 Billion Russia Arms Credit Line (Update 1)." Bloomberg.com, September 14, 2009.

"Captured Colombia Rebel Sent Home." BBC News, January 4, 2004.

Cardona, Libardo. "Colombian Rebel Turncoat Claims Betrayal." SignonSanDiego.com, February 20, 2009.

Cardoso, Fernando Henrique; César Gaviria; and Ernesto Zedillo. "The War on Drugs Is a Failure." *Wall Street Journal*, February 23, 2009.

Carlin, John. "Revealed: Chávez Role in Cocaine Trail to Europe." Guardian.co.uk, February 3, 2008.

Carlsen, Laura. "A Primer on Plan Mexico." Americas.irc-online.org, May 5, 2008.

Ceaser, Mike. "Colombia's Efforts Have Rebels 'Falling Apart.'" *San Francisco Chronicle*, April 18, 2008.

Central Intelligence Agency. "Colombian Counterinsurgency: Steps in the Right Direction." Office of African and Latin American Analysis, intelligence memorandum, January 26, 1994; available at www.gwu.edu/~nsarchiv.

———. "The World Factbook: Colombia." Cia.gov, April 23, 2009.

Charles, Robert B. "State Department's Air Wing and Plan Colombia." On-the-record briefing, U.S. Department of State, Washington, D.C., October 29, 2003; available at www.state.gov and at docs.google.com.

"Chávez's Hostage Mission Collapses." Msnbc.com, December 31, 2007.

Chrisafis, Angelique. "FARC Defector Starts New Life in France After Asylum Deal." Guardian.co.uk, December 11, 2008.

"Clara Rojas y su versión del cautiverio." ElPaís.com, January 23, 2009.

"Coca Cultivation in Andean Countries on the Rise, UN Survey Shows." UN News Center, June 18, 2008; available at www.un.org.

"Cocaine Prices in the U.S.A." Narcoticnews.com, October 2, 2009.

Cockes, Douglas C., and Paul C. Hooper. "Concerns Over the Need to Protect Our Professional Credentials and Reputations," letter to Kent Kresa, December 5, 2002.

———. "Northrop Grumman Corporation/California Microwave Systems SOUTHCOM Reconnaissance System Program, Bogotá, Colombia, Safety of Flight Issues Rebuttal Letter to: 'Documentation of Written Warning' letter to Douglas Cockes, Employee #5966—October 24, 2002 [and] 'Documentation of Written Warning' letter to Paul Hooper, Employee #5964—October 24, 2002," letter to James G. Cassady, Roslyn Smith, cc: Douglas L. Tait, November 14, 2002.

"Colin L. Powell Holds News Briefing." Colin L. Powell, U.S. secretary of state, Santiago, Chile, June 9, 2003. FDCH Political Transcripts. Available at lexisnexis.com.

"Colombia: Pastrana Ends Peace Talks, Orders Army to Attack the FARC." STRATFOR Global Intelligence. February 21, 2002.

"Colombia to Pay Ex-Rebel Reward." BBC News, March 14, 2008.

"Colombia Transfers Imprisoned Leftist Rebels Ahead of Mass Release." *International Herald Tribune*, June 1, 2007.

"Colombian Hostage Crisis Ends Bloodlessly." *New Zealand Herald*, July 5, 2008.

"Colombian Rebel Taken to Top Jail." BBC News, January 10, 2004.

"Colombia's Leader Defends Presence of G.I.'s." *New York Times*, February 10, 1994.

"A Compendium of Drug-War Statistics." Cipcol.org, April 14, 2009.

"Conmovedor testimonio de Íngrid: 'Duerme uno en cualquier hueco, tendido en cualquier sitio, como cualquier animal.' " Semana.com, November 30, 2007.

"Countering the Lies Concerning the Escape of the 15 Prisoners of War." machetera.wordpress.com, July 11, 2008.

Daniel, Frank Jack. "Weapons Put Provocateur Chávez Back in U.S. Spotlight." Reuters.com, September 16, 2009.

Davis, Jack. "The Bogotazo." Cia.gov, May 8, 2007. From the CIA's *Studies in Intelligence* 13, no. 4 (1969).

De Córdoba, José, and Jay Solomon. "Chávez Aided Colombia Rebels, Captured Computer Files Show." WSJ.com, May 9, 2008.

De la Garza, Paul, and David Adams. "Military aid . . . from the Private Sector." *St. Petersburg Times*, December 3, 2000.

De La Vega, Garcilasso. *The Royal Commentaries of Peru, in Two Parts.* Translated by Sir Paul Rycaut, Kt. London: Miles Flesher, 1688.

"Declaración y rueda de prensa del Presidente Álvaro Uribe, desde Villavicencio." Press release, February 3, 2009; available at web.presidencia.gov.co.

"Defense Chief in Colombia Resigns." *New York Times*, August 3, 1995.

Del Rosario Arrázola, Rosario, and Juan David Laverde. "La nueva estrategia de 'Cano.' " *El Espectador* (Bogotá), September 27, 2008.

Drug Enforcement Administration, Intelligence Division. "Coca Cultivation and Cocaine Processing: An Overview." September 1993; available at www.druglibrary.org.

————. The Drug Trade in Colombia: A Threat Assessment." U.S. Department of Justice. March 2002.

Dudley, Steven. "Jungle Escape: A Tale of Abduction and Rescue." *Reader's Digest,* March 2009.

"El País Guerrilla." *Cambio,* May 19, 2003, p. 38.

"El poder del guerrillero que entregó al niño Emmanuel." Las Voces del Secuestro, January 7, 2008.

Ellingwood, Ken. "Corruption Hurting Mexico's Fight Against Crime, Calderón Says." Latimes.com, December 10, 2008.

Emanuelsson, Dick. "Entrevista con Lucero Palmera, guerrillera FARC y esposa de Simón Trinidad." Elcorreo.eu.org, September 15, 2005.

Entregas voluntarias desmovilizados del 01-ene al 02-sep-2008. Bogotá: Ministerio de Defensa Nacional, Programa Atención Humanitaria al Desmovilizado, 2008.

Entregas voluntarias desmovilizados segundo gobierno Dr. Uribe del 07-ago-2002 al 02-sep-2008. Bogotá: Ministerio de Defensa Nacional, Programa Atención Humanitaria al Desmovilizado, 2008.

Entregas voluntarias desmovilizados segundo gobierno Dr. Uribe del 07-ago-2006 al 02-sep-2008. Bogotá: Ministerio de Defensa Nacional, Programa Atención Humanitaria al Desmovilizado, 2008.

Evans, Michael. " 'Body Count Mentalities'—Colombia's 'False Positives' Scandal, Declassified." The National Security Archive. January 7, 2009; available at www.gwu.edu./~nsarchiv.

"Entrevista con el comandante Iván Márquez." Agencia Bolivariana de Prensa ABP (abpnoticias.com). February 20, 2008.

Exclusivo: El video de las FARC sobre la operación Jaque. Noticias Uno, Bogotá, Colombia, 2008. Video filmed by the FARC; available at www.noticiasuno.com.

"FARC Communique: 'Warmongers Win.' " BBC News, January 13, 2002.

"FARC Has Offered to Free Betancourt: Uribe." Available at Afp.google.com, June 13, 2008. Originally from AFP.

"FARC Statement Ending Peace Talks, January 13, 2002." Press release, the Center for International Policy's Colombia Program, January 13, 2002; available at www.ciponline.org.

"FARC: 'Terrorists' or 'Belligerents.' " World War 4 Report, January 20, 2008.

Ferro Medina, Juan Guillermo, and Graciela Uribe Ramón. *El Orden de la guerra: Las FARC-EP entre la organización y la política.* Bogotá: Centro Editorial Javeriano, Pontificia Universidad Javeriana, Facultad de Estudios Ambientales y Rurales, Colciencias, 2002.

Fichtl, Eric. "Washington Has Lost Its Way in Colombia." *Colombia Journal,* August 30, 2004.

Forero, Juan. "Ammo Seized in Colombia; 2 G.I. Suspects Are Arrested." NYTimes.com, May 5, 2005.

————. "Colombia Rebels Quitting Safe Havens as Peace Talks Fail." *New York Times,* January 14, 2002.

————. "Colombia's Army Chief Steps Down." *Washington Post,* November 5, 2008.

————. "Deep in the Colombian Jungle, Coca Still Thrives." NPR.org. December 31, 2007. Part 2 of *The Forgotten War on Drugs* series.

————. "15 Hostages Rescued in Colombia." *Washington Post,* July 3, 2008.

————. "From Colombia's Upper Class, Rebel and His Foil Diverged." NYTimes.com, December 20, 2004.

————. "In Colombia Jungle Ruse, U.S. Played a Quiet Role." Washingtonpost.com, July 9, 2008.

————. "Private U.S. Operatives on Risky Missions in Colombia." *New York Times,* February 14, 2004.

———. "South American Leaders Assail U.S. Access to Colombian Military Bases." Washingpost.com, August 29, 2009.

"Former FARC Captive Believes Rebels Will Free All Hostages Soon." ThaiIndian News, June 11, 2008. Originally from IANS.

"Freed Rebel Ruins Hopes of Peace with Call to Fight." Washingtontimes.com, June 21, 2007.

"A Friend to Iran." *Washington Post*, September 10, 2009.

Fundación País Libre. *Estadisticas secuestro a 2006;* available at www.paislibre.org.

Garza, Antonio O., Jr. Message from the ambassador of the United States, *Newsletter from the Ambassador,* Embassy of the United States: Mexico. June 30, 2008.

Gechem Turbay, Jorge Eduardo. *¡Desviaron el vuelo!—Viacrucis de mi secuestro.* Bogotá: Editorial La Oveja Negra Ltda., Quintero Editores, 2008.

Gedda, George. "Powell seeks EU Backing for Common Front on Cuba." Associated Press, June 9, 2003.

Gerth, Jeff. "Management Woes Hobble U.S. Air Fleet in Drug War." *New York Times,* June 13, 1990.

Gonsalves, Marc et al. *Out of Captivity.* New York: William Morrow, 2009.

"Gov. Richardson Is the Candidate Who Can Restore America's Image . . ." Democrats.org, December 27, 2007.

Green, Eric. "U.S. to Offer Reward for Information on Captured Americans in Colombia, State Dept. Developing a Campaign for $5-Million Reward." U.S. Department of State, October 21, 2003; available at www.america.gov.

Griswold, Deirdre. "Behind Stock Exchange/FARC Meeting." Workers.org, July 8, 1999.

Gumbel, Andrew. "Chiquita Banana Company Is Fined $25m for Paying Off Colombian Paramilitary Groups." *The Independent,* March 16, 2007.

Gunson, Phil. Manuel Marulanda obituary. Guardian.co.uk, May 26, 2008.

Hanratty, Dennis M., and Sandra W. Meditz. *Colombia: A Country Study.* Washington, DC: GPO, 1988.

Harrison Narcotics Tax Act, 1914 (full text). DRCNet Online Library of Drug Policy.

Held Hostage in Colombia. Directed by Jorge Enrique Botero, Karin Hayes, and Victoria Bruce. Urcunina Films, 2003.

"High-Ranking Member of Colombian FARC Narco-Terrorist Organization Extradited to U.S. on Drug Charges." Press release, U.S. Department of Justice, March 10, 2005; available at www.usdoj.gov.

"High-Ranking Member of Colombian FARC Narco-Terrorist Organization Extradited to U.S. on Terrorism, Drug Charges." Press release, U.S. Department of Justice, December 31, 2004; available at www.usdoj.gov.

"Hostages to Heroes." Robin Meade interview with Marc Gonsalves, Keith Stansell, and Thomas Howes in San Antonio, Texas. CNN, July 11, 2008.

Human Rights Watch. "Human Rights Watch World Report 2001: Colombia: Human Rights Developments." Available at www.hrw.org.

———. "Statement to the 61st Session of the U.N. Commission on Human Rights: Human Rights in Colombia." Press release, Hrw.org, April 12, 2005.

"I Handed Over More Than 30 Young Men as 'False Positives.'" Semana.com, March 24, 2009.

"Ingrid Betancourt." Interview by Terry Gross. *Fresh Air.* NPR, January 8, 2002.

Internal Displacement Monitoring Centre. "Current IDP Figures," July 3, 2009; available at www.internal-displacement.org.

Isacson, Adam. "Uribe Falls to Earth." Foreignpolicy.com, July 3, 2009.

James, Ian. "Freed Colombian Hostages Relate Ordeal." USAToday.com, January 12, 2008. Originally from AP.

Jarry, Emmanuel, and Estelle Shirbon. "France Renews Contact with FARC Leaders on Hostage." Reuters.com, June 19, 2008.

Joubert-Ceci, Berta. "U.S. Judge Sentences Trinidad to 60 Years." IACenter.org, February 3, 2008.

Kaplan, Robert D. *Imperial Grunts: The American Military on the Ground.* New York: Random House, 2005.

Karch, Steven B. *A Brief History of Cocaine,* 2d ed. Boca Raton: CRC P/Taylor & Francis Group, 2006.

Keen, Col. P. K. Letter to Thomas Howes, July 4, 2003, Bogotá, Colombia.

Keylor, William R. *A World of Nations: The International Order Since 1945.* New York: Oxford University Press, 2008.

The Kidnapping of Ingrid Betancourt. Directed by Victoria Bruce and Karin Hayes. Urcunina Films, 2003. First broadcast on HBO/Cinemax, 2004.

"Kill Them and Let's Get Out of Here: FARC." Semana.com, February 9, 2009.

Kirincich, Elizabeth A. "Letter on Behalf of U.S. Government" to Shane Gonsalves, February 26, 2003. United States Department of State, Office of American Citizens Services and Crisis Management, Washington, D.C.

Kirk, Robin. *More Terrible than Death: Massacres, Drugs, and America's War in Colombia.* New York: PublicAffairs, 2003.

Klare, Michael, and David Andersen. *Scourge of Guns: The Diffusion of Small Arms and Light Weapons in Latin America.* Washington, D.C.: Federation of American Scientists, 1996.

Kraft, Scott. "On the Borderline of Good and Evil." *Los Angeles Times,* April 3, 2009.

Kraul, Chris. "Colombian Military Atrocities Alleged." *Los Angeles Times,* August 21, 2008.

Kruzel, John J. "Colombian Military Rescues Hostages, Including U.S. Contractors." U.S. Department of Defense, July 3, 2008; available at www.defense.gov.

Kushner, Adam B. "The Truth About Plan Colombia." Newsweek.com, January 3, 2009.

Lackey, Sue, and Michael Moran. "Russian Mob Trading Arms for Cocaine with Colombia Rebels." MSNBC.com, April 9, 2000.

"Las cuentas de las FARC." Semana.com, January 30, 2005.

Lecompte, Juan Carlos. *Buscando a Ingrid.* Bogotá: Aguilar, 2005.

Leech, Garry. "Plan Colombia: A Closer Look." *Colombia Journal,* July 2000. This special report originally appeared in *Colombia Report,* an online journal that was published by the Information Network of the Americas (INOTA).

Leonard, Thomas M., and John F. Bratzel, eds. *Latin America During World War II.* New York: Rowman & Littlefield, 2006.

Livingstone, Grace. *Inside Colombia Drugs, Democracy and War.* New Brunswick, New Jersey: Rutgers University Press, 2004.

"Luis Eladio Pérez dice que las Farc liberarán a varios secuestrados." ElEspectador.com, June 9, 2008.

"Madre de Íngrid Betancourt, indignada por difusión de carta de su hija secuestrada." ElTiempo.com, December 1, 2007.

"Major General Keith Huber Delivers Remarks Regarding Americans Rescued in Colombia." Transcript of the statement Huber gave at Fort Sam Houston, San Antonio, Texas, July 3, 2008; available at www.accessmylibrary.com.

Markey, Patrick. "Colombia's FARC Deserters Sap Rebel Army." Kuwaittimes.net, October 30, 2008. Originally from Reuters.

———. "Colombia's Uribe Says FARC Reaches Out on Hostages." Reuters.com, June 13, 2008.

SOURCES AND REFERENCES   293

Marks, Thomas A., *Colombian Army Adaptation to FARC Insurgency.* Strategic Studies Institute, January 2002; available at www.strategicstudiesinstitute .army.mil.

Marosi, Richard. "Families Want Answers from Man Who Says He Dissolved 300 People." Latimes.com, February 8, 2009.

———. "Less Cocaine on U.S. Streets, Report Says," Latimes.com, December 16, 2008.

———. "7 Police Officers Die in Tijuana Attacks." Latimes.com, April 29, 2009.

Marulanda Vélez, Manuel. *Cuadernos de campaña.* The book, published in 1973, is available at www.scribd.com.

McNamara, Martin. "US Considers Intervention in Colombia." Guardian.co.uk, February 23, 2003.

McQuaid, John. "Spy Program Cloaked in Bureaucratic Web." *Times-Picayune,* November 10, 2003.

Meade, Robin. "Robin Meade Expressed." Edition. CNN.com, July 11, 2008.

Menge, Margaret. "Former Hostage Gonsalves Files for Divorce in Key West." *Florida Keys Keynoter,* July 18, 2008.

Merida Initiative, Program Description Reference Document, Mexican Security Cooperation Plan. February 29, 2008. Available at www.wilsoncenter.org.

"Mexico Under Siege." *Los Angeles Times,* March 3, 2009.

Meyer, Josh. "Gun Flow South Is a Crisis for Two Nations." Latimes.com, June 17, 2009.

Michel, Victor Hugo. "Invasión burocrática de EU." Impreso.milenio.com, April 16, 2009.

"Mindefensa confirma la muerte de líder de Farc." Semana.com, May 25, 2008.

Mitchell, Chip. "Special Reports: Untold Stories." Cpj.org, October 20, 2005.

Muse, Toby. "US Troops 'Tried to Smuggle Cocaine.' " Guardian.co.uk, April 9, 2005.

Muse, Toby, and Frank Bajak. "Kidnapper Sends Letter of Apology to Candidate's Family." USAToday.com, April 16, 2008. Originally from Associated Press.

National Drug Intelligence Center. "Cocaine—National Drug Threat Assessment 2009." U.S. Department of Justice, December 2008; available at usdoj.gov.

National Human Development Report 2003: Solutions to Escape the Conflict's Impasse. United Nations Development Program, October 8, 2004; available at www.pnud.org.co.

Negroponte, John D. "Helping Colombia Is in Our National Interest." Bogota .usembassy.gov, May 22, 2007. Originally published in the *Miami Herald.*

Nesvisky, Matt. "Smoking, Drinking, and Drug Use Respond to Price Changes." The National Bureau of Economic Research, September 18, 2009; available at www.nber.org.

Novak, Robert. "Ground the Flying Diplomats." CNN.com. September 25, 2003.

"Nuevo Arco Iris (2): The FARC." Center for International Policy's Colombia Program, December 3, 2008; available at www.cipcol.org. English translation by Anthony Dest. Original article from Colombian think-tank Corporación Nuevo Arco Iris.

Ocampo López, Javier. *Historia Básica de Colombia,* 4th ed. Santafé de Bogotá: Plaza & Janés Editores, 1994.

"Online NewsHour: Colombia's Struggle." PBS.org, October 6, 2003.

Operación Jaque. National Geographic Channel, October 18, 2008.

"Operación Jaque, Parte 1–5." *Noticias RCN,* RCN TV, Bogotá, August 5, 2008.

"Operación prueba de vida." Semana.com, December 1, 2007.

Orozco, Cecilia. " 'La Cruz Roja fue clara: cese total de operaciones militares.' " *El Espectador* (Bogotá), February 2, 2009.

Orth, Maureen. "Inside Colombia's Hostage War." *Vanity Fair,* November 2008, p. 192ff.

Otis, John. "Betancourt No Hero, Say Fellow Former Hostages." TIME.com, March 1, 2009.

———. "Cache of Cash Becomes a Curse / Euphoria Turns to Fear for Colombian Troops Who Discovered a Fortune Hidden by Guerrillas." *Houston Chronicle,* March 28, 2004.

Padgett, Tim. "Chávez's New Diplomatic Defeat." TIME.com, January 1, 2008.

"Paramilitary Demobilization." U.S. Office on Colombia, September 25, 2008.

"Peace Initiatives in Colombia: Dialogues with the FARC." Ciponline.org, August 10, 2007.

"Peace Timeline: 1999." Ciponline.org, February 22, 2001.

"Peace Timeline: Pre-1999." Ciponline.org, February 22, 2001.

Pérez, Luis Eladio, and Darío Arizmendi. *7 años secuestrado por las FARC.* Bogotá: Aquilar, 2008.

"Person of the Year: Juan Manuel Santos." Semana.com, December 22, 2008.

Piette, Betsey. "Colombian Prisoner Wins Second Round in U.S. Courts." Workers.org, March 30, 2007.

Pinchao, John. *Mi Fuga Hacia la Libertad.* Mexico: Planeta, 2008.

Powell, Lee, and Rich Matthews, producers. *Hostages Re-enter Life After Colombian Raid.* Youtube.com, July 3, 2008.

"Powell Says Little Progress on Finding US Hostages in Colombia." Agence France Presse, March 13, 2003.

"President Bush and President Uribe of Colombia Participate in a Joint Press Availability." White House press release, March 11, 2007; available at georgewbush-whitehouse.archives.gov.

President of the Republic. "Statement of President Pastrana Rejecting FARC Offer, January 12, 2002." Press release, Center for International Policy's Colombia Program, January 12, 2002; available at www.ciponline.org.

Proof-of-life video. Bogotá, Colombia, November 30, 2007.

Quinones, Sam. "Phoenix, Kidnap-for-Ransom Capital." Latimes.com, February 12, 2009.

Rabasa, Ángel, and Peter Chalk. *Colombian Labyrinth: The Synergy of Drugs and Insurgency and Its Implications for Regional Stability.* Santa Monica, California: Rand, 2001.

Radu, Michael. "E-Notes: Victory for Colombia, Theater in Caracas." Foreign Policy Research Institute (FPRI), March 25, 2008; available at www.fpri.org.

"Remarks by President Bush and President Uribe of the Republic of Colombia in Joint Press Availability." White House Rose Garden, Washington, D.C., September 22, 2008; available at www.america.gov.

Rescate de Clara Rojas y Consuelo González. Telesur, Caracas, Venezuela, January 10, 2008; available at www.youtube.com.

Richter, Paul, and Greg Miller. "Colombia Army Chief Linked to Outlaw Militias." Latimes.com, March 25, 2007.

Riding, Alan. "In Colombia, Drug Money Talks at the Highest Levels." *New York Times,* July 17, 1988.

Romero, Simon. "Manuel Marulanda, Top Commander of Colombia's Largest Guerrilla Group, Is Dead." *New York Times,* May 26, 2008.

Romero, Simon, and Damien Cave. "Carefully Planned Colombia Rescue Exploited FARC Weaknesses." Nytimes.com, July 4, 2008.

Rueda, Manuel, and Alfredo Cohen, producers. "Anti-FARC on Facebook." Current.com, February 25, 2008.

Rueda, María Isabel. "Juan Carlos Lecompte dice que no descarta que se haya acabado todo con Íngrid Betancourt." ElTiempo.com, July 8, 2008.

Santos, Juan Manuel. "Fuerza Pública propinó el golpe más contundente a las FARC hasta el momento." Ministerio de Defensa de Colombia, March 1, 2008; available at www.mindefensa.gov.co.

———. "Rueda de prensa del ministro de Defensa, Juan Manuel Santos" (announcement of Manuel Marulanda's death—intercepted recordings). Ministerio de Defensa de Colombia, May 25, 2008; available at www.mindefensa.gov.co.

———. "Rueda de prensa del ministro de Defensa, Juan Manuel Santos" (audio file of press conference). Ministerio de Defensa de Colombia, May 25, 2008; available at www.mindefensa.gov.co.

Schmidt, Sharon. Letter to Senator Patrick Leahy, November 14, 2003.

Schmitt, Richard B. "DEA Arrests 175 Mexican Drug Trafficking Suspects." Latimes.com, September 18, 2008.

Scruggs, Richard, et al. *Report to the Deputy Attorney General on the Events at Waco, Texas, February 28 to April 19, 1993.* Washington, D.C.: U.S. Department of Justice, 1993. Redacted version available at www.usdoj.gov.

"Second Senior FARC Rebel 'Killed.' " BBC News, March 7, 2008.

Secretariado del Estado Mayor Central de las FARC-EP. "Comunicado de las FARC-EP." web.archive.org/web/20031217020442/www.farcep.org, February 21, 2003.

———."Comunicado de las FARC-EP." web.archive.org/web/20031217020442/www.farcep.org, February 24, 2003.

———. "Comunicado de las FARC-EP." web.archive.org/web/20031217020442/www.farcep.org, March 2, 2003.

———. "Carta abierta de las FARC-EP a los expresidentes liberales." web.archive.org/web/20031217020442/www.farcep.org, April 27, 2003.

———. "Comunicado de las FARC-EP." web.archive.org/web/20031217020442/www.farcep.org, July 12, 2003.

———. "Comunicado de las FARC-EP, La hora del canje." web.archive.org/web/20041229065054/www.farcep.org.

———. "Comunicado de las FARC-EP." web.archive.org/web/20041229065054/www.farcep.org.

"Senadora Piedad Córdoba en Aló Presidente con Hugo Chavez." *Aló Presidente*, Venezolana de Televisión, Caracas, Venezuela, August 17, 2007. YouTube.com, August 17, 2007.

Sequera, Vivian. "Colombia Says Rebel Leader Killed by Own Chief of Security in Another Blow." Associated Press, March 7, 2008.

Simons, Geoff. *Colombia: a Brutal History.* London: SAQI, 2004.

Smith, David, and Sybilla Brodzinsky. "Stone: My Part in Hostage Baby Saga." *The Observer*, January 6, 2008.

Smith, Gaddis. *The Last Years of the Monroe Doctrine 1945–1993.* New York: Hill & Wang, 1995.

Solano, Gonzalo. "As U.S. Closes Military Post, Ecuador Hails Restoration of 'Sovereignty.' " Washingtonpost.com, September 19, 2009. Originally from AP.

"Special Investigation of Non-Commissioned Officer." Interview by Carlos Mow, 2004.

"Special Report: History of the Massive Kidnappings in Colombia." Fondelibertad.gov.co, May 29, 2009.

Strohm, Chris. "Officials Seek to Transfer State Drug Program to Justice Department." GovernmentExecutive.com, October 7, 2003.

Tate, Winifred. "Paramilitaries in Colombia." *The Brown Journal of World Affairs* 8 (2001): 163–175. Available at www.watsoninstitute.org.

"3 Colombians Held in U.S. Drug Smuggling." NYTimes.com, May 19, 2005.

Torpy, Bill. "Families Want Scrutiny of Drug War in Colombia." *Atlanta Journal-Constitution*, May 8, 2004; available at www.november.org.

Torres, Juan Carlos. *Operación Jaque: La Verdadera historia*. Bogotá: Planeta, 2008.

Tovar, Adriana. "22 miembros de la fuerza pública siguen secuestrados." Laopinión.com.co, January 30, 2009.

"Trial Begins for 'Sonia'—Colombian Revolutionary." Fightbacknews.org, January 5, 2007.

Ubags, Wies. "Hostage Families Demand Action—from the FARC and the Government." Colombiareports.com, October 4, 2009.

United Nations Office on Drugs and Crime. *Coca Cultivation in the Andean Region: A Survey of Bolivia, Colombia and Peru*. June 2008; available at www.unodc.org.

United States of America, Appellee v. Ricardo Palmera Pineda, also known as Simon Trinidad, Appellant. No. 08–3012. United States District Court for the District of Columbia, October 5, 2009. Document no. 1209534.

United States of America, Plaintiff v. Juvenal Ovidio Ricardo Palmera Pineda, aka Simon Trinidad, Defendant. U.S. District Court for the District of Columbia, Cong., 1 (2006). (Testimony of Derek Harvey, James Hollaway, Gustavo Enrique Avendana Miranda, Juan Carlos Sánchez, Jorge Enrique Botero, Dr. Maximo Duque, Carlos Garcia, Alejandro Barbeito, Elias Ochoa, Carmen Alicia Medina Ochoa, and Simón Trinidad.)

United States of America v. Pedro Antonio Marin et al. United States District Court for the District of Columbia, April 29, 2005. No. 04–446. (FARC indictments.)

"Uribe's second term." Economist.com, May 29, 2006.

U.S. Army South, Office of Public Affairs. "Public statement by Marc Gonsalves, Thomas Howes and Keith Stansell." Army.mil, July 5, 2008.

U.S. Army South, Office of Public Affairs. "Robin Meade of Headline News to Interview Gonsalves, Howes and Stansell No. 014–08." Press release, Fort Sam Houston, San Antonio, Texas, July 10, 2008.

"US Code: Title 18,1203. Hostage taking." Legal Information Institute at Cornell Law School, January 3, 2007; available at www.law.cornell.edu.

U.S. Department of Justice. "High Ranking Member of Colombian FARC Narco-Terrorist." Press release, July 2, 2007; available at www.usdoj.gov.

———. "Senior Member of FARC Narco-Terrorist Organization Found Guilty of Hostage-Taking Conspiracy." Press release, Federal Bureau of Investigation, July 11, 2007; available at washingtondc.fbi.gov.

U.S. Department of State. "Andean Counterdrug Initiative, International Narcotics and Law Enforcement: FY 2007 Budget Justification," April 2006; available at www.state.gov.

———. *Colombia: An Opportunity for Lasting Success* (brochure, Bureau of Public Affairs). State.gov, September 16, 2008.

———. "International Terrorism: American Hostages" (press release, Richard Boucher, Bureau of Public Affairs). State.gov, February 20, 2002.

———. "Remarks After Meeting with Colombian President Alvaro Uribe" (press release). State.gov, September 30, 2003.

———. *2007 International Narcotics Control Strategy Report*, vols. 1 and 2; available at www.state.gov.

———. *2008 International Narcotics Control Strategy Report*, vols. 1 and 2; available at www.state.gov.

———. *2009 International Narcotics Control Strategy Report*, vol. 1; available at www.state.gov.

U.S. Government Accountability Office (GAO). *Plan Colombia: Drug Reduction Goals Were Not Fully Met, but Security Has Improved; U.S. Agencies Need More Detailed*

Plans for Reducing Assistance—Summary. Report no. GAO-09-71, October 6, 2008; available at www.gao.gov.

U.S. Government General Accounting Office (GAO). *Report to Congressional Requesters, Drug Control—Efforts to Develop Alternatives to Cultivating Illicit Crops in Colombia Have Made Little Progress and Face Serious Obstacles.* Report no. GAO-02-291 Alternative Development, February 2002; available at www.gao .gov.

"U.S. May Deploy Troops if Mexico Border Violence Escalates." Latimes.com, March 13, 2009.

U.S. Naval Forces Southern Command. Redacted SRS Aircraft Mishap, February 13, 2003.

———. Redacted SRS Aircraft Mishap, March 25, 2003.

"U.S. Strips Colombian President of His Visa." *New York Times,* July 12, 1996.

"US to Dismiss Cocaine Charges Against Colombian Rebel Leader." Associated Press Worldstream, May 6, 2008.

U.S. v. Simon Trinidad. No. 04-232-02. U.S. District Court of the District of Colum- bia, October 1, 2006. (Audio transcript no. 1, date of collection: February 2, 2003). Government exhibit no. 104C.

———. No. 04-232-02. District Court of the District of Columbia, October 7, 2006. (Audio transcript, Mayday radio communications, February 13, 2003). Govern- ment exhibit no. 12B.

Vaicius, Ingrid. "The U.S. Military Presence in Colombia." Center for International Policy, February 26, 2003; available at www.ciponline.org.

Veillette, Connie. *Plan Colombia: A Progress Report.* Congressional Research Service report no. RL32774, June 22, 2005; available at www.fas.org.

Venton, Jill, et al. "Cocaine Increases Dopamine Release by Mobilization of a Synapsin-Dependent Reserve Pool." *Journal of Neuroscience* 26 (2006): 3206-3209.

Vieira, Constanza. "Colombia: Hostage Rescue, According to Captured Guerrilla Leader." Ipsnews.net, July 16, 2008.

———. "Rights-Colombia: UN Warns of Civilian Killings by Military." Ipsnews.net, November 3, 2008.

———. "Colombia: The Farmers Who Abandoned Coca for Cocoa." IPS.org, June 4, 2009.

Villalón, Carlos. "Cocaine Country." *National Geographic,* July 2004, pp. 34-55.

Wallace-Wells, Ben. "How America Lost the War on Drugs." *Rolling Stone,* Decem- ber 13, 2007.

Wang, Ting. "Caught in the Accountability Blindspot: American Military Contrac- tors Held Hostage in Colombia." Master's thesis, Yale University Law School, 2004.

Washington Office on Latin America (WOLA). " 'Chemical Reactions': A WOLA Report on the Failure of Anti-Drug Fumigation in Colombia." Press release, February 29, 2008; available at www.wola.org.

"A Welcome Flip-Flop." *Washington Post,* June 11, 2008.

Wilkinson, Tracy. "10 Mayors, Other Mexico Officials Detained." Latimes.com, May 27, 2009.

Wilson, Scott. "Colombian Fighters' Drug Trade Is Detailed." *Washington Post,* June 26, 2003; available at www.latinamericanstudies.org.

Wimbish, Michael. "SOUTHCOM remembers U.S. Hostages Held by the FARC." Southcom.mil, February 14, 2008.

———. "Former Hostages Honored at SOUTHCOM, Awarded Defense of Free- dom Medal." Southcom.mil, March 12, 2009.

Wolf, Paul. *Simon Trinidad: A Conspiracy of One.* Washington, DC: Paul Wolf, 2006.

———. "FARC Negotiator Gets Colombia's Max—in US prison." Ww4report.com, January 28, 2008.

———. "Judge Hogan Resigns from Simón Trinidad Case." Prensarural.org, March 26, 2007.

Youngers, Coletta. "U.S. Entanglements in Colombia Continue." *NACLA Report on the Americas* 31, no. 5 (1998).

Interviews and Personal Communications

Angela Botero, November 22, 2008.
Phill Bragg, September 18, 2009.
Brig. Gen. (retired) Remo Butler, October 30, 2008.
Alfonso Cano, May 1997.
Douglas Cockes, June 4, 2008; August 31, 2009.
Piedad Córdoba, March 4, 2009.
Lt. Col. John L. Dorrian, July 15, 2008.
Shane Gonsalves, August 12, 2003.
Consuelo González de Perdomo, December 8, 2008.
Suzanne K. Hall, August 14, 2008.
Paul Hooper, June 7, 2008.
Adam Isacson, May 30, 2008.
Maj. Gen. P. K. Keen, July 15, 2008.
Alain Keler, August 2002.
Kenneth Kohl, September 5, 2008.
Adair Lamprea, March 14, 2002.
Juan Carlos Lecompte, March and May 2002; June 13, 2008.
Damien Loras, July 16, 2008.
Iván Marquez, December 2007; February 2008.
Patricia Medina, May 20 and July 29, 2008.
Mauricio Mesa, March 14, 2002.
Gary Noesner, January 28 and June 14, 2004; June 24, July 17, and November 19, 2008.
Albert Oliver, November 12, 2008.
Frank Pearl, September 3, 2008.
Malia Phillips, August 14, 2003.
Louis Ponticelli, November 14, 2008.
Raúl Reyes, September 2007, January 2008.
Rodolfo Ríos, August 30 and September 5, 2008.
Anayibe Rojas Valderrama (aka "Sonia"), March 2007.
Jo Rosano, May 12, July 11, and August 2003.
Jaime Rueda, November 22, 2008.
Vice President Francisco Santos, September 12, 2003.
Sharon Schmidt, January 2004.
Simón Trinidad, July and December 2001; February 2002.
Robert Tucker, February 5, 2009.
Carlos Villalón, October 2008.
Maria Alejandra Villamizar, November 29, 2008.
Christopher Voss, October 15, 2008.
Paul Wolf, November 3, 7, 21, 2006; May 21, June 26, 28, and July 11, 2007; April 21, 2008.

INDEX

Page numbers in *italics* refer to illustrations.

A NOTE ABOUT THE AUTHORS

Victoria Bruce is the author of *No Apparent Danger: The True Story of Volcanic Disaster at Galeras and Nevado del Ruiz* (Harper-Collins, 2001).

Karin Hayes produced and directed (with Bruce) the Alfred I. duPont–Columbia University Award–winning documentary film *The Kidnapping of Ingrid Betancourt* (HBO/Cinemax, 2004).

Jorge Enrique Botero, the Colombian journalist and best-selling author, is the only journalist who ever gained access to the American hostages held by the FARC.

A NOTE ON THE TYPE

This book was set in Janson, a typeface long thought to have been made by the Dutchman Anton Janson, who was a practicing type-founder in Leipzig during the years 1668–1687. However, it has been conclusively demonstrated that these types are actually the work of Nicholas Kis 1650–1702), a Hungarian, who most proba-bly learned his trade from the master Dutch typefounder Dirk Voskens. The type is an excellent example of the influential and sturdy Dutch types that prevailed in England up to the time William Caslon (1692–1766) developed his own incomparable designs from them.

Composed by North Market Street Graphics,
Lancaster, Pennsylvania

Printed and bound by Berryville Graphics,
Berryville, Virginia

Designed by Soonyoung Kwon